Dante and his "Divine Comedy." Fresco
by Michelino, Florence, Cathedral.

Companion
to Dante's
DIVINE COMEDY

A COMPREHENSIVE GUIDE FOR THE STUDENT AND GENERAL READER

by

Aldo S. Bernardo *and* Anthony L. Pellegrini

Revised Edition

Published under the auspices of the
Center for Medieval and Renaissance Studies

Global Academic Publishing
Harpur College
Binghamton University
2006

Copyright © 2006

Library of Congress Cataloging-in-Publication Data

Bernardo, Aldo S.
  Companion to Dante's Divine comedy: a comprehensive guide for the student and general reader / Aldo S. Bernardo and Anthony L. Pellegrini.--Rev. ed.
      p. cm.
  "Published under the auspices of the Center for Medieval and Renaissance Studies."
  First ed. published under the title : A critical study guide to Dante's Divine comedy. Totowa, N.J. : Littlefield, Adams, c1968. (ERA key guides; PQ130)
  Includes bibliographical references and index.
  ISBN-13: 978-1-58684-263-5 (pbk. : alk. paper)
  1. Dante Alighieri, 1265–1321. Divina commedia. I. Pellegrini, Anthony L., 1921– . II. Bernardo, Aldo S., 1920– . Critical study guide to Dante's Divine comedy. III. Title. IV. Series.
  PQ4390.B5755 2006
  851'.1--dc22
                                    2006006799

Text typeset in Times New Roman, with titles in
Abadi MT Condensed Light.
Printed in the USA.

Published by Global Academic Publishing
Binghamton University, LNG 99
Binghamton, New York 13902-6000 USA
Phone: (607) 777-4495; Fax: (607) 777-6132
E-mail: gap@binghamton.edu
Website: http://academicpublishing.binghamton.edu/

Dedication

In grateful recognition of their faithful attentiveness, the authors dedicate this revised edition to the adult reading group who over the past five years have, at their repeated request, shared with us six separate journeys — thus far — through Dante's great poem.

The Authors

Aldo S. Bernardo, B.A., M.A., Brown University, Ph.D., Harvard University; Distinguished Service Professor Emeritus of Italian and Comparative Literature, SUNY-Binghamton and Founder of its Center for Medieval and Renaissance Studies; also served as longtime Chairman of the Humanities Division of Harpur College (SUNY-Binghamton); major scholarly focus: Petrarch, Dante, and Boccaccio.

◆

Anthony L. Pellegrini, A.B., M.A., Ph.D., Harvard University; Professor Emeritus of Romance Languages and Literatures, Harpur College (SUNY-Binghamton); served multiple terms as Department Chairman; major areas of interest: Medieval Italian and French Literature, and Romance Philology, with primary focus on Dante. Served for three decades as bibliographer of American Dante Studies and as Founding Editor of *Dante Studies* for the Dante Society of America.

◆

Special Tributes

Profound thanks are due the publishers Rowman and Littlefield for their gracious transfer of copyright to this book to the authors.

We also wish to express our warm gratitude to Professor Sandro Sticca, Director of our Medieval Center, for his encouragement to proceed with this revised edition and for his assistance in seeing it through to publication.

We owe a further warm debt of gratitude to John L. Pellegrini for the endless hours he dedicated so skillfully to scanning the original edition, cleaning it of extensive but now extraneous matter, and reformatting the entire text.

CONTENTS

ILLUSTRATIONS

PREFACE

DURING OUR HALF-CENTURY of teaching Dante's masterpiece, first as part of a Great Books course, then as a free-standing offering in Italian or English, we witnessed an increasingly entrenched philosophy of materialism, a vulgarization of the culture, the rise of situational ethics, etc. But all the while, it was possible to maintain the poem's value as a supreme work of art. As such, beyond a gripping narrative adventure, it rewarded our students with an incomparable aesthetic experience that only the greatest works achieve. Dante's poem also offered a powerful program of moral and ethical and religious edification. Furthermore, the journey through the *Divine Comedy* constituted an exceptionally profound spiritual experience for both the believer and the non-believer. All these effects were expressly or tacitly acknowledged by our students. They have lost none of their validity even now.

In more recent years, however, this was no longer enough. Under the pressures of modern life, today's students insist upon something more from this unique creation of the Middle Ages to justify its inclusion in an already crowded academic program. Happily, a fresh, singularly pragmatic justification presented itself in a 1992 issue of a well-known business magazine, with a career-counseling article under the self-descriptive title of "Dante, M.B.A." The article features a highly successful corporate executive who maintains that business students ignore the humanities at great cost. And more specifically, that Dante's poetic creation of a whole universe, with all the parts organized and fitted together in an incredible structure of perfect proportion and balance, is a model, arguably, of "the best long-term business strategy ever articulated." Anyone aspiring to a career in business might well take note.

Still more recently, in their book, *Dante's Path: A Practical Approach to Achieving Inner Wisdom* (2003), psychotherapists Bonney and Richard Schaub have patterned their method on Dante's poetic journey from a condition of bondage (Hell) to liberation (Purgatory) to illumination (Paradise). It is a proven method for unlocking our potential for supreme love as well as profound inner wisdom, and thus for learning to cope in a challenging, even chaotic, world.

This last reference only serves to confirm our unwavering conviction that Dante's poem encapsulates in its cosmic vision the essential core of a sound, well-balanced liberal arts education.

In further tribute to our poet, we note that Pope Benedict XVI has spoken of the strong influence of Dante he underwent during his youth and, furthermore, for his very first encyclical "Deus caritas est" (God is Love), he acknowledges having embraced the poet's holistic vision and definitive treatment of "love," human and divine, in the *Divine Comedy*, and particularly in the *Paradiso*.

* * *

In the present guide-book, we authors have sought to light the way through the poem, leaving the personal encounter with the work itself to the reader. We therefore recommend that the reader have in hand a good copy of Dante's text, preferably, for the first time around, in an edition not unduly burdened with notes (e.g., the Huse translation see BIBLIOGRAPHY). We suggest, further, that the reader consider the various elements of guidance we provide as points of departure for venturing into the pertinent items cited in the select, and purposely short, BIBLIOGRAPHY.

The canto summaries and commentaries are intended to help the reader with the multi-faceted nature of the poem, to help in seeing the whole forest beyond the trees. We have striven to focus on the main thread of the poet-wayfarer's journey, while outlining the essential and dominant elements of both literal and allegorical meaning. The reader must do his or her own fleshing out with a careful reading of the poem itself. In successive readings, moreover, the reader will gradually put aside this guide and re-create Dante's *Comedy* for him- or herself, plumbing ever new depths of meaning and aesthetic satisfaction.

As a parting word, it should be clear that this guide is geared primarily to the English-speaking reader with no knowledge of Italian. The bibliography consists therefore of readings exclusively in English. It is our hope that anyone reading the poem in the original language may also find the guide abundantly useful.

* * *

Concerning the present edition, over the years, we have received many inquiries about our original *A Critical Study Guide to Dante's "Divine Comedy,"* as it was titled, which has long been out of print, since 1968, in fact. It was then published in the ERA series of

"Key-Indexed Guides." More recently, we have been further encouraged by our experience with a Dante reading group of mature adults to bring out a revised edition. Hence the present *Companion to Dante's "Comedy,"* a new title designed to reflect its larger scope beyond the focus of college students, to whom even the original edition was not exclusively limited. We are confident of the enhanced usefulness of this edition for the student at any level — high school, college, or graduate school — as well as for the general reader. Here, each can find her or his own level of needed guidance to Dante's poem, whether in the original Italian or in English.

The Authors

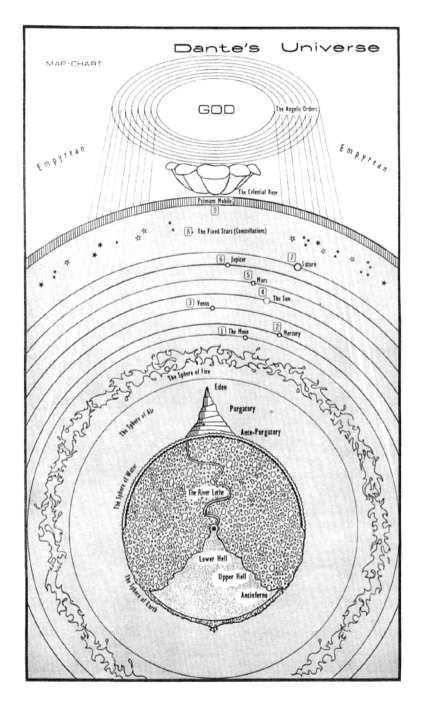

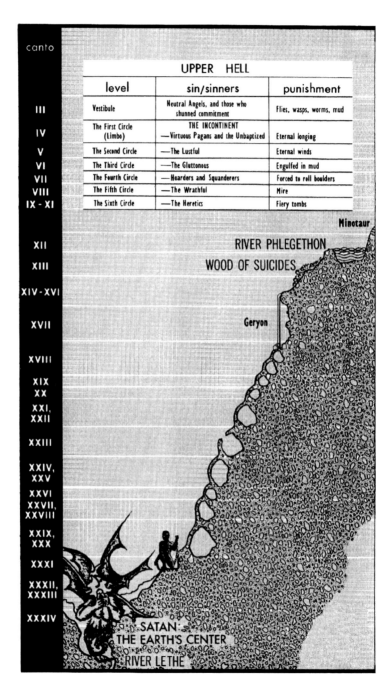

canto

	UPPER HELL		
	level	sin/sinners	punishment
III	Vestibule	Neutral Angels, and those who shunned commitment	Flies, wasps, worms, mud
IV	The First Circle (Limbo)	THE INCONTINENT —Virtuous Pagans and the Unbaptized	Eternal longing
V	The Second Circle	—The Lustful	Eternal winds
VI	The Third Circle	—The Gluttonous	Engulfed in mud
VII	The Fourth Circle	—Hoarders and Squanderers	Forced to roll boulders
VIII	The Fifth Circle	—The Wrathful	Mire
IX - XI	The Sixth Circle	—The Heretics	Fiery tombs

Minotaur

XII

XIII

RIVER PHLEGETHON

WOOD OF SUICIDES

XIV-XVI

XVII   Geryon

XVIII

XIX
XX

XXI,
XXII

XXIII

XXIV,
XXV

XXVI
XXVII,
XXVIII

XXIX,
XXX

XXXI

XXXII,
XXXIII

XXXIV

SATAN:
THE EARTH'S CENTER
RIVER LETHE

INFERNO

canto

HELL GATE

RIVER ACHERON — Charon — III

Minos — IV

Cerberus — V

WALLS MARSH Plutus — VI

OF THE OF — VII

CITY STYX Phlegyas — VIII

OF DIS — IX - XI

LOWER HELL

level	sin/sinners	punishment	canto
The Seventh Circle 1st Ring	THE VIOLENT — against neighbors	Souls in boiling blood	XII
2nd Ring	— against themselves	Souls become bleeding plants and trees	XIII
3rd Ring	— against God and Nature	Burning sand, rain of fire	XIV - XVI
Precipice			XVII
The Eighth Circle 1st Ditch 2nd Ditch	THE FRAUDULENT — Panders, Seducers — Flatterers	Whipped and prodded, Immersed in excrement	XVIII
3rd Ditch	— Simoniacs	Head-down in holes	XIX
4th Ditch	— Soothsayers	Heads twisted backwards	XX
5th Ditch	—Grafters, Swindlers	Immersed in boiling pitch	XXI, XXII
6th Ditch	— Hypocrites	Weighed down by leaden robes Staked to ground	XXIII
7th Ditch	— Thieves	Agonies and metamorphoses caused by serpents	XXIV, XXV
8th Ditch	— Evil counselors	Concealed in flames	XXVI
9th Ditch	— Sowers of Discord	Bodies repeatedly mutilated	XXVII, XXVIII
10th Ditch	— Falsifiers alchemists, impersonaters, counter-feiters, and liars	Diseases: leprosy, madness, dropsy, high fever	XXIX, XXX
(Well of Giants: Nimrod, Ephialtes, Briareus, Antaeus, etc., chained)			XXXI
The Ninth Circle Division 1 (Caina) Division 2 (Antenora) Division 3 (Tolomea)	—Traitors : to kin — to country — to guests —	Bodies in ice : heads, hands exposed heads exposed heads bent back	XXXII, XXXIII
Division 4 (Giudecca)	to lords, benefactors	totally submerged	XXXIV

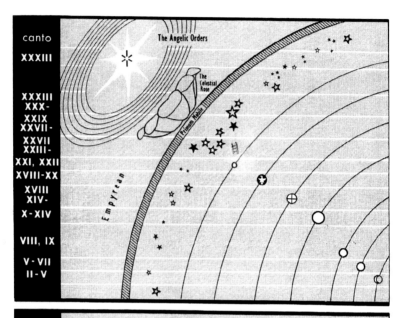

PURGATORIO

canto	level	sin/sinners			disciplining torment
XXXIII / XXVIII-	Garden of Eden	The Mystical Procession — Beatrice — Pagent of the Church and Empire			Innocence Restored
	The Mountain				
	level	**sin/sinners**			**disciplining torment**
XXVII / XXV-	Seventh Terrace	Lust	Sins of the flesh	Love excessive for worldly goods	Purging Fire
XXV / XXII-	Sixth Terrace	Gluttony			Hunger and Thirst
XXII / XIX-	Fifth Terrace	Avarice, Prodigality			Souls Bound Prostrate
XIX / XVII-	Fourth Terrace	Sloth	Spiritual sloth	Love deficient for the good	Souls Rushing About
XV, XVI	Third Terrace	Wrath	Sins of the spirit	Love distorted for exalting self over neighbor	Eyes Blinded by Smoke
XIII, XIV	Second Terrace	Envy			Eyes Sealed with Wire
X-XII	First Terrace	Pride			Souls Bearing Heavy Stones
IX	Gate of Purgatory				
	Ante-Purgatorio				
VI-VIII	Valley of the Princes	Negligence — the Preoccupied			Detained for Time Equal to Mortal Lifespan
IV, V	Slope / Sloping ledge	Negligence — The Unshriven (who have suffered violent death) — The Indolent			Detained for Time Equal to Mortal Lifespan
III	Foot of Mountain	The Excommunicated			Detained 30 Times the Years of Contumacy
I, II	Mountain Isle Shore				

PARADISO

canto

	The Final Vision of God		XXXIII
level (sphere)	**souls represented**	**angelic orders**	
Tenth Heaven: Empyrean	(The Holy Trinity, The Virgin, The Angels, The Blessed)		XXXIII XXX -
Ninth Heaven: the Primum Mobile		Seraphim	XXIX XXVII -
Eighth Heaven: the Fixed Stars	Christ: The Church Triumphant—Faith, Hope, Charity	Cherubim	XXVII XXIII -
Seventh Heaven: Saturn	The Contemplatives—Temperance	Thrones	XXI, XXII
Sixth Heaven: Jupiter	The Just Rulers—Justice	Dominations	XVIII-XX
Fifth Heaven: Mars	The Warriors— Fortitude	Virtues	XVIII XIV -
Fourth Heaven: the Sun	The Theologians—Prudence	Powers	X - XIV
Third Heaven: Venus	The Sensual Lovers—Temperance	Principalities	VIII, IX
Second Heaven: Mercury	The Ambitious—Justice	Archangels	V - VII
First Heaven: the Moon	The Weak and Inconstant—Fortitude	Angels	II - V

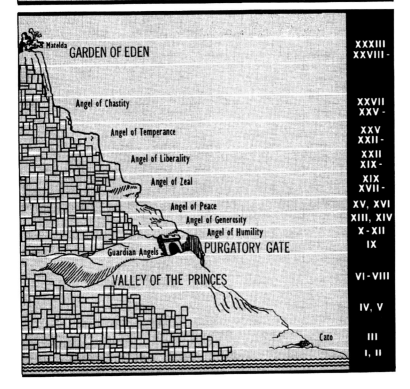

	canto
Matelda GARDEN OF EDEN	XXXIII XXVIII -
Angel of Chastity	XXVII XXV -
Angel of Temperance	XXV XXII -
Angel of Liberality	XXII XIX -
Angel of Zeal	XIX XVII -
Angel of Peace	XV, XVI
Angel of Generosity	XIII, XIV
Angel of Humility	X - XII
PURGATORY GATE	IX
Guardian Angels	
VALLEY OF THE PRINCES	VI - VIII
	IV, V
Cato	III
	I, II

DANTE'S JOURNEY to GOD

The structure and action of the poem may be followed schematically on this chart from the bottom upward. From internal evidence in the poem, it is clear that Dante set the ideal time of the poetic journey in the year 1300, and more specifically, during Easter. The pilgrim-protagonist enters Hell the evening of Good Friday, which in 1300 fell on April 8. These facts, along with other time references in the poem, yield the approximate timetable indicated below. The pilgrim's journey to the pit of Hell took Friday night and all of Saturday. After crossing the earth's center of gravity, the pilgrim finds himself back at the beginning of Saturday. It takes him all of the "second" Saturday and Saturday night to "climb out" from the earth's center to the other side. It is the noblest part of the day, noon, of Easter Wednesday, when the pilgrim rises from Earthly Paradise to Heaven.

guide	time	location
ST. BERNARD Guidance of Intuition in the ultimate mysteries. [The mystical vision; ineffableness. Ecstatic in tone.]	**WEDNESDAY** **April 13** —— **NOON** ——	**Empyrean**
BEATRICE Guidance of Revelation, the Light of Grace, in the knowledge of divine things. [Effects of light, movement, and music; transhumanizing; sweetness of manner and style. Lyrical in tone.]		**Nine Spheres**

paradiso

Vision of beatified souls
and knowledge of ultimate reality:
God in His essence.

[In glory with God.]

	WED	TUESDAY April 12	MONDAY April 11	SUNDAY April 10	SATURDAY April 9	FRIDAY April 8	THURS
	MORN	NOON / EVE / MORN	NOON / EVE / MORN	NOON / EVE / MORN	NOON / EVE / MORN	NOON / EVE / MORN	EVE

BEATRICE

VIRGIL

Guidance of Reason in life as well as in Purgatory, with grace restored.

(Open air, sunshine; hopefulness and courtesy; lighter style. Pastoral in tone.)

VIRGIL

Guidance of Reason in the physical world, where man, primarily on his own, is involved in the "human comedy" of passion and strife. (Somber darkness; despair; harshness of manner and language. Dramatic in tone.)

purgatorio

- Garden of Eden
- Terrace VII
- Terrace VI
- Terrace V
- Terraces III, IV
- Terrace II
- Terrace I
- Purgatory Gate
- Valley of the Princes
- Purgatory Shore

Atonement of redeemed souls to restore spiritual harmony with God.

[En route to God.]

inferno

- Circle IX
- Circles VI, VII, VIII
- Circle V
- Circles II, III, IV
- Gate, Circle I
- Mountain; Three Beasts
- Prelude: Dark Wood of this Life

Full understanding of sin and evil, exemplified by the damned who variously denied God.

[Eternal exile from God.]

DANTE ALIGHIERI

BIOGRAPH

DATE	AGE	BIOGRAPHIC HIGHLIGHTS	MAJOR PUBLICATIONS	CONTEMPORARY EVENTS	LITERARY EVENTS
1265		MAY (?), BORN IN FLORENCE UNDER THE SIGN OF GEMINI		FLORENCE (GUELPH) DEFEATED BY SIENA (GHIBELLINE) IN BATTLE OF MONTAPERTI 1260	
1274	9	[PROBABLY FIRST MEETS BEATRICE (PORTINARI?)]		SAINT LOUIS OF FRANCE DIES 1270	
1277	12	FATHER ARRANGES DANTE'S FUTURE MARRIAGE TO GEMMA DONATI		ST. THOMAS AQUINAS DIES, AND ST. BONAVENTURE 1274	
1283	18	FATHER DEAD. DANTE COMES OF AGE [PROBABLY MEETS BEATRICE AGAIN]		GHIBELLINES ARE EXILED FROM FLORENCE 1275	POET GUIDO GUINIZELLI DIES 1276
				GIOTTO BORN 1276?	
1289	24	JUNE 11, FIGHTS WITH GUELPH CAVALRY IN BATTLE OF CAMPALDINO DEC. 31, DEATH OF BEATRICE'S FATHER, FOLCO PORTINARI (?)		POPE NICHOLAS III ELECTED 1277	
				GHIBELLINES RETURN TO FLORENCE 1279	
				POPE MARTIN IV ELECTED 1281	
				SICILIAN VESPERS 1282	
1290	25	JUNE 8, BEATRICE DIES. DANTE BEGINS PHILOSOPHIC STUDIES		PHILIP III OF FRANCE DIES 1285	
1291?	26	MARRIES GEMMA DONATI		GUELPH FLORENCE AND LUCCA VICTORIOUS AT CAMPALDINO 1289	
1292	27	COMPOSES THE Vita nuova. HAS WRITTEN AND CIRCULATED MANY LYRIC POEMS BY THIS TIME	THE Vita nuova 1292?	CAN GRANDE DELLA SCALA BORN 1291	ROGER BACON DIES 1292?
				POPE CELESTINE V ELECTED 1293	
1294	29	SPRING, MEETS CHARLES MARTEL IN FLORENCE		POPE BONIFACE VIII ELECTED 1294	POET GUITTONE D'AREZZO DIES 1294
1295	30	JULY, ENTERS POLITICAL LIFE MORE LYRIC POEMS IN THE MEANTIME		MARCO POLO RETURNS TO VENICE 1295	DANTE'S DEAR TEACHER BRUNETTO LATINI DIES 1295
1300	35	(IDEAL DATE OF THE Divine Comedy) JUNE, IS ELECTED A PRIOR OF FLORENCE [VISITS ROME FOR THE JUBILEE?]		MODEL PARLIAMENT IN ENGLAND BONIFACE VIII PROCLAIMS JUBILEE YEAR 1300	DANTE'S POET FRIEND FORESE DIES 1296
				THE ARTIST CIMABUE DIES	DANTE'S POET FRIEND GUIDO CAVALCANTI DIES 1300
1301	36	OCTOBER, IS SENT ON EMBASSY TO POPE BONIFACE VIII IN ROME		CHARLES VALOIS ENTERS FLORENCE 1301	
				EXPULSION OF WHITES FROM FLORENCE 1302	
				DEATH OF BONIFACE VIII 1303	

DATE	AGE	BIOGRAPHIC HIGHLIGHTS	MAJOR PUBLICATIONS	CONTEMPORARY EVENTS	LITERARY EVENTS
1302	37	JAN. 27, in absentia IS CONDEMNED TO EXILE BY THE BLACKS. TAKES FIRST REFUGE IN VERONA		POPE BENEDICT XI ELECTED	PETRARCH BORN JULY 20, 1304
1303	38	MORE DIVERS POEMS BY THIS TIME		POPE CLEMENT V ELECTED 1305	
1304-1307		CONTINUES STUDIES AND WRITING	THE Convivio AND De vulgari eloquentia 1304-1307	EDWARD I OF ENGLAND DIES 1307	DUNS SCOTUS DIES 1308
1306	41	IN PADUA		HENRY VII OF LUXEMBOURG ELECTED EMPEROR	
1307	42	[?BEGINS WRITING THE Divine Comedy]		"BABYLONIAN CAPTIVITY" OF PAPACY 1309	JEAN DE MEUN, CONTINUER OF Roman de la Rose, DIES 1310?
1308	43	IN VERONA. [?VISITS PARIS]		HENRY VII'S ARMY IN ITALY 1310	BOCCACCIO BORN 1313
1310	45	WRITES EPISTLE TO HENRY VII	THE Monarchia 1310?	HENRY VII DIES; CAMPAIGN COLLAPSES 1313	
1314	49	WRITES EPISTLE TO ITALIAN CARDINALS TO BRING PAPACY BACK TO ROME FROM AVIGNON	AT LEAST THE Inferno COMPLETE 1314	CAN GRANDE DEFEATS PADUANS 1314	JOINVILLE DIES 1316?
1315	50	FLORENCE OFFERS TO REPEAL DANTE'S SENTENCE IF HE ACKNOWLEDGES GUILT. HE REFUSES		BANK OF THE BARDI IN FLORENCE RICHEST IN EUROPE 1318	
1315-1316		IN ROMAGNA		CAN GRANDE CHOSEN HEAD OF GHIBELLINE LEAGUE IN LOMBARDY 1318	
1316?	51	IN RAVENNA		FLORENCE AT WAR WITH LUCCA 1320	Defensor pacis BY MARSIGLIO OF PADUA 1324
1320	55	LECTURES AT VERONA ON SCIENTIFIC PROBLEM	Quaestio de aqua et terra 1320	EDWARD II OF ENGLAND DIES 1327	
1321	56	GOES ON EMBASSY TO VENICE FOR GUIDO NOVELLO OF RAVENNA. SEPT. 13 (or 14), DIES IN RAVENNA	THE Divine Comedy COMPLETE 1321	GIOTTO DIES 1337	CHAUCER BORN 1340?
			FIRST PRINTED EDITION OF 1472 DANTE'S Comedia		
			FIRST EDITION WITH THE TITLE Divina commedia 1555		GUTENBERG BIBLE IS FIRST BOOK PRINTED FROM MOVABLE TYPE c. 1445
			FIRST PRINTED EDITION OF THE Vita nuova 1576		

BIOGRAPH

CHRONOLOG

ITALIAN LITERATURE

- FAZIO DEGLI UBERTI ?-c.1368
- ST. CATERINA 1347-1380
- FRANCESCO DA BARBERINO 1264-1348
- DANTE ALIGHIERI 1265-1321
- GUIDO CAVALCANTI c.1255-1300
- GUINIZELLI c.1240-1276
- GUITTONE D'AREZZO c.1225-1294
- JACOPONE DA TODI 1236-1306
- FRANCESCO PETRARCA 1304-1374
- FRANCO SACCHETTI 1335-1400
- CECCO ANGIOLIERI 1258?-1313
- CINO DA PISTOIA c.1270-1337
- GIOVANNI BOCCACCIO 1313-1375
- BRUNETTO LATINI 1220-1295
- DINO COMPAGNI c.1255-1324
- PIER DELLE VIGNE ?-1249

WORLD LITERATURE

- JOHN GOWER 1325?-1408
- JEAN FROSSART 1333?-1400?
- WILLIAM LANGLAND 1332?-1400?
- GEOFFREY CHAUCER 1340?-1400
- JEAN DE MEUN c.1250-1310?
- RUTEBEUF fl. 1250-1280
- JEAN DE JOINVILLE 1224?-1316?
- DE LORRIS fl. 1230
- WALTHER VON DER VOGELWEIDE 1170?-1230?
- ST. THOMAS AQUINAS 1225-1274
- ST. BONAVENTURE 1221-1274
- ROGER BACON 1214?-1292?
- ST. FRANCIS 1182-1226
- ROBERT GROSSETESTE c. 1175-1253

CONTEMPORARIES

- WILLIAM OF OCCAM 1300?-1349?
- JOHN WYCLIFFE 1320?-1384
- GIOTTO DI BONDONE 1276?-1337
- BRUNELLESCHI 1377?-1444
- GHIBERTI 1378-1456
- GIOVANNI CIMABUE c.1240-c.1302
- MARCO POLO c.1254-1324

1200   1250   1300   1350   1400

DANTE ALIGHIERI

A S WITH MANY GREAT WRITERS, including the more recent Shakespeare, we have very little exact biographical information about Dante. Biographies, even of considerable length, have indeed been written about him, but these have frequently been romanticized accounts inflated by an indiscriminate culling of references from his poetic works and by equally unreliable anecdotal accounts of later writers, or even near-contemporaries, such as Boccaccio. In truth, the firm facts we possess concerning Dante's life are extremely few.

Dante's Life

Dante lived in a period of political strife marked by intense internecine warfare among the Italian city-states as well as factional struggles within the individual cities themselves. This was the day of intense conflict between two political factions, the Guelphs, who generally supported the power of the Papacy, and the Ghibellines, who were for the Empire. In Florence proper, there was the further complicating power struggle between the White and the Black factions into which the Guelphs had split.

It is fairly certain that Dante was born in 1265 in Florence, and we definitely know that he died in 1321 in Ravenna. A life span of fifty-six years was not an inconsiderable accomplishment for the times, when life expectancy averaged in the low twenties. We know from the *Divine Comedy* that the poet was born under the sign of Gemini, probably in May of the year. He was born to a Florentine family of good standing, which could lay ancient claim to the minor nobility.

Virtually nothing is known of Dante's early years. His mother seems to have died in his childhood. If we take literally a passage at the beginning of the *Vita nuova,* a first meeting with his beloved Beatrice (probably of the Portinari family) occurred when he was nine years old, or in 1274. There is documentary evidence that in 1277, when Dante was twelve, and in keeping with the contemporary practice of arranged marriages, his father betrothed him to Gemma Donati, daughter of a fairly prominent Florentine family of the old nobility.

By 1283, when Dante came of age at eighteen, his father was already dead. In this same year, nine years after his presumed first encounter, Dante met Beatrice for the second time, again if we are to take at face value a passage in the *Vita nuova*.

The next firm piece of information we have about the poet is that on June 11, 1289, at the age of twenty-four, Dante fought successfully with the cavalry of the Guelph league of Florence and Lucca at the Battle of Campaldino, where they defeated the Ghibellines of Arezzo and Pisa. It seems he also participated in another expedition against the Ghibellines of Pisa and witnessed the surrender of Caprona.

It was in the same year that Beatrice's father (Folco Portinari?) died. On June 8, 1290, Beatrice herself died. There is evidence that Dante now entered a period of intense study focused primarily on philosophy. He had participated in the activity of fashionable young men of writing love poetry addressed to various ladies. By this time he had also accumulated and circulated a number of love lyrics and other occasional pieces.

By 1291 Dante was certainly married to Gemma Donati. While probably not marked by much happiness, the marriage produced two sons, Piero and Jacopo, and one or two daughters.

In March of 1294, Dante was privileged to meet Charles Martel, a powerful French ruler of the day, whose arrival in Florence was received with great magnificence. It is said that Charles Martel praised Dante very highly, among other things, for his calligraphy. The poet later immortalized their friendship in Canto VIII of the *Paradiso*.

Dante's dedication to things of the intellect did not preclude his participating in the political life of his beloved city. In July of 1295, he joined the Guild of Physicians and Apothecaries, in order to qualify for public service. By November of that year he was a member of the Council of the Captain of the People, in which capacity he served until spring of 1296, when he became a member of the Council of One Hundred. Other offices followed, and by the end of the decade he could be considered a fairly important figure in local politics.

After a successful mission to San Gimignano for the Guelph League in the spring of 1300, he served a short term as one of the six Priors of Florence during the ensuing summer. In this office he shared responsibility for banishing the leaders of both the White and Black parties, among whom unfortunately was his "first friend," the poet

Guido Cavalcanti. He served again on the Council of One Hundred and in October of 1301, he was sent with two other envoys to Rome to invoke the help of Pope Boniface VIII in the feud between the Whites and the Blacks.

All this is mentioned, in order to give some idea of Dante's importance in the active life of Florence. The record, moreover, reveals nothing to indicate that Dante's service was anything but competent and objective in every way. Indeed the nature of his assignments is evidence itself of the high regard in which he was held.

During Dante's absence in Rome, the Blacks, who had seized power in Florence that fall, embarked on a series of cruel reprisals. On January 27, 1302, they issued a first sentence condemning Dante, on charges of barratry, to exile and a heavy fine. In March, his exile was made permanent for life under pain of death. Dante ignored the trumped up charges and made no reply to the action. He was never to see his beloved Florence again.

Thus, from that year began the poet's long and painful wanderings, as he sought asylum at various hospitable courts throughout northern Italy. Most generous of all seems to have been the famous Can Grande della Scala of Verona, where Dante spent an extended sojourn at the start of his banishment and again possibly in 1314 and later. In 1306, he seems to have stopped in Padua, and later that year in Lunigiana with the Malaspina family. It is impossible, however, to follow the exile's meanderings with any precision or detail. Moreover, it is quite debatable whether he actually journeyed to Paris sometime between 1307 and 1309, as some have claimed on the authority of Boccaccio and Villani.

For a time, Dante's hopes soared with the election of the idealist Henry VII of Luxembourg to the imperial crown in 1308. Two years later it seemed as if his expectation would indeed be realized, for in 1310 the Emperor descended with an army into Italy to bring order and peace to the strife-ridden land. When in 1311 Henry was crowned at Sant'Ambrogio in Milan, some believe that Dante may even have been present. In any case, in May of 1311, the poet addressed a Latin epistle to Henry, hailing the emperor on his holy mission. Meanwhile, opposition to Henry by Guelph Florence was reinforced by the leaguing together of other Guelph cities of Tuscany. Some minor successes of Henry's forces were doomed to come to naught. He himself died in

1313, and the whole campaign collapsed. With that were also destroyed Dante's fervent hopes of seeing Italy's ills resolved. And his own unhappy lot was thereby sealed as well.

But Dante's concern over contemporary affairs did not flag entirely. The transfer in 1305 of the Papal See to Avignon by the French Clement V under the influence of the French monarch, Philip IV, eventually prompted Dante in 1314, after the latter's death, to compose a Latin epistle urging the cardinals of Italy to bring the Papacy back to Rome.

Meanwhile, in 1315, the city of Florence offered amnesty to Dante, among others, but on conditions amounting to his acknowledgement of wrong-doing. Unwilling to demean himself, Dante refused. And on November 6, the Florentines confirmed his exile on pain of death, this time including his two sons in the death sentence. Dante's children had by now joined him, while his wife seems to have remained in Florence.

In the last two or three years of his life, Dante was offered refuge in Ravenna by Guido Novello da Polenta, a nephew of Francesca da Rimini immortalized by the poet in Canto V of the *Inferno*. He seems to have been reasonably happy there surrounded by scholars and others who shared his interests. With the Bolognese teacher Giovanni del Virgilio he even exchanged some Latin eclogues. In 1320, Dante went to Verona to deliver a Latin treatise, *Quaestio de aqua et terra,* before a learned audience of churchmen. It was on a much debated problem of medieval physics and theology about the irregular relationship between dry land and water on the surface of the world.

In 1321, we find Dante on one last embassy to Venice in behalf of Guido Novello. Upon his return to Ravenna, whether it was disappointment over the failure of his mission or some disease that brought him low with fever, the poet died on September 13, 1321.

Dante's Works

Despite the hardships, especially psychological, if not always physical, for a man of Dante's proud temperament, the last two decades of his life were active and fruitful where his literary production was concerned. The specific works have not been mentioned along the way of the above account, because of the virtual impossibility of dating them all with any exactness. In any case, during the period of his exile he developed from a great poet to the greatest of poets.

Dante probably composed the *Vita nuova* ("New Life") in 1292. This is a composition in alternating prose and verse telling the story of the poet's love for Beatrice. From the pattern of this experience, now manifest only from hindsight, the poet-lover draws the most profound significance. For by Christological analogy the figure of Beatrice has led him to God. In fulfillment of his expressed intention at the end of the *Vita nuova,* Dante entered a period of intensified study, in order that he might eventually "write of her what has never been said of any woman." The final achievement was of course the *Divina commedia.*

The *Convivio* ("Banquet") and the *De vulgari eloquentia* ("On the Vernacular Language"), both unfinished, appear to belong to the period, 1304–1307, when Dante was still pursuing his studies very intensively. The first is a philosophical work in Italian, of which only four (of the fifteen projected) "treatises" were finished, comprising an introduction and three allegorical explications of three long doctrinal *canzoni* (odes). It is easy to speculate that in the *Convivio,* where he seeks to re-interpret the figure of Beatrice of the *Vita nuova,* the poet must eventually have come to the realization that philosophy, while a noble science, could not of itself provide the ultimate answers. And so his diminishing interest led him to abandon the work.

The *De vulgari eloquentia* is a theoretical work in Latin on language and its literary use. This may be considered the first known treatise on Romance philology. In the far-ranging treatment, Dante upholds the dignity of the Italian language, as against Latin, for literary use.

It is generally accepted that Dante wrote the *De monarchia* ("On Monarchy") in 1310. This Latin treatise deals with government and its relationship to the Church. In it, Dante argues the independence of the Emperor to govern in worldly matters, while the Pope governs in spiritual matters. The ideal is universal peace to make possible the full realization of man's potential under the harmonious guidance of the dual leadership.

Among the remaining works that have come down to us are numerous Italian poems which modern scholars have collected together under the general title of *Rime*. These are simply "poems," mostly lyrical, consisting of (1) youthful pieces antedating the *Vita nuova;* (2) poems subsequently incorporated in, or written expressly for, the *Vita nuova;* (3) a *tenzone,* or debate in verse, with a poet friend, Forese Donati, whose shade the pilgrim encounters in *Purgatorio* XXIII; (4) allegorical and doctrinal poems, including the three doctrinal *canzoni* found in the *Convivio;* (5) more love poems and verse epistles written after the time of the *Vita nuova;* (6) the so-called *rime petrose* ("stony rhymes"), four *canzoni* (including a sestina and a "double" sestina), telling of the unrequited passion of the poet-lover before the cruelty of a beloved "lady of stone"; and (7) other verses written during the poet's exile. Except for a few individual pieces which may be dated approximately, these divers compositions defy attribution to particular years or even relative chronology of any certitude.

   Other works in Latin comprise a number of epistles written on various occasions. For example, these include Dante's letter to Henry VII, hailing him as the savior and peacemaker of Italy and the epistle to the Italian cardinals, pleading for restoration of the Papacy to Rome. Another letter, generally accepted as authentic, serves as a dedication of the *Paradiso* to Can Grande della Scala, who showed much generous hospitality to the exiled poet. This composition is especially valuable, because in it Dante analyzes the subject, purpose, structure, and allegory of his poem. A pair of eclogues, also in Latin, are part of a poetic exchange between Dante and Giovanni del Virgilio, mentioned above. Finally, there is the *Quaestio de aqua et terra* ("The Question of Water and Earth"), the scientific treatise which Dante delivered in Verona in 1320, also mentioned above.

   Where the masterpiece itself is concerned, we are not at all certain as to the date of inception. There is some indication that Dante probably began writing the *Comedy* in 1307, which may be taken as the earliest possible date. At any rate, the poem must have occupied him with varying periods of intensity for the rest of his life. The *Inferno* may have been essentially completed in 1314. The *Comedy* as a whole was very likely still receiving its last touches in 1321, the year of the poet's death.

Summary List of Dante's Works and Approximate Dates

1283–1307   *Rime* / Lyric poems (Including the 31 in the *Vita nuova* and 3 in the *Convivio*.)

1292 (1294?)   *Vita nuova* / The New Life (In prose and lyrics, inspired account of his love for Beatrice; prelude to the *Comedy*.)

1303–04   *De vulgari eloquentia* / On the Vernacular Language (First treatise on Romance philology.) Left unfinished.

1304 ... 1316   *Epistolae* / Epistles (13 in all, addressed to various notable persons.)

1304–07   *Convivio* / The Banquet (Philosophical-encyclopedic commentary on a series of odes.) Left unfinished; only the introduction and 3 chapters completed of 14 projected.

1306–09   *Inferno* / Hell (First canticle of the *Comedy*.)

1308–12   *Purgatorio* / Purgatory (Second canticle of the *Comedy*.)

1317   *Monarchia* / Monarchy [i.e., Government] (Treatise on universal world government, coordinated under two leaders, one political, the other spiritual.)

1319–20   *Egloghe* / Eclogues (2, in an exchange with Giovanni Del Virgilio.)

1320   *Quaestio de aqua et terra* / The Question of Water and Earth (Scientific treatise on the nature and relationship of the two elements.)

1315–21   *Paradiso* / Paradise (Third canticle of the *Comedy*, bringing the poem to completion.)

BACKGROUND

Why Dante?

A S A POETIC MASTERPIECE, Dante's *Divina commedia* has no peer. T. S. Eliot has observed that the Florentine poet and Shakespeare "divide the modern world between them; there is no third." If one wag was able to quip that the history of philosophy is but a series of footnotes to Plato, another, taking a chronologically reverse view, might point out that all the various achievements of poetry since 1300 may already be found in Dante's poem. In a different vein, it may be noted that the vast bibliography on Dante is probably second to that of no other literary figure or work after the Bible. Indeed, recent decades have seen a quickening of scholarship, critical writing, and general interest relating directly or indirectly to Dante and his works.

There are two important reasons for the abiding vitality of Dante's masterpiece. There is first and foremost the incomparable power of his poetry. Tribute is invariably paid to it in terms of a "miracle" of artistic creation. Beyond its primarily aesthetic value, the second very important aspect of Dante's *Comedy* is its complete and intimate involvement with existence. Anyone who has read the poem with understanding and sensitivity agrees that it embraces all of creation and its relationship to God in a most profound and essential way. This is what the critics mean when they speak of "complete vision."

Dante sought answers to the "big questions" that thinking men have been asking themselves throughout history. What is man? What is life? Why are we here? Where are we going? Does God exist? What is justice? How can men live in peace? These, and many other questions, Dante asked, explicitly or implicitly, in his own terms, and they continue to be our own. Indeed, many of Dante's concerns scarcely require translating into what we would consider our terms. The notions familiar to us are many, ranging from the personal to the cosmic level: "self-identity," "realization of one's potential," "peace of mind," "United Nations," "One World." If Dante's "vocabulary" seems different from ours at times, this need be no real obstacle to communication. What is particularly remarkable is the consistency of answers and solutions which he found in terms of his universe, thanks to the completeness and unity of his vision, historical, philosophical, spiritual, and poetic. In the course of reading his great poetic synthesis, we find ourselves re-discovering the Ancient and the Christian worlds, and at the same time all that which is universal and perennial in our own "modern" world.

The Medieval Vision

Viewed against the background of his times, Dante's master-piece may be seen as a poetic synthesis of all that went before. The *Comedy* has been compared to a vast ocean into which flow the great rivers and various tributaries of all previous literature, mythology, history, knowledge, and modes of thought of Graeco-Roman antiquity and the Judaeo-Christian world that followed. Dante's was the age of the great compendia — the summas of philosophy and theology, the specula of universal history, the specula of natural science, that is, the bestiaries, herbals, and lapidaries, all universal and encyclopedic in scope. Even the medieval cathedral, at least in its more signal examples, such as Chartres, was a kind of architectural summa, presenting in its symbolic structure and in its storied sculpture what may be called the Christian epic. This was the Bible in stone, through which the populace was constantly and visually aware of the Two Cities, the earthly and the heavenly, the City of Man and the City of God.

So much that the modern reader would have to consider "background" for the intelligent reading of the *Divine Comedy* Dante could simply assume on the part of his contemporary reader, without giving it second thought. As indicated above, for example, his medieval audience was intimately familiar with the Bible and Christian doctrine, which were part of the very fabric of their culture. While many readers of today still have some acquaintance with the Christian Story, along with the concept of the Two Cities, many others do not. Since these matters are at the core of Dante's poem, it will be helpful for all readers to have conveniently before them the great Christian "myth" as briefly and effectively summarized by the philosopher George Santayana:

There was in the beginning, so runs the Christian story, a great celestial King, wise and good, surrounded by a court of winged musicians and messengers. He had existed from all eternity, but had always intended, when the right moment should come, to create temporal beings, imperfect copies of himself in various degrees. These, of which man was the chief, began their career in the year 4004 B.C., and they would live on an indefinite time, possibly, that chronological symmetry might not be violated, until A.D. 4004. The opening and close of this drama were marked by two magnificent tableaux. In the first, in obedience to the word of God, sun, moon, and stars, and earth with all her plants and animals, assumed their appropriate places, and nature sprang into being with all her laws. The first man was made out of clay, by a special act of God, and the first woman was fashioned from one of his ribs, extracted while he lay in a deep sleep. They were placed in an orchard where they often could see God, its owner, walking in the cool of the evening. He suffered them to range at will and eat of all the fruits he had planted save that of one tree only.

But they, incited by a devil, transgressed this single prohibition, and were banished from that paradise with a curse upon their head, the man to live by the sweat of his brow and the woman to bear children in labour. These children possessed from the moment of conception the inordinate natures which their parents had acquired. They were born to sin and to find disorder and death everywhere within and without them.

At the same time God, lest the work of his hands should wholly perish, promised to redeem in his good season some of Adam's children and restore them to a natural life. This redemption was to come ultimately through a descendant of Eve, whose foot should bruise the head of the serpent. But it was to be prefigured by many partial and special redemptions. Thus, Noah was to be saved from the deluge, Lot from Sodom, Isaac from the sacrifice, Moses from Egypt, the captive Jews from Babylon, and all faithful souls from heathen forgetfulness and idolatry. For a certain tribe had been set apart from the beginning to keep alive the memory of God's judgments and promises, while the rest of mankind, abandoned to its natural depravity, sank deeper and deeper into crimes and vanities. The deluge that came to punish these evils did not avail to cure them.

Henceforth there were two spirits, two parties, or, as Saint Augustine called them, two cities in the world. The City of Satan, whatever its artifices in art, war, or philosophy, was essentially corrupt and impious. Its joy was but a comic mask and its beauty the whitening of a sepulchre. It stood condemned before God and before man's better conscience by its vanity, cruelty, and secret misery, by its ignorance of all that it truly behoved a man to know who was destined to immortality. Lost, as it seemed, within this Babylon, or visible only in its obscure and forgotten purlieus, lived on at the same time the City of God, the society of all the souls God predestined to salvation; a city which, however humble and inconspicuous it might seem on earth, counted its myriad transfigured citizens in heaven, and had its destinies, like its foundations, in eternity. To this City of God belonged, in the first place, the patriarchs and the prophets who, throughout their plaintive and ardent lives, were faithful to what echoes still remained of a primeval revelation, and waited patiently for the greater revelation to come. To the same City belonged the magi who followed a star till it halted over the stable in Bethlehem; Simeon, who divined the present salvation of Israel; John the Baptist, who bore witness to the same and made straight its path; and Peter, to whom not flesh and blood, but the spirit of the Father in heaven, revealed the Lord's divinity. For salvation had indeed come with the fulness of time, not, as the carnal Jews had imagined it, in the form of an earthly restoration, but through the incarnation of the Son of God in the Virgin Mary, his death upon a cross, his descent into hell, and his resurrection at the third day according to the Scriptures.

To the same city belonged finally all those who, believing in the reality and efficacy of Christ's mission, relied on his merits and followed his commandment of unearthly love.

All history was henceforth essentially nothing but the conflict between these two cities; two moralities, one natural, the other supernatural; two philosophies, one rational, the other revealed; two beauties, one corporeal, the other spiritual; two glories, one temporal, the other eternal; two institutions, one the world, the other the Church. These, whatever their momentary alliances or compromises, were radically opposed and fundamentally alien to one another. Their conflict was to fill the ages until, when wheat and tares had long flourished together and exhausted between them the earth for whose substance they struggled, the harvest should come; the terrible day of reckoning when those who had believed the things of religion to be imaginary would behold with dismay the Lord visibly coming down through the clouds of heaven, the angels blowing their alarming trumpets, all generations of the dead rising from their graves, and judgment without appeal passed on every man, to the edification of the universal company and his own unspeakable joy or confusion. Whereupon the blessed would enter eternal bliss with God their master and the wicked everlasting torments with the devil whom they served.

The drama of history was thus to close upon a second tableau: long-robed and beatified cohorts passing above, amid various psalmodies, into an infinite luminous space, while below the damned, howling, writhing, and half transformed into loathsome beasts, should be engulfed in a fiery furnace. The two cities, always opposite in essence, should thus be finally divided in existence, each bearing its natural fruits and manifesting its true nature. (George Santayana. *The Life of Reason, or The Phases of Human Progress.* Vol. 3: *Reason in Religion.* New York, Charles Scribner's Sons, 1930, from the chapter on "The Christian Epic," pp. 92–97.)

The Medieval Literary Mode

Relating to this Christian context, there developed a whole body of tropes and metaphors in the philosophical, theological and exegetical literature of the Middle Ages. This figurative language enjoyed a tradition going back several centuries to St. Augustine and even before. The same metaphors were part of Dante's own "vocabulary" employed in the *Comedy*. For example, the opening figure of a dark wood needed no translation for his contemporary reader, who would recognize it immediately for a state of sin. The sun's rays illumining the top of the mount as a sign of God's light would also have spoken directly to him. The figure of the circle employed so frequently by the poet in the *Paradiso* was a symbol of divinity of very long tradition. To cite the most obvious example, the journey itself, on which the narrative of Dante's *Comedy* is cast, was a common metaphor among the theologians. St. Bonaventure (1221–1274), for instance, gave to one of his works the title, *Itinerarium mentis ad Deum,* or "Journey of the Mind to God."

Dante's own opening verse in which he speaks of "the journey of our life" is fraught with meaning, reflecting the view of earthly life itself as a pilgrimage. Centuries before, in his *De doctrina christiana,* St. Augustine had employed the journey metaphor to define the condition of man according to the medieval Christian world-view — life as a pilgrimage to a higher goal:

Chap. 3. Some things are for use, some for enjoyment.

... if we set ourselves to enjoy those [things] which we ought to use, [we] are hindered in our course, and sometimes even led away from it; so that, getting entangled in the love of lower gratifications, we lag behind in, or even altogether turn back from, the pursuit of the real and proper objects of enjoyment.

Chap. 4. Difference of use and enjoyment.

For to enjoy a thing is to rest with satisfaction in it for its own sake. To use, on the other hand, is to employ whatever means are at one's disposal to obtain what one desires, if it is a proper object of desire; for an unlawful use ought rather to be called an abuse. Suppose, then, we were wanderers in a strange country, and could not live happily away from our fatherland, and that we felt wretched in our wandering, and wishing to put an end to our misery, determined to return home. We find, however, that we must make use of some mode of conveyance, either by land or water, in order to reach that fatherland where our enjoyment is to commence. But the beauty of the country through which we pass, and the very pleasure of the motion, charm our hearts, and turning these things which we ought to use into objects of enjoyment, we become unwilling to hasten the end of our journey; and becoming engrossed in a factitious delight, our thoughts are diverted from that home whose delights would make us truly happy. Such is a picture of our condition in this life of mortality. We have wandered far from God; and if we wish to return to our Father's home, this world must be used, not enjoyed, so that the invisible things of God may be clearly seen, being understood by the things that are made (Rom. 1:20) — that is, that by means of what is material and temporary we may lay hold upon that which is spiritual and eternal. (St. Augustine, *On Christian Doctrine,* Bk. I. See BIBLIOGRAPHY.)

The Medieval Universe

There is another area in which we modern readers of a medieval work such as Dante's must exercise our historical imagination together with suspension of disbelief, and that is, in the area of medieval cosmography. So different is our own view of the universe, in accordance with the findings and theories of modern science, that it is easy for us to look pridefully down upon medieval "science" as simple,

primitive, superstitious. It takes but an additional joggle of our historical imagination (which, incidentally, is a fairly recent faculty acquired
by man) to foresee perhaps a future generation of men that, in a similar
attitude, will look back on our science as myth. The fact remains that
medieval science, based on deductive reasoning from a set of axio-
matic "first principles," was actually highly rational and expertly
worked out. The trouble is, logical reasoning without hard facts based
on observation can be misleading. Within its own rational system,
however, medieval science, particularly astronomy, was perfectly valid
and consistent.

Astronomical observation, moreover, was also based on "common sense," which tells us that the sun does rise in the morning and
travels in an arc across the sky over the earth, which seems to stand
stationary at the center of the solar revolutions. This former view sur-
vives in our language, which still speaks of the rising and setting of the
sun and moon. We have to do here with Ptolemaic astronomy. According to this system, the universe is geocentric, that is, the earth is considered to be at the center, while the planets revolve about it, even as
we can observe that they apparently do.

Medieval science and philosophy, whether Byzantine, Arab,
Judaic, or Latin Christian, was based on the large mass of thought and
folklore handed down by the last centuries of classical antiquity from
ancient Greece. Science and philosophy, it must be remembered, were
still essentially one, not differentiated as they have become in more
recent times, beginning with the Renaissance. Because of the Neo-
Platonic core of medieval thought, it was possible to move easily from
the material world to the spiritual. Physics and metaphysics were not
far apart. In fact, they blended together harmoniously in both ancient
and medieval cosmology. The archetypal example of the relation of the
physical and the spiritual in Christian times was of course Christ, who
in His dual nature combines the human and the divine. This duality
obtained throughout the medieval cosmos.

According to medieval cosmology, at the center of the universe
as created by God (Genesis 1) is the world, or the planet of the creature
which He made in His image, man, who now lives out the drama of
salvation on it. (Most scholars, incidentally, considered the earth to be
round, contrary to the strictly popular notion that it was flat.) About the
earth rotate nine concentric spheres of imponderable crystalline sub-

stance called aether. Imbedded in and carried by each of these spheres are, in ascending order, the heavenly bodies Moon, Mercury, Venus, Sun, Mars, Jupiter, Saturn, Fixed Stars (or Constellations), respectively, with a ninth sphere, the Primum Mobile, containing no heavenly body as such, but characterized by pure motion. The Primum Mobile takes its primal motion from God and in turn imparts motion to all the spheres below. The nine spheres are in the custody of a hierarchy of spiritual intelligences, or Angels, respectively. Beyond this whole physical universe is the realm of pure spirit and perfect tranquillity, the Empyrean, where the angelic hierarchy has its true place around God, along with the blessed of Paradise. The combined influence of the angelic intelligences over the spheres is what constitutes the force called Nature in the sub-lunar world of generation and corruption. Standing between the realm of brute matter and the Angels and combining both matter and spirit, something in the manner of Christ, is man with his immortal soul. The spheres circle above, beckoning to man with their manifest reflection of the Creator's hand, if man will but contemplate them. This, in sum, is the stage on which man lives out his life's pilgrimage and acts out the drama of salvation, as outlined in the previously quoted passages from Santayana and St. Augustine.

The Medieval Symbolism

Even in the natural world of earth itself, there are everywhere vestiges of the Lord's creative hand, so many signs in things and events pointing beyond themselves to spiritual meanings. They are there for the contemplative eye to read for man's edification. Along with the principles of order, harmony, and hierarchy of God's creation, and along with the signs and events to be interpreted symbolically and allegorically in man's immediate natural world, there went a whole number mystique. The number one, of course, stands for the unity of all things in God's scheme and for the unity of the three persons of the Trinity in the Godhead. The number two, among other things, represents the duality of the cosmos, the material and the spiritual; the two natures of Christ, the divine and the human; the two covenants, the Old and the New Testaments; and the general principle of antithesis, or opposites. Three, a particularly mystical number, represents the Trinity of the Father, the Son, and the Holy Spirit; also, the three theological virtues, Faith, Hope, and Charity, or Love. Four is the earthly number par excellence, representing as it does the four elements, the four winds, the four cardinal directions, and the four humors in man, but it also recalls the biblical four corners of the world, the four Evangelists (Matthew, Mark, Luke, and John), the four cardinal virtues (Prudence, Temperance, Fortitude, and Justice), and so on. Five recalls the wounds of Christ received on the cross.

Skipping a bit, we may cite the number seven, standing for the seven days of God's act of creation, according to Genesis. Nine is, for one thing, the number of miracles, since such events involve the direct action of the Trinity as factor of itself. Ten is considered the perfect number, and one hundred even more exalted, having as its root the perfect number ten as factor of itself. Twelve of course suggests the Twelve Apostles of Christian history and twenty-four, the books of the Old Testament as counted in the Middle Ages.

This is only a partial account of the various significances attaching to numbers in the world of Dante. There is also the symbolism associated with various colors. For example, in medieval art, the colors of white, green, and red stand for the theological virtues of Faith, Hope, and Charity, respectively. Gold (or the blue of the heavens) is commonly found as the background of religious paintings to signify eternity. This brief discussion of number and color significances will suffice to alert the reader to some of the related symbolism to be found in the *Divine Comedy*.

The Medieval Synthesis: Dante's *Comedy*

In this connection, a word must be said about the structure of Dante's poem. The poet was, as we said, concerned with total vision, including both the human and the divine, the material and the spiritual. Even as the universe was ultimately and essentially God-centered, spiritually speaking, so did he conceive his poem in the same way. The perspective is unmistakably God-oriented. This is obviously reflected in the cosmological structure, but it is also reflected in the very metrical form of the poem. (See CRITICAL ANALYSIS, "Some Matters of Style.")

As for the question of subject and meaning, or intent, of Dante's poem, it has often been repeated of late that the *Divine Comedy* can be read on several levels. This is true. But it does not follow that we may be satisfied to choose any one level and settle for it alone. For it would be tantamount to a betrayal of the poet to read the *Comedy,* for example, simply as an interesting adventure story, as one scholar has seriously proposed! Of equal distortion would be a reading at the purely doctrinal or exclusively moral levels. Dante's *Comedy* is first and foremost a poem, a work of art, albeit a work of art patently concerned with complete vision, as we have said before. It behooves us, therefore, to seek to recapture Dante's masterpiece on his own terms, that is, completely, or as completely as possible. Here we may be properly reminded of F. O. Matthiessen's injunction to the literary critic to approach the work of art with a complete mind, not just a part of it. This is good advice, as we seek to read the *Comedy* on all levels, or try to, since it may take successive readings, each richer than the last, until the complete vision comes through to us polysemously.

What was Dante's own view of the work he created? This is found in a fairly complete statement in his Latin epistle dedicating the *Paradiso* to Can Grande. The key passages for us are the following:

> ... the sense of this work is not simple, but on the contrary it may be called polysemous, that is to say, "of more senses than one"; for it is one sense which we get through the letter, and another which we get through the thing the letter signifies; and the first is called literal, but the second allegorical or mystic. And this mode of treatment, for its better manifestation, may be considered in this verse: "When Israel came out of Egypt, and the house of Jacob from a people of strange speech, Judaea became his sanctification, Israel his power." For if we inspect the letter alone the departure of the children of Israel from Egypt in the time of Moses is presented to us; if the allegory, our redemption wrought by Christ; if the moral sense, the conversion of the soul from the grief and misery of sin to the state of grace is presented to us; if the anagogical, the departure of the holy soul from the slavery of this corruption to the liberty of eternal glory is presented to us. And although these mystic senses have each their special denominations, they may all in general be called allegorical, since they differ from the literal and historical.

When we understand this we see clearly that the *subject* round which the alternative senses play must be twofold. And we must therefore consider the subject of the work as literally understood, and then its subject as allegorically intended. The subject of the whole work, then, taken in the literal sense only, is "the state of souls after death," without qualification, for the whole progress of the work hinges on it and about it. Whereas if the work be taken allegorically the subject is "man, as by good or ill deserts, in the exercise of the freedom of his will, he becomes liable to rewarding or punishing justice." (P. H. Wicksteed, trans. Temple Classics.)

In this passage we have outlined for us the four-fold method of exegesis common in the Middle Ages, particularly among the theologians: the literal or historical, the allegorical, the moral or tropological, and the anagogical or spiritual. Dante seems to settle, of course, for the literal and the allegorical, the latter term being simply defined in terms of an "other" or different sense. It is interesting that Dante stresses the importance of the first, or literal, sense, since the whole work depends on it.

This same letter to Can Grande contains two more points related to our purpose here. Dante himself entitled his poem *Comedia* ("Comedy"); it was a Renaissance editor who embellished it with the adjective "divine" and modernized the spelling to *Divina commedia*. The title "Comedy," the poet explains in the letter, is based on the fact that, with respect to its content, the poem begins with evil and horror of Hell and ends in goodness and joy of Paradise. Also, with respect to language and style, it is lowly and humble. What is more, it is written in the common tongue, or vernacular (Italian), as opposed to the more dignified Latin, traditionally reserved for serious writing.

Finally, the poet states, in this same letter, the end or purpose of his poem. Though it may be considered manifold, he says, it may be summed up briefly "that the end of the whole and of the part is to remove those living in this life from the state of misery and lead them to the state of felicity." Thus, even as Dante's *Comedy* is a poetic work of art, and it should be read as such, it bears with it, like most great works of art, a powerful didactic dimension. Dante, to say the least, was imbued with a profound sense of mission.

Important Note

In the following section of summaries/commentaries, we confess to having violated Dante's artistic strategy of withholding certain items of information in order for these to emerge along the way of his intended unfolding form of the poem. For example, we are not told the supposed date of the wayfarer's journey until well into the poem, in Canto XXI of the *Inferno*. Unfortunately, annotated editions and translations of the *Divine Comedy* invariably state these things prematurely from page one! With the cat already out of the bag, so to say, we have had little choice but — reluctantly — to do the same. In this awareness, we hope that the reader's appreciation of the poet's strategy of unfolding form may not be unduly diminished.

In reading this most Christian of artistic masterpieces we urge the non-believer, for example, to exercise the usual "suspension of disbelief" demanded of any work of art. It is the only way to be rewarded with the full aesthetic experience, and more, that the work of art has to offer.

Incipit Comedia Dantis Alagherii florentini natione, non moribus

(Here begins the Comedy of Dante Alighieri, a Florentine by birth, but not by character)*

CAPSULE SUMMARY

Inferno I: The *Prelude*   CANTO I OF THE *Inferno* may be compared to a prelude in every sense of the term. Not only does it echo all the themes of the poem, but it establishes a double perspective which obtains throughout the journey. By speaking of *our* life in the very first verse, the poet invites our participation. By alluding to "my weary body," he reminds us that he, as *a living individual,* is the protagonist. From this point on, the reader senses that whenever the poet uses the first person singular he could be referring either to himself as a specific individual or to himself as typical of Everyman.

Furthermore, as we behold the scene of the first canto, we have difficulty imagining an actual geographic location in which it is taking place. There is something terribly unreal about the "dark forest," the *hill* (or mountain) topped by the sun, and the mysterious *valley* — especially when the poet speaks of "the pass which no one before had ever left alive." The sudden appearance of the three beasts and of Virgil add to this sense of mystery.

The entire opening scene is but a figurative prototype of the human condition at the moment of one's achieving a positive identity. Although the experience could be analyzed in psychological terms, the nature of the poem demands that it be done in Christian terms. But first it is essential that the reader suspend disbelief. He must try to *understand* Dante's doctrinal position, not *question* it. What we have in this

---

* Thus does Dante present his poem in Latin, the literary language normally reserved for all serious works in the Middle Ages, even as he composed the poem in the vernacular, Italian, for the common reader. The present expanded title of the poem in modern Italian, *Divina commedia*, stems from the addition of the adjective, "divine," by a Venetian editor in 1555.

first canto is the moment of initial conversion when a soul freely turns away from sin or evil and toward the good. Having once recognized the good (the sun's light on the summit of the mountain), the soul desires to reach it directly. But it is not that simple. Certain impediments must first be removed (the three beasts or what they symbolize). No individual is capable of achieving this alone. He must first be endowed with the grace which affords him the insight necessary to turn to his reason for proper guidance (the entire movement from Mary through Beatrice to Virgil). With enlightened reason as its guide, the soul longing for the good must first undertake to learn what the good is *not,* and why it is so easy to pursue false images of the good. It is for all this that Virgil as reason must presumably lead Dante down before he can go up. He must first thoroughly understand the nature of sin, or evil, before he can ascend to the good at the top of the mountain.

Inferno II–IV: The Entrance   The reader must take careful note of the tone of Canto II in which Dante's journey actually begins. It is dusk, the time when all living creatures normally retire. Dante alone is preparing for an arduous task. The solitude of the moment, the humility of the wayfarer, the allusions to Aeneas and St. Paul, and, finally, Virgil's response to Dante's hesitation, all contribute to the sense of cosmic significance implicit in the episode. The description of the powers that had motivated Virgil's appearance was easily recognized by a reader of Dante's day as a portrayal of the Christian concept of divine grace without which no soul can achieve salvation. Although Dante had descended to depths of sin which were akin to death itself, divine grace had come to his assistance. One must also note that the entire movement is one of love. Beatrice's words "Love moved me and makes me speak," mark the moment of fusion between Beatrice, Dante's beloved, and Beatrice, symbol of Revelation.

The mysterious words inscribed over the gate of Hell must also be seen within the context of doctrinal interpretation. They proclaim the perfection of Divine Justice which cannot ultimately recognize "those who have lost the good of the intellect." If intellect is what distinguishes man from other creatures, those who have refused to use it properly while alive cannot expect mercy after death. This is why Beatrice herself is fearless and unmoved by the dreadful spectacle of Hell.

On the other hand, man cannot play it safe or remain neutral. He must truly live by getting involved in things, and not merely exist. Those who refuse to do so have really lost all their humanness. They belong in a category apart, outside the general scheme of things. They are worth less than sinners. They are truly insignificant. All this is reflected in Dante's contemptuous attitude towards the category of souls first encountered, in the ante-Hell, or vestibule, this side of the Acheron.

Contrariwise, Dante's Limbo (Canto IV) reflects a profound human pathos. It is here the poet feels compelled to place the great men of antiquity. These had indeed not shunned involvement, but rather had died while still under the stain of original sin. Except for the Hebrews, the ancients had been incapable of believing in the coming of Christ. Their intellect and virtue, however, won them a place at the very top of Hell. This is an example of the kind of moment where the reader must suspend disbelief. A basic tenet of Christianity is faith in Christ. Without it no one can achieve salvation. By placing ancient greats in his Limbo, Dante succeeds in producing moments of deeply felt pathos.

Inferno V–IX: Upper Hell

From Canto V to Canto IX we follow Dante through Upper Hell in which are punished sins of incontinence. Especially noteworthy is how the punishments befit the sins. These sinners freely chose to pursue excess in material things, although aware of the dangers involved. It is fitting, therefore, that the very excesses they enjoyed most while alive now constitute the basis of their punishments in eternity. "Wherewith a man sinneth, by the same also shall he be punished" (Wisdom 11:16).

Inferno X–XXXIII: Lower Hell

The sins of Lower Hell are directed against justice, and are due to some form of malice stemming, ordinarily, from envy and pride. Unlike sins of incontinence, sins of malice are generally directed outwardly, against someone or something. They are therefore much more serious. In fact, as the degree of malice increases, the human identity of the sinners encountered by Dante becomes more blurred. Not only do they appear in increasingly mutilated condition, but they become more and more identified with dirt or matter in which they tend to be immersed. The symbolism reflects primarily the increasing absence of any recognizable form of love with its inherent warmth, until it disappears completely in the bottommost pit where the souls are embedded in ice. The use of mythological monsters as guardians and images of the principal categories of sin is likewise an indication of the distortions to which sinners are subject.

Inferno XXXIV: Hell Personified

The ultimate distortion is, of course, seen in the figure of Satan. He is stuck fast in the dead center of the world of matter on which all the inert weight of the universe thrusts. In addition, his triune nature epitomizes the Ultimate Negative just as the Trinity epitomizes the Ultimate Positive. Most importantly, the fact that Satan's six wings are responsible for the cold winds that produce the ice in which he is thereby self-imprisoned signifies the self-perpetuating condition of sin.

When finally Virgil assists Dante in making a complete turn at Satan's waist, which marks the exact center of the Universe in Dante's cosmology, we sense the full import of Dante's journey thus far. Not only has he examined the nature of sin as closely as possible under the guidance of reason, but his reason now helps him turn away from sin and see it as it really is — a perversion. The sight of Satan stuck upside down in brute matter reminds us that all of Hell is like that. In short, the implication is clear that man must be a fool indeed to surrender to sin.

Purgatorio I–VIII: The Ante-Purgatory

Dante's second realm, unlike the Inferno, has no negative characteristics. Rather than a void extending to the center of the earth, it is a fairly steep mountain isle in the midst of an ocean located in the southern hemisphere of the earth. Now echoes of things seen and heard rush back to mind as we join Dante and Virgil in this portion of the journey.

The mountain and the rising sun remind us of the opening scene of the poem. The waters bring back memories of the shipwrecked seafarer of *Inferno* I and of Ulysses' ill-fated journey in *Inferno* XXVI. Easter morn sets the tone of hope just as did Good Friday in the opening moments. The four stars "never seen except by the first people" stand in sharp contrast to the three beasts of the opening canto. The sudden appearance of Cato parallels the arrival of Virgil back there. The casual reference to Beatrice produces a similar echo. Finally, the washing of Dante's face at the foot of the mountain and the symbolic act of girding him with a humble plant recall Dante's condition when he emerged from the dark forest and felt unworthy of the journey which only Aeneas and St. Paul had previously undertaken while still alive.

The bright colors and brilliant light of the rising sun contrast sharply with the darkness that had dominated the Inferno. Similarly, the angelic boatman recalls Charon by contrast. The singing souls are the antithesis of the cursing souls that piled into Charon's boat.

In short, we seem to be once again back in the opening scene of the poem, but this time there are no beasts to cope with. There is no need to turn back. Instead, there is need of encouragement and even goading to go forward. The most serious obstacle to progress is the human disposition to dally. The agreeable trance created by Casella's lovely song is quickly dispelled by the booming voice of Cato who reminds the souls that absolutely nothing, not even a supreme moment of art, must interfere with their duty to cleanse themselves in the ascent up the mountain. Progress is the effective motif of Purgatory.

As with the Inferno, Dante's Purgatory too has a kind of vestibule or ante-Purgatory which contains souls who do not fit clearly into the general scheme. Here Dante daringly includes the souls of the excommunicated who were victims of human judgment but who had managed to make their peace with God by the final moment of their lives. Together with the negligent they must wait an allotted time before beginning their ascent.

Purgatorio IX–XV: The Pilgrim in Purgatory

In Canto IX, Dante enters Purgatory proper. His mysterious flight to the gate of Purgatory in Canto IX is fraught with overtones of mythic and psychic insights. The symbolic entrance through the portals is similarly steeped in Christian doctrine. Once again suspension of disbelief on the part of the reader is essential. This portion of Dante's journey must be viewed as a new beginning for the soul that has put away its pride and is willing to communicate with its Creator. The system of *goads* and *checks* introduced by the poet on each ledge of the mountain are vivid representations of what might be called "God-talk." The messages contained therein could not be clearer. If happiness and peace are man's ultimate goal, the infallible path that leads thereto has been clearly set forth in the "official records" of

Scripture. Unless mankind is willing to examine and learn from such records without prejudice, it cannot hope for real progress.

The journey through Purgatory proper is superficially not unlike the journey through Hell, but the difference in orientation, spirit, and atmosphere is absolute. In contrast to the damned of Hell, these souls all repented before death and thus bear the stain of vices rather than sins. However, even these vices, which represent dispositions to sin, must be cleansed in order for them to complete the journey. So we find the souls of this realm undergoing torments rather than punishments. Each torment represents a particular form of discipline necessary to expiate one of the seven capital vices. *Goads* and *checks* abound to help the souls realize what is to be shunned and what is to be pursued. Everywhere may be seen similar evidence of God's helping hand available to the willing soul. As Dante obtains the necessary insight into each vice, one of the seven P's (for the Latin "peccata" — sins) symbolically inscribed on his forehead by the guardian angel of the gate is removed. Each time this happens he feels lighter, as if a weight has been lifted from his shoulders.

Purgatorio XVI–XVIII: The Center of the Poem

The most important single lesson takes place in the exact center of the poem. In Cantos XVI–XVIII, Dante learns from Virgil that the cosmic force which determines all things is love. The fate of every soul depends on how and where it directs this mysterious force from within and on its capacity to receive its influence from without. Love is indeed responsible for evil as well as good. Both Hell itself and the classification of vices in Purgatory depend upon the manner in which man freely chooses to make use of this God-given force.

Purgatorio XIX–XXXIII: The Final Purification

Having once fully grasped all the implications of this crucial lesson under the guidance of reason, Dante enters, as it were, the world of the purely positive. The inherent rottenness of the tempting siren of the wayfarer's dream in Canto XIX, who personifies sins of the flesh, is readily exposed. By contrast, the poet, Statius, who appears in Canto XXI, reflects the infinite ramifications of a love which can lead even a presumably pagan poet to conversion as a full-fledged member of the Christian community.

Beginning with Canto XXVII, Dante undergoes a series of experiences signifying the recovery of innocence. His dream of Leah in Canto XXVII recalls the state of original innocence which man enjoyed before the fall. Virgil's parting words in the same canto imply the restoration of perfect freedom to Dante's now rectified will, which henceforth will turn naturally to God without the guidance of reason. The entrance into the Garden and the girlish figure of original innocence introduce the theme of joy that will mark the subsequent journey. The appearance of Beatrice, the personal confession and contrition, the immersions in the two streams, are all moments in the process of purification and restoration of order in the soul.

As for the symbolic pageant, the modern reader would gain much by viewing it as the evolution of society or mankind rather than of the Church only. For the medieval mind the Church was but the organization of society as willed by God. Therefore, the pageant represents history as willed by God, as marred by man, and as the true Christian should see it. Having once grasped the essence of the human condition, and having rid himself of all memory of sin, Dante begins quite naturally to rise upward into the realm of the spirit.

Paradiso I–XXXIII: The Ultimate Metaphor

Until recently, Dante's planet-hopping journey through Paradise proved rather awkward for readers to accept. The current developments in space programs may afford a measure of support to the modern reader's imagination. Nevertheless, there still remains the problem of perspective. The entire journey through the nine heavens of Dante's last realm is best viewed as an exerted effort by the wayfaring soul to adjust its sight. From the moment his flight begins, Dante has actually entered Paradise proper, but his limited human mind must be guided upward step by step by Revelation in order to understand what he sees.

The souls encountered in the various heavens are all enjoying the beatific vision to the fullest extent of their individual capacities as determined by grace. As Dante eventually learns, they are disposed throughout the various rows of a huge amphitheater from which they contemplate God directly in eternity. The amphitheater is, of course, but a metaphor used by the poet to help us *see* a purely spiritual and divinely ordered scene. Through this device he is able to introduce the concept of "degrees of blessedness," which in turn enables him to preserve the individuality of souls to the very end. Similarly, the distances between planets signify the enormous leap that the mind must make under the guidance of Revelation in order to achieve a simple intuition of the nature of the Divinity.

For making this purely spiritual experience (which is called "transhumanizing" in Canto I) as *tangible* as possible for the reader, the poet has recourse to a variety of other artistic devices as well. Particularly noteworthy is the use of music, color, motion, light, and geometric forms to represent the ever-changing "reality" that confronts the reformed soul as it seeks to "see" the ultimate essence of the Godhead. As everything becomes increasingly ineffable, the use of metaphor increasees. Perhaps the most effective is the figure of circularity and of circular motion which will become the essential quality of the final vision.

From the very beginning of his heavenly journey, therefore, Dante is actually beholding God. In order to adjust to the overwhelming vision, the mind undergoes a series of kaleidoscopic experiences whereby it first beholds such forms as a huge cross of stars, an eagle of lights, a golden ladder, a river of light, a white rose, and an enormous amphitheater. Even as late as Canto XXX Beatrice informs Dante that these images are but "shadowy prefaces of the reality." While these are significant in themselves, his vision is not yet sufficiently exalted to see the *reality* behind such images.

This ultimate reality lies beyond reason. In order to grasp it, the intellect must understand the truths of the Christian faith as revealed through Scripture and doctrine. This really amounts to the fullest comprehension and acceptance of the three theological virtues of Faith, Hope and Charity and the four cardinal virtues of Prudence, Temperance, Fortitude and Justice. To achieve this, Beatrice, with the aid of other willing souls, leads Dante through complex discussions of such subjects as Incarnation, Predestination, Justice, Heredity, etc. When Dante finally grasps the correspondence between these spiritual truths and the human condition, he is at last able to glimpse the very essence of God. In the final, fleeting vision, achieved intuitively, Dante beholds how Love binds the human and divine in an indissoluble unity with all of Creation.

COMPREHENSIVE SUMMARY

Inferno

Canto I   IN A TERRIFYING WOOD, a man at midpoint of life's journey comes to after having lost his way. Speaking in the
first person, he would like to share his experience with us to tell of the
good that resulted from his frightful journey. He cannot recall how he
became lost, because he was burdened with sleep when he strayed from
the straight path. Reaching the foot of a lofty mount whose top is
bathed in the sun's rays, he feels his fear subside somewhat. We are
told that it is springtime and early morn. After resting briefly, he attempts to climb the mountain, but his progress is impeded successively
by a spotted leopard, a lion, and a she-wolf. The latter beast actually
crowds the wayfarer back towards the depths, where close to despair he
descries the figure of an elderly man who identifies himself as Virgil.
Our hero entreats his favorite author to assist him, whereupon he is told
another road is necessary. He is rather to be taken on a downward path
through hell, where he will behold suffering souls, then to a place
where souls suffer gladly on the way to eternal bliss, and finally he
may pass to a loftier realm where Virgil himself cannot enter. Our hero
(who will be identified as "Dante" only in *Purgatorio* XXX) is most
willing to follow Virgil on such an itinerary.

COMMENTARY: This canto serves as a formal introduction to and symbolical adumbration of the whole mysterious journey.
Its various elements, seen here only in a vague, strange half-
light, gradually come into focus and clarity of meaning; indeed, to change the image, they are echoed time and again
throughout the poem.

The full poem is composed in *terza rima,* or triple
rhyme; it is divided into three major parts, or *cantiche,* each
consisting of 33 cantos for a total of 99, in addition to the introductory canto which brings the whole to the perfect 100.
The pervasive number 3 indicates the presence of a triune God

everywhere in the poem, just as the medieval mind felt His presence everywhere in creation.

Dark and somber in tone, but with a faint glimmer of light and hope, the opening canto already begins to reflect the post-lapsarian Christian story and the drama of salvation. For example, the poet lends a prominent place as rhyme-words to *life* and *death* in the first and seventh verses. Further, while in this canto we learn that it is springtime, the poem later reveals that the journey occurs specifically at Eastertide and the action echoes much of the drama of Holy Week, beginning with the Last Supper. Still later the date is pinpointed as April of 1300, the year itself bearing numerological implications. Indeed, the moment of Creation is distinctly implied by the allusion to the position of the planets being the same as in that springtime when the universe was first created.

The very first verse invites us to participate in the action of the poem by referring to the midpoint of *our* life. We thus have the image of a wayward man who has skirted perdition and has undergone an initial conversion, thanks to Illuminating Grace from Heaven. In his struggle to emerge from the dark wood of sin, he has reached a mountain whose summit reflects the rays of the source of all light. To reach that goal, however, man must first understand his plight; he must realize the full import of having turned away from the light and what it means to return to it. In short, he must learn the full meaning of sin and its effect on human nature. The three beasts encountered are but symbols of the major categories of sin: Fraud, Violence, and Incontinence. Presumably, our wayfarer has already understood the nature of fraud and violence, inasmuch as he successfully bypasses the first two beasts. But incontinence, the all-besetting sin in the form of a she-wolf, he must yet understand and master.

To achieve this, our hero, or Man, must have help. Being a fallen creature yet inherently capable of understanding, he must turn consciously to that portion of his being which distinguishes him from animals and brute matter, namely his reason. This psychological moment is signified by the appearance of Virgil, the singer of the Roman Empire which, uniquely, gave the world a universal peace as necessary preparation for the advent of a Savior. Indeed, according to medieval belief, Virgil had "predicted" the coming of Christ. Virgil is a highly appropriate guide for the wayfarer, yet the implication is already present that, even in his primary meaning of Reason, Virgil has his limitations. He can lead Dante, by way of a basic rational process involving an initial downward path, only to a circumscribed destination. Beyond that, he must depend on an unnamed soul who will serve as guide for the last portion of the journey.

Canto II   As evening falls and the two poets are about to begin their journey, there is some hesitation as Dante inquires of Virgil whether indeed he is worthy of such an undertaking. He recalls only two cases in history of mortal men being permitted to visit the hereafter, namely, Aeneas and Saint Paul. Virgil reassures Dante at some length, explaining how and why he came to Dante's aid. He had been prompted by three heavenly ladies: Beatrice, Saint Lucy, and the Virgin Mary. Beatrice, avowedly moved by love, had approached Virgil directly, because of his well-known powers of persuasion, to request that he rescue her friend from his predicament before the she-wolf. She in turn had been urged by Saint Lucy who had apprised her of Dante's dire state first noted by the Virgin who was concerned for his welfare. Virgil thereupon berates Dante for hesitating to respond to the wishes of three such ladies. His confidence restored, Dante readily agrees to follow his guide without further ado.

COMMENTARY: The soul ready for the journey of salvation must be humble and aware. The process of consciously turning from evil to good is psychologically complex. In Christian doctrine, Divine Grace initiates the process, involving an illumination by which the soul first grasps the essential significance of Divine Mercy. Symptomatic of this initial stage of conversion is an experienced humility, born of a sense of having miraculously escaped eternal damnation and of recognizing the possibility of eternal beatitude. The inception of this process is reflected on a number of levels in Canto II.

It is the eve of Good Friday, the soul is overwhelmed
with awe at the impending journey, and the poet must appeal to
the Muses for assistance in describing the ineffable experience.
Also, two highly significant time references reflect the sweep
of human history: the great Aeneas, founder of Rome and consequently father of all the rich associations attaching thereto,
had, according to Virgil's *Aeneid,* been privileged to visit the
afterlife; Saint Paul, the chosen vessel, had undergone a comparable Christian experience. Both heroes were involved in the
establishment of the City of God on earth. Pleading humility,
Dante questions his worthiness for such a privilege. But Virgil
convincingly explains that God's love overlooks no man, that
salvation is indeed an individual matter.

Having now understood the movement from Mary, as
Divine Mercy, to Lucy, as Illuminating Grace, to Beatrice, as
Revelation for this particular man, and then to Virgil, as the
necessary Reason for controlling the will, Dante turns eagerly
and resolutely to the journey.

Canto III   Virgil escorts Dante over a steep and woody path leading to
a huge gate, mysteriously inscribed as being the entrance to
eternal grief and damnation. Again the presence of the Christian Almighty is felt in the designation of the gate's triune Creator as Divine
Power, Infinite Wisdom, and Primal Love. Virgil identifies the place as
the abode of those who lost "the good of the intellect" (sight of God).
Crossing the threshold, our pilgrim hears the wailing of countless tortured souls echoing near and far from below. Virgil explains this to be
the most horrifying zone of creation: here are those sluggardly souls
who in life shunned all commitment, were neither good nor bad, and
contributed nothing to society; and also those fallen angels who in their
cowardice took sides neither for nor against God. In Dante's estima-
tion, these are the most contemptible of creatures; indeed Virgil suggests they barely note them and pass on. However, Dante notices that
these souls eternally scurry after a whirling banner ever beyond reach.
Among them, he recognizes a late 13th-century pope. From the bites of
flies and wasps constantly plaguing them, their blood drips to the
ground where worms feed on it.

Reaching a shore, Dante and Virgil see a large group of souls eager to cross a river, and suddenly a boat appears with an old, frightful helmsman who berates the souls to prepare to cross the river of death. He yells to Dante, as one still alive, to move along, but Virgil's explanation changes his attitude. The souls embark uttering curses and imprecations. As Virgil identifies them as irrevocable sinners sinking in their evil, the terrain quakes violently with a flash of lightning and Dante falls in a faint.

COMMENTARY: The converted wayfarer now turns to the netherworld of damning evil with sharpened awareness of the presence of Divine Justice. Hungry to understand, he turns to Reason and learns that here must abide in torture, grief, and suffering those who abused the greatest gift of creation, the intellect. The first lesson to be grasped is the importance of engagement in life's drama, for without such involvement the human creature is virtually cast aside from the universe, indeed is something less than brute matter. Another basic lesson attaches to the inherent attractiveness of evil for its devotees and their actual desire to be ferried across the River of Death. The shock of such realizations is comparable to the earthquake preceding Christ's descent into Hell and virtually numbs the mind overwhelmed by deeper understanding.

Canto IV A thunder-clap wakes our poet-pilgrim, who finds himself mysteriously transported to the brink of a dark precipice from which emerge sounds of constant wailing. Again Dante hesitates to venture into this blind realm, since Virgil himself has turned pale. Virgil reassures him that his look reflects pity, not fear, as they approach the first circle of Hell, Limbo, which we soon learn is where Virgil himself is located. He explains that the souls here are not sinners as such, but happened not to receive Christian baptism or to live before Christ. Thus they languish in desire without hope. Their pathetic situation prompts Dante to ask if ever any were permitted to leave this place. Whereupon Virgil describes, from his limited understanding, the harrowing of Hell by "a Powerful One" (Christ who, after His crucifixion, descended here and freed from Limbo all worthy Old Testament figures).

Pushing on, Dante notices to one side a faint light and certain souls of great dignity and majesty. These Virgil identifies as virtuous pagans of old who had excelled in wisdom and virtue. He singles out Homer, Horace, Ovid, and other famous poets of antiquity. Their state is symbolized by a palace whose grounds the group enters through seven encircling walls, representing the four moral virtues (prudence, temperance, fortitude, justice) and three intellectual virtues (understanding, knowledge, wisdom). Inside, Virgil identifies for Dante several other virtuous pagans who had excelled in mind or body. Led beyond the castle, Dante is once again engulfed in frightful darkness and tortured cries.

COMMENTARY: Reason itself cannot help being moved as it contemplates the consequences of sin. The pilgrim heading towards salvation and undergoing "re-formation," is confronted with a basic tenet of Christian doctrine: belief in Christ is an absolute prerequisite to ultimate salvation. All ancient knowledge and wisdom prove inadequate under the Christian scheme. Without such faith in Christ, the sages of antiquity were still essentially victims of ignorance. Hence Dante placed them in the topmost zone of Hell with the unbaptized children they resemble, whose minds remained only in potential, and with whom they shared the guilt of a shortcoming beyond their control.

Dante's Limbo is a place of darkness echoing with sighs rather than shrieks, since its denizens lack God's light of knowledge and they suffer a deep longing, impossible of satisfaction. Those few who combine wisdom with virtue do enjoy a limited light with their peers in not unpleasant surroundings. But situated well within the gate, on the brink of the infernal abyss, they must nevertheless be reckoned among the irrevocably damned. The pilgrim is now ready to leave this twilight zone and to enter the realm of sin and evil proper.

Canto V   At the threshold of the second circle stands Minos converted by Dante into a hideous demon who judges each damned soul and assigns it to its designated circle according to the circlings of his tail about his body. Like Charon, Minos questions Dante's presence in the realm of the dead but accepts Virgil's explanation. The sound of anguished cries increases as Dante enters a dark and wind-lashed place, where he dimly perceives souls swept along on the blast. The souls seem to hesitate momentarily at a point marked by some strange ruins, where their outcries multiply as do their imprecations. Dante learns these are the lustful, those carnal sinners who placed sensual desire above reason.

At Dante's request, Virgil identifies several souls from the past now being whirled about in the gale, and the pilgrim feels deep pity at the sight of so many ancient personages who failed to control their amorous passion. He asks permission to talk with two who seem particularly attached to one another even as they are buffeted about. They are Paolo and Francesca whose illicit and tragic love has been made legendary by this brief scene. Queried by Dante, the poet of Love, Francesca reveals how love trapped them into a situation which led to their destruction. Her moving account causes Dante once again to fall in a swoon.

COMMENTARY: The soul now begins the downward path into the abyss of sin in an apparent descent which is psychologically in keeping with the soul's submersion in sin as it surrenders to its passions and senses. The gravity of sin is also reflected in that the circles become successively tighter as the descent continues. The use of Minos as penal arbiter of the damned implies the timeless unity of the spiritual world, for in ancient as in more recent times sin and evil have always been the same. Indeed sinfulness inherently bears its own punishment, as obviously exemplified in the stormy blast of this circle which reflects the comparable uncontrolled passion typical of the lustful.

In the episode at hand, compassion touches our poet-pilgrim who would acknowledge love as the noblest of human emotions. But the story of Paolo and Francesca underscores the inexorability of Divine Justice. Despite Francesca's undying passion, her gentleness, her modest reticence, and despite the persistence of her love even in Hell where all is hatred, she is eternally damned. She remains an adulteress who let passion rule her life, which she lost before she could repent. The sensitive soul, conscious of the potential beauty of love, cannot endure the thought that an instant of indiscriminate indulgence should lead to perdition. The poet's swoon actually helps to relieve the tension created by Francesca's account, which distills the matter to what may be called the quintessence of lust.

Canto VI   Awakening, Dante finds himself in the third circle which is marked by rain, hail, snow, slime, and general putrefaction. The guardian of this circle is the classical monster Cerberus, with three heads and filthy appearance. Its dog-like howling echoes the howls of the sinners being clawed by it. Virgil throws a handful of dirt into one of the demon's mouths to subdue its threatening gestures as the wayfarers approach. The souls themselves lie engulfed in mud and filth, a condition singularly appropriate for representing gluttony which is punished on this terrace.

The first soul encountered by Dante is a Florentine by the name of Ciacco, meaning "pig." At Dante's query concerning the ultimate outcome of the internecine strife plaguing Florence, Ciacco foretells the changing political scene of the next few years. Dante then inquires after the fate of other members of factions, and Ciacco reveals their locations in the afterlife. As Ciacco returns to his prone position in the mud, Virgil reveals that he will not rise again until the Last Judgment. This prompts Dante to inquire whether the punishments will increase or decrease upon resumption of the body on Judgment Day. Virgil explains that an increase is inevitable according to the doctrine of greater or less perfection. The soul with the body it assumes is more complete, or "perfect," than without. Consequently, the enjoyment or suffering it is undergoing will be multiplied accordingly after resumption of the body.

COMMENTARY: The wayfaring soul is now ready to face sin in all its horror. The multiform Cerberus, hideous, filthy, and barking incoherently, along with the positioning of the souls in cold slime, reflects the depth to which a soul can sink in its pursuit of evil. Like the preceding circle of lust and the following circle of avarice and prodigality, gluttony falls within the upper zone of Hell, since it involves essentially a weakness rather than a perversion of the will. The basic nature of such sins is excessive attachment to temporal things for selfish motives. Even Dante cannot help experiencing a sense of compassion for a soul like Ciacco, who had evidently been an active citizen of Florence.

In this canto, Dante introduces two developments whose importance will emerge in subsequent cantos. The first is a reference to the ability of the damned to see into the future. This is simply a device Dante employs for reasons that will become clear later. We must keep in mind that while he began the poem around 1307, Dante places his journey back in 1300. Consequently, it is possible, on the fictive journey, for souls to foresee events occurring after 1300.

The second development is the allusion to the nature of the souls themselves. Dante refers to his walking over the empty shades* which look like real people. We shall find throughout the journey in Hell that the souls, while weightless, are not only visible and audible, but tangible as well. Both devices are used by Dante for artistic purposes.

Finally, there is the point of doctrine at the end of the canto which is also important for the wayfarer trying to understand the consequences of evil. The horrible punishments the shades undergo in Hell will increase manyfold when they regain their bodies on Judgment Day.

Canto VII   The fourth circle contains both misers and spendthrifts, or, generally speaking, those excessively concerned with worldly goods to the point of distorting their own nature. Again the sin is symbolized by a classical monster, Plutus, whose inflated and puffy nature, prone to collapse when thwarted, is an apt symbol of wealth. Its unintelligible clucking sounds which seem to resemble human words likewise contribute to the disfiguring qualities of avarice and prodigality. When Plutus retreats at the words of Virgil, Dante sees souls in greater number than in any other circle.

Their punishment is to roll terribly heavy weights with their chests, as in rite-like fashion they wend their way around the circle in

---

* "shade" is used to signify a bodyless soul with the same outward form it had in life.

two discrete groups which meet at a certain point and yell imprecations at one another, before turning about and laboriously working their way to the opposite side, where the encounter is repeated. Their loud outcries at each encounter resemble a "bark" which says "why hoard" and "why squander?" Many of the misers are clearly clerics, with whom Dante especially associated this sin. Virgil comments that it is impossible to discern any particular souls here since their personal identity has been completely submerged in their vice.

Following a discussion of Lady Fortune's guardianship of earthly possessions, Virgil urges Dante to follow him down to the next terrace, since they must not linger. As they cut across the circle they come upon a body of boiling water that pours over a cliff into the abyss below through a gulley. The filthy water forms part of the classical River Styx, which here spills into a marsh where Dante sees mired souls beating one another with great violence. Virgil reveals that these are the wrathful who sink further into the marsh according to the degree of their own besetting wrath. As the two wayfarers circle the bubbling pool, they unexpectedly come in sight of a tower visible in the distance.

COMMENTARY: The image of the depths to which a soul sinks in pursuit of evil continues in this canto, as we observe the souls "putting their hearts" into the rolling of huge weights. This most serious form of incontinence disfigures the soul beyond recognition. The futile activity here, which will continue eternally, likewise fittingly represents the endless and useless efforts of humanity to transfer worldly possessions. Interestingly, Dante exhibits none of the gentleness or consideration he did among the lustful and even the gluttonous. The Italian verses themselves bristle with harsh, derisive terms.

Once again we receive important information that must be marked for future reference. On the transfer of worldly possessions, Dante has Virgil explain that Fortune serves this function as a special minister of God. She is like an angel of earth whose mission is to shift prosperity at random, insuring that it not remain too long with any one person, family, or nation. Dante's inability to address any shade in this circle indicates the extent to which avarice or prodigality may destroy the person.

The subsequent scene of souls mired at various levels in a swamp and venting their rage on one another is a fitting representation of wrath, which belongs to the second major division of Hell, that of Violence. The degrees of wrath are reflected in the levels occupied by the souls within the marsh. So do the sinful continue their willful descent into brute matter which they increasingly resemble, according to the gravity of their sin.

Canto VIII   Observing the tower, our two wayfarers see two flashes of light to which two others appear to respond from another point in the darkened horizon. As Dante inquires about the mysterious signals, he notices a boat coming swiftly toward them. The helmsman, and guardian of the fifth circle, is the wrathful Phlegyas of antiquity whose rage against Apollo led to his death at the hands of the god. His assumption that Dante is a damned soul is quickly corrected by Virgil who indicates that he is simply to ferry them across the swamp. During the crossing, a soul attempts to come alongside the boat to speak to Dante. He is sternly repulsed and rebuked by Dante who expresses a desire to see him undergo even greater torment. The desire is satisfied as a number of souls pounce upon the offender, identifying him as Filippo Argenti.

Following this scene, Virgil informs Dante that they are approaching the battlements of the City of Dis, or Lower Hell, ruled over by Satan and his minions. Disembarking, Dante notices upon the battlements countless demons who are disturbed by Dante's presence and agree to speak only to Virgil. Dante's fear at being left alone is somewhat overcome by Virgil's comforting words. There follows a surprising scene in which Virgil is refused admission and the gates are closed in his face. He returns to Dante irritated and upset.

COMMENTARY: The erring soul in its attempt to probe the hidden recesses of human wickedness, is now ready to understand the further extent to which human nature can sink to inhuman depths. Whereas the avaricious and prodigal had their hearts and minds set upon the possession of what is essentially matter, the wrathful are now actually sunk in matter in the form of a swamp. Dante's display of righteous indignation aroused by the sight of such wickedness, apparently approved by Virgil, is an indication of the revulsion a human being should feel at the sight of sinful rage.

The moment has now arrived for the soul to probe sin even more deeply. The vast battlements encircling the City of Dis, or Lower Hell, enclose the sinners guilty not of simple incontinence of desire or temper, but of permanent evil disposition classified under Bestiality and Malice. The relevant sins result from basic pride and envy, the worst dispositions. The demons' refusal to admit the wayfarers marks a moment where further advance seems impossible to the horrified searcher. Reason itself seems to be non-plussed and incapable of affording help. The only hope is for heavenly assistance.

Canto IX   Dante's terror increases at the sight of Virgil's disturbance over this unexpected turn of events. To a discreet question whether ever before a soul from Limbo had traveled to the depths of Hell, Virgil responds, reassuringly, that he had taken the trip and thus knows the way. He informs Dante that the only means of gaining access to the City of Dis without divine assistance is by rage and violence.

At this moment Dante observes on the walls of the city three Furies plotting how best to ensnare the visitors. They suggest calling on the Medusa to turn Dante into stone, whereupon Virgil hastens to make Dante turn his back to the walls. As he does so, Dante hears what appears to be a powerful blast approaching over the dark mire. At Virgil's bidding, he strains his sight to behold coming swiftly over the Stygian waters a heavenly messenger who proceeds directly to the gates of Dis and with a touch of his small wand forces them open. Pausing only to rebuke the guardians of the wall for thinking they could obstruct that which is ordained by heaven, he disappears without a word to our wayfarers, who in turn hasten through the gate.

Once inside, Dante notices sepulchers as far as his eye can see. And in each grave he further notes hot flames. Since all are uncovered, the tortured cries of the occupants echo forth with bloodcurdling effect. Here, Virgil informs Dante, are buried the heretics of all times. Each tomb holds heretics of similar kind and burns with a flame whose intensity depends on the degree of heresy involved.

COMMENTARY: The soul seriously begins to despair of Reason as a safe guide. Close questioning, however, reassures Dante that Virgil has indeed probed every depth of sin to the bottom of Hell. Dante realizes the nature of the obstacle involved when the Furies appear on the ramparts, threatening to overcome him with a madness which would preclude his return to earth. Reason saves him from this fate by having him turn his back on such madness and face in the opposite direction, whence assistance quickly comes in the form of an angel bearing Divine Grace. The ease with which the heavenly agent proceeds to the walls reflects the actual power of that Grace. The only passing impediment seems to be the murky atmosphere symbolizing ignorance and spiritual blindness.

Inside the walls, the arch-heretics and their followers who had willfully defied the Creator now exist in a kind of living death: they suffer eternal burial for having denied future life. Because their sin is essentially one of outright pride rather than weakness, they fall within the City of Dis. Their location above the first great precipice that divides the Upper from the Lower Hell bespeaks the fact that heresy belongs to the speculative intellect and hence is not a sin of the lower appetite nor of the will.

Canto X   As Dante questions Virgil regarding the occupants of the graves in this sixth circle, a voice dramatically booms from one of them requesting that Dante linger a moment since the shade has recognized him to be Florentine. The solemn and majestic words are those of Farinata, a leader of the Florentine Ghibellines who had been responsible for saving Florence from destruction following a famous battle against the Guelphs. The haughty spirit, who seems to be scornful of Hell itself, inquires after Dante's lineage. The ensuing exchange is rather caustic, inasmuch as Dante and his family had been Guelphs.

Suddenly there is another dramatic interruption by a second shade of much less imposing aspect than Farinata. This is Guido Cavalcanti's father, who expected his son to be with Dante since he was

Dante's intellectual equal, as well as friend and fellow poet. He quickly withdraws into his grave upon misunderstanding Dante's words which seem to imply that Guido has died a confirmed skeptic.

The dramatic dialogue continues as Farinata once again interrupts to inquire about the bitter hatred among Florentine factions. As the conversation progresses, Dante in turn asks why the souls in Hell can foretell the future, yet know nothing about the present. The answer is that this "power" is really a form of punishment. After the Last Judgment they will forever live in total blindness. Dante requests that Farinata tell Guido's father that he had misinterpreted his remark and that his son still lives. Having pointed out other famous shades, Virgil reassures Dante that only with Beatrice will he discover what his future holds.

COMMENTARY: Although all forms of heresy are presumably punished in this Circle of Hell, Dante focuses attention on epicureanism, whose free thinking philosophy that considered the comfortable life as the highest good he regarded the most dangerous. The grim irony reflected in the eternal entombment of sinners who believed that the spirit perishes with the body is especially impressive. By selecting the few examples that he uses in this canto, Dante once again indicates the inexorableness of Divine Justice, since each example is representative of the best minds of the times. Pride of intellect can indeed lead to perdition. Meanwhile, the poem's objectivity continues to be poignantly reflected in the presence here among the damned even of such worthy men as Farinata, "savior of Florence." For anyone, however secretly flawed, will be found wanting in the scales of Divine Justice.

Canto XI   Preparing to leave the circle of the heretics, Dante notes the grave of a heretic pope whose presence is revealed only by an inscription on his tomb.

As they continue their descent, the great stench prompts Virgil to slow the pace, to enable their senses to adjust. This affords him time to explain the structure of Hell to his pupil, by describing the three circles yet to come. In the seventh circle, immediately below, subdivided into three concentric rings, are those, respectively, who had been violent against a neighbor, against themselves, and against God. The lowest, remaining area of Hell, inhabited by the fraudulent, is in two parts, or circles, since fraud is of two types: fraud complex perpetrated against a person whose confidence one enjoys and fraud simple practiced against a person not thus involved. The latter encompasses sins of deceit, punished in ten concentric ditches of the eighth circle; the former, sins of treachery, in which category Satan himself is located and holds court, in the bottom-most pit, or ninth circle.

His curiosity thus far satisfied, Dante asks Virgil why wrath is not included within the walls of Dis, Satan's city. Virgil patiently reminds him of what past teachers, such as Aristotle, had to say on this. Incontinence is not so offensive to God as malice and bestiality, because the latter deliberately seek to do harm to a fellow creature. Fraud in particular is peculiar to man, who has the gift of reason, and treachery involves a breach of trust. Dante next asks why usury, included in the circle of the violent, is such a serious offense. Again Virgil refers him to Aristotle's teachings, explaining that human industry is but a reflection of divine industry. Since usury is an unnatural use of human industry, it offends God. It now being three hours after midnight, Virgil urges they move on.

COMMENTARY: The soul on its journey to salvation is now ready to examine the worst forms of sin of which man is capable. The example of the heretical Pope who is burning in the hot fire of divine retribution and is identified only by an inscription on his tomb is an example of the degree to which man is capable of losing human identity.

The lowest area of Hell must now be faced. The unbearable stench reflects the putrefaction of the souls guilty of the sins to come. Reason now feels it best to mark time in order to prepare the soul for the impending shock. Significantly, the analysis of the sins punished in the forthcoming three circles is given in both Classical and Christian terms. The discussion also offers occasion to distinguish three general categories of sins punished in Hell and thus to show the relation of what Dante has seen and learned so far to the total picture. Dante's concern for the human condition is further evinced by the implication that what is most displeasing to the Creator is harm done to fellow creatures. By the time Virgil's disquisition is over, Dante has at least an intellectual grasp of what are the consequences of sin. There now remains the need to see these consequences in their most vivid forms.

Canto XII   On the brink of the seventh circle, Dante focuses our attention first upon a landslide along the slope and then upon the Minotaur, guardian of this circle. The nature of this classical monster, half man and half bull, as well as his blind fury and his perverted progeny, aptly typifies bestial violence. His uncontrollable rage is self-defeating and cannot block the wayfarers' passage. Consequently, the wayfarers bypass the monster with comparative ease.

Virgil anticipates Dante's question by explaining that the landslide over which they now climb down resulted from the earthquake caused by the "Powerful One" who descended here. It obviously marks the path followed by Christ Himself in the harrowing of Hell.

He then directs Dante's attention into the valley, traversed by a river of boiling blood that contains sinners guilty of violence. On the banks run Centaurs whose part-human, part-equine nature also suggests the bestial implications of violence. Their main responsibility is to keep sinners at their proper depth in the boiling blood. A short dramatic scene ensues in which the Centaurs threaten the travelers with their arrows until Virgil satisfactorily describes their mission. At this point, a Centaur is assigned to guide the wayfarers along the shore of the river. He identifies a number of shades of submerged murderers whose level of submersion is indicative of the degree of their guilt. The examples encompass both classical and contemporary figures.

COMMENTARY: As the pilgrim soul now enters the lower reaches of sin, a reminder of Divine Justice and retribution confronts it in the form of a landslide closely associated with Christ's Passion. The sins of violence punished in the seventh circle are symbolized both by the presiding monster and by his minions: in either case, they are half man and half beast. The submersion of the sinners in the river of blood is further symbolic of the nature of violence, as is the immobility of the Minotaur, stymied by his own blind rage.

As we learned in the last canto, the seventh circle is divided into three concentric rings, the first of which contains the souls guilty of violence against others. The bloody behavior of such sinners toward their fellowmen is emphasized by their location in the river of blood. Psychologically, the soul is left speechless at such a sight, hence this is one of the few cantos in which Dante does not speak. Finally, in the image of the Centaur serving briefly as guide to our wayfarers, we have an indication of how Reason at times can let sin identify itself when it is so obvious.

Canto XIII   The Centaur-guide departs and our wayfarers find themselves in a somber, strange wood presided over by ugly, filthy Harpies. As wails and laments emanate from all sides, Virgil explains that this is the second ring of the seventh circle. To help Dante pinpoint the source of the outcries, Virgil suggests he break a twig on one of the trees. Dante does so, whereupon, instead of sap, blood trickles out, like tears, from the break, as a voice from the trunk complains bitterly at the hurt. Sadly continuing its plaint, it explains that all plants in the forest were once men and so deserve some consideration. While Dante reacts with fear and wonder, Virgil assumes responsibility for the action, declaring that he had encouraged Dante to snap a twig to convince him of the incredible situation.

As requested, the shade identifies himself as Pier delle Vigne, personal confidant of Emperor Frederick of Sicily, and relates how he had taken his own life to escape the ruler's wrath. Pier vows he never broke faith with his master and requests that Dante render some comfort to his memory upon his return to the world. Our pilgrim is still so overcome that Virgil must inquire after the eventual fate of these souls. Pier explains that the soul of a suicide is immediately thrown into the seventh circle by Minos at random, there to take root and gradually form a tree or plant. The Harpies constantly pluck at them and through the breaks the constrained souls give vent to their intense pain in the form of blood and outcries. On Judgment Day they too will resume their bodies, but only to drag them here and dangle them from their branches forever.

There is a sudden sound of the hunt, which is soon followed by the rush of two shades, naked and bleeding, chased by black hounds through the forest. The ghastly chase ends as one shade turns into a bush which the hounds proceed to mangle. The voice from this bush identifies the shade as a Florentine who had squandered his possessions. Squanderers are also relegated to this circle with the suicides.

COMMENTARY: The pilgrim now learns why suicide, like murder, is a crime against God: in both cases a life is cut short before its divinely allotted term. By abusing this freedom of action to deprive himself of bodily movement, the suicide is not much different from a plant. Having forsaken their humanity, and thus violated God's eternal plan, the shades here have placed themselves outside God's law and assumed the form of wild vegetation. They will never again deserve to re-possess their bodies, even after the Last Judgment, since they did not respect them in life. The voices that issue forth with tears of blood reflect the painful injury done to the body, while the very immobility and brittleness of the shades in their present state mirror the suicide's paralysis of will. That Pier's suicide seems almost condonable renders even more poignant the inexorability of Divine Justice. Everything here, from the voracious Harpies with maidens' faces to the strange vegetation and the canto's general tone of negation, emphasizes the unnaturalness of suicide. Finally, the sudden eruption of the reckless squanderers chased by hounds reminds us that squandering of possessions, of which taking one's life is but the extreme instance, is like a mad race through life pursued by the hounds of Ruin and Death.

Canto XIV   The third ring of circle seven, flanked on one side by the frightening forest of the suicides, on the other by the gaping abyss leading to lowest Hell, consists of desert sand on which rain flakes of fire. It is covered by naked souls occupying different positions, some lying, some sitting, some running. The running shades are the most numerous, while the prostrate ones are the fewest. The constant rain of flames seems to set the sand afire, while the slapping hands create a constant din, as the shades try to extinguish the flames that plague them.

Dante's attention is attracted by a soul of gigantic proportions who seems to lie proud and scornful of the singeing flames. It is Capaneus of classical mythology who had blasphemed against Jupiter and continues haughtily to do so, defying the deity to make him cry out. Virgil angrily reminds Capaneus that his main punishment is his very rage.

As the wayfarers carefully wend their way along the boundary between the strange forest and the fiery plain, Virgil points out the torrent of boiling blood which seems to issue from the forest and traverse the desert. In the air above the river no raining flames appear. Virgil informs Dante that next to Hell's gate this river is most noteworthy: the source of the river is really a statue of an old man located on a mountain in Crete, consisting of a golden head, silver arms and torso, and copper midriff. The rest is of iron with the exception of the right foot of clay. Facing Rome, the whole statue, except for the golden portion, is rent by a crack, through which flow tears that eventually form the rivers in Hell. Learning that there are four such rivers, Dante inquires about their location and learns that the one they now view is Phlegethon. He wonders why, if all four rivers have a common source, this is the first time they should encounter Phlegethon. Virgil explains that they have not yet completed a full circumlocution on their downward path.

COMMENTARY: The sandy, barren plain where a rain of fire falls, poignantly images the denial of nature involved in the sins of this third ring of the seventh circle. The blasphemers, the sodomites, and the usurers do violence, respectively, to God, to Nature considered as God's minister, and to human industry, Nature's offspring. Neither size nor might can justify blasphemy against God, as Capaneus with his arrogant pose testifies.

The symbolic statue of Humanity located in Crete and indicated as source of the Rivers of Hell is also a highly appropriate device. Crete represents a half way station between the Old World and the New. Both Aeneas and Saint Paul had made a stop there. Until the forces represented by these two figures, the Empire and the Cross, become one, Humanity will continue to be imperfect. By facing Rome the Old Man anticipates this union in Rome. The crack in the statue focuses on the continuing schism while the tears from it forming the waters of

Hell represent the grief inherent in human nature's awareness of its own imperfections. On the other hand, the intact golden head is probably a reminder of the hopeful potentiality in man. The quenching of the rain of fire over the boiling river of blood and tears appears to signify the appeasing of God's anger by human suffering.

Canto XV   Moving away from the forest on the narrow river bank in the lee of the fiery rain, our pilgrims encounter a group of shades on the sand below, who look at them squintingly because of the dense vapor from the boiling river. One of them recognizes Dante. Despite his terribly burned appearance, he is in turn recognized by Dante as Brunetto Latini, a very dear teacher of his and a renowned intellectual. Dante volunteers to linger with him to talk awhile. But Brunetto indicates it is best to continue walking, while he follows along at Dante's feet as Dante and Virgil walk on the raised shore. Dante explains what has brought him to this point in his journey, and Brunetto predicts from his knowledge about him that Dante's salvation is practically assured, despite the many obstacles, especially political, that he must overcome.

There follows a bitter attack against Florentine politics and a lofty homage to Brunetto for having taught Dante "how man becomes eternal." Dante then proceeds to inquire after Brunetto's companions and learns that the greatest portion were men of letters and thinkers of great note whose only guilt consisted of the perverted love inherent in sodomy. The closing scene of the elderly Brunetto dashing off in a most unbecoming fashion to rejoin his companions brings the canto to an impressive close.

COMMENTARY: Focusing almost exclusively on the person of Brunetto Latini, this canto too underscores the inexorableness of Divine Wrath. That Dante must express his gratitude toward his former teacher in this fashion adds immeasurably to the artistic dimensions of the canto. Brunetto's charred countenance, his walking "at the feet" of his former student, the various indications of his breadth of learning, and Dante's confession that it was from Brunetto that he had learned an important lesson in life, all tend to emphasize the point that a single deadly fault is enough to damn an otherwise noble man. Brunetto's undignified flight at the end of the canto serves to enhance the pathos involved in the great teacher's case.

Canto XVI   As the pilgrim soul proceeds cautiously along the third ring of the seventh circle towards the edge of the abyss to Lower Hell, we note a fine example of the manner in which different portions of the poem are interlocked through a process of anticipation and/or reminiscence, so that a question or a point raised earlier is unfailingly picked up later. Back in Canto VI Dante had asked Ciacco of the whereabouts of two of their fellow Florentines "who had set their mind to doing good." Ciacco had informed him that he would meet them lower down in Hell. Some now appear to Dante among the sodomists, badly disfigured; and in their haste to avoid the searing heat of the flames by standing still too long, they indulge in a kind of round-dance which suggests a group of children at play rather than the highly dignified men of state they had been. So great is Dante's respect for them that he is tempted to join them, but the thought of the fire-rain restrains him. The conversation once again prompts Dante to apostrophize against Florence for its decadence.

The "dancing" souls suddenly depart, and Dante follows Virgil to the brink of the chasm from which rises the thunder of the bloody Phlegethon as it plunges into the abyss. Virgil asks Dante to remove the cord he wears about his waist. As he does so, Dante remarks that he had once thought of overcoming the spotted leopard with the cord. Virgil throws the cord into the abyss. In a few moments Dante beholds a vision which he says defies description: a huge shape looms into sight like a diver returning to the surface.

COMMENTARY: Dante's meeting with former Florentine companions for whom he had the highest respect because of their dedication to the public welfare emphasizes yet again the tension between human and divine judgment. An otherwise upright man is doomed to damnation for a seemingly pardonable weakness, which in the eyes of God, however, destroys the essence of human dignity. While such a doctrine may appear unacceptable to the modern mind imbued with recent medical discoveries, we must bear in mind that the basic issue for

Dante is that leaders such as those he encounters should have possessed the discipline to resist or at least repent their involvement in sodomy. The dramatic episode that ensues, with its mysterious actions and overtones, now prepares the inquiring soul for what is to come. Virgil's symbolically throwing the cord over the precipice represents Dante's stripping himself of the self-confidence which could jeopardize the soul's progress toward salvation. It is only with humility that man can properly face the further instances of divine justice pertaining to the ugliest forms of sin.

Canto XVII   Dante's sight is finally able to focus on the weird form that perched at the edge of the precipice: it is the monster which infects the entire world with its sting. "The filthy image of fraud," with the face of a just man, the body of a serpent, and tail of a scorpion, is a composite drawn from several sources dealing with the classical monster, Geryon. Here, Geryon "lands" on the shore, with its tail hovering in the void. Carefully following Virgil along the sheltered bank, Dante approaches the waiting monster, when he suddenly beholds more shades sitting on the sandy shore. Virgil encourages him to linger a moment with them while he arranges for the descent.

Dante learns that the sinners in this last ring of the seventh circle are guilty of usury. Unrecognizable because of the disfiguring downpour of flames, they each carry hanging from the neck pouches of moneybags on which are inscribed their family crests in vivid colors. One of the shades identifies himself and other companions as members of illustrious families.

Recalling Virgil's admonition against tarrying too long, Dante returns quickly to find him ready to climb on Geryon's back. The frightened Dante manages to seat himself with Virgil holding onto him tightly from behind. Virgil thereupon orders Geryon to start the descent recommending that he go slowly. The vivid description of the sensations felt by Dante during such an "air-borne" trip is most impressive. From below, burning fires and loud wailing intensify the sense of horror experienced by the pilgrim soul as it now probes more deeply into the nature of sin. After discharging its passengers deep in the abyss, Geryon vanishes.

COMMENTARY: The disfigured appearance of the squatting usurers recognizable only by their moneybags and coats of arms is appropriate. Notwithstanding their noble stock, the inordinate love of gold has consumed their individuality. That Virgil permits Dante to linger alone with the shades seems to imply Dante is now able to cope with certain forms of sin without dependence on Reason. The act of climbing directly upon Geryon's back may suggest the need for the closest possible scrutiny of sin in order to grasp it in its totality. Virgil's positioning himself between the venomous tail and Dante serves to emphasize the role of Reason in one's self-defense against fraud. The gradual helicopter-like descent emphasizes both the distance that separates the forthcoming forms of sin from the preceding ones, and the need for care in approaching and understanding the nature of the most serious forms of sin.

Canto XVIII We thus follow the wayfarers into the eighth circle which Dante calls Malebolge, "Evil Pouches." The circle is divided into ten concentric ditches, where the various types of fraud are punished. Each of the ditches slopes downward from the one before and is connected to it by a series of bridge-like strips of stone as spokes of a wheel, over which our travelers walk. Beyond the inner-most ditch, towards the center, gapes the ultimate pit of Hell, the ninth and last circle (see VISUAL AIDS, pp. 12–13).

Having disembarked from Geryon's back, Dante sees in the first ditch the betrayers of women, panders and seducers, who are naked and file ceaselessly in two opposing rows along the bottom of the ditch where devilish fiends prod them relentlessly. As the wayfarers cross over the ditch, Dante speaks to one of the shades who identifies himself as coming from Bologna. His words are cut short by one of the demons who pushes him away with his whip. From the other side of the ditch, Dante is able to see the other band of seducers who had previously been walking away from him. As the shades file by, Virgil identifies several from classical times.

The pilgrims next come to the second ditch whose stench is almost unbearable, for the shades here are immersed in human excrement.

COMMENTARY: The gross and vile language not only used by the poet
                himself but also attributed to the fraudulent encountered
        here, reflects most appropriately the nature of seducers and
        panders. Similarly, the comparison of their double march to the
        throngs of pilgrims visiting Rome during the Jubilee year af-
        fords an ironic commentary on the state of these sinners. Tor-
        menting fiends rather than guardians, the horned devils relent-
        lessly scourge them even as betrayers of women are in life
        goaded on by their mean passions.
                The filth and stench that engulf the flatterers in the
        second ditch reflect their unclean manner of life. The gross
        language used to describe their plight is equaled only by the
        vileness of the words they utter. While they are not tormented
        by fiends, they are by the filth in which they wallow, a fitting
        correlative of their unctuous words.

Canto XIX   The sin punished in the third ditch of Malebolge is simony.
                As Dante and his guide cross over one of the ledges, our
wayfarer sees the ground on either side along the ditch, as far as the
eye can reach, perforated by round holes in which shades are rammed
upside down, with only their feet and calves protruding. The sight
prompts Dante to cry out in admiration of the scope of Divine "art"
and, with ironic twist, to compare what he beholds to the multi-basined
baptismal font in the Baptistry of Florence.
        Each hole here presumably contains a specific type of simonist
who is shoved deeper into the rocky crevices of the hole as another
sinner arrives. On the soles of the protruding feet lick flames as on an
oily surface. Dante's attention is drawn to the feet and legs of a 13th-
century simoniac pope, Nicholas III, whose soles seem to be particularly scorched by the flames.
        The dramatic dialogue that ensues starts with the pope's mis-
taking Dante for his successor, Boniface VIII, whom Dante considered
also guilty of simony. Discovering that it is Dante instead, Nicholas
reveals his identity and his guilt and predicts that Boniface will be even
more guilty. This prompts a strong, though reluctant, invective by
Dante against simoniac popes, reminding them of the trust committed
to them when Christ passed on his "keys" to Peter. Dante's stinging

rebuke receives the approval of Virgil who not only embraces him but literally carries him to the next ditch.

COMMENTARY: The third ditch of the eighth circle presents to the questing soul a form of sin which once again involves the principle of perversion of a human creature to the level of inert matter. The use of ecclesiastical office for private material gain really goes beyond mere fraud. It was in Dante's time also considered an offense against the Holy Spirit. For this reason even a pontiff has his entire body immersed in matter, while the soles of his protruding feet are seared by tongues of flame representative of God's wrath. The apostrophe to Emperor Constantine, who by his unfortunate "donation" to the papacy originated the medieval claim to temporal power by the Church, suggests a modern theme which will recur time and again in the Comedy: the desirable separation of Church and State.

Canto XX   In the fourth ditch of the eighth circle Dante beholds another heart-rending sight. Countless shades march slowly, as in a religious procession, around the ditch in silence and tears. Closer scrutiny reveals that each shade has his head twisted backwards so that he blindly walks forward while staring behind. Such distortion of the human body brings tears to Dante's eyes, at which Virgil rebukes him sharply for displaying compassion here. Virgil advises the pilgrim rather to understand rationally the manner of retribution. He then proceeds to identify many soothsayers and augurs of antiquity as well as reputed sorcerers and astrologers of more recent times. The wayfarers move on to the next circle after Virgil observes that above on earth it is early morning.

COMMENTARY: In this canto spiritual perversion is portrayed by bodily distortion. The shades of the soothsayers, guilty of probing the future to deceive their naive fellows, must now eternally walk in the opposite direction from the one they face. They thus move blindly into the future, foreknowledge of which is the domain of God alone. The agony they suffer because of their wrung necks is depicted in their silent tears that flow ironically down between their buttocks. Dante's momentary weakness at the sight of such torment is chided by Reason, because the fate of the damned, as prescribed by Divine Justice, should arouse satisfaction not pity.

Canto XXI   In its wryly comical treatment of the fate of swindlers or grafters, this canto affords some relief from the grimness encountered thus far in the eighth circle. The fifth ditch presents to Dante's sight a lake of boiling pitch. His wonderment is coupled with fright at the sudden entrance of a horned demon with a shade slung over his shoulders in the fashion of a butcher carrying a carcass of meat. Dropping his prey into the boiling pitch, he dashes off for more, while his fiendish cohorts ply their sharp hooks to ensure that the newcomer, along with many others submerged in the pitch, keep beneath the surface.

A moment of horseplay ensues, as the devils menacingly surround Virgil and Dante before acceding to Virgil's request for safe passage. The leader of the band advises the wayfarers to pursue another path, since they will shortly find their present one blocked by a landslide (again, from Christ's harrowing of Hell). Dante's fear of the threatening demons is allayed by Virgil's words that their anger is directed at the sinners, not at them. Whereupon Dante obediently follows Virgil behind a band of ten demons who volunteer to show them the way.

Canto XXII   The mock-heroic theatricality of Canto XXI continues in XXII, as Dante and Virgil follow the band of demons along the edge of the boiling pitch. The fiends' gross language and gestures intensify the grim slapstick spirit of the scene. True to character, the submerged swindlers seek to foil the devils by surfacing hither and yon in the pitch and quickly disappearing when the demons approach.

One shade who fails to submerge in time is snatched up on one devil's hook. This provides Dante occasion to speak to the sinner who proves to be a nobleman from Navarre. As the demons prepare to mangle the shade, it identifies a fellow-sinner from Pisa, Friar Gomita, who happens to be the only Italian grafter known to him under the pitch. He promises, however, to bring forth others in exchange for his freedom from the demons' hooks. While the latter confer on striking a bargain with their prisoner in hopes of capturing others whom he will bring to the surface, the prisoner suddenly dives into the pitch. Despite their nimbleness, none of the fiends is able to recapture him. There ensues a grotesque squabble between two of them who finally fall into the pitch themselves and must be extracted with grappling irons by the others.

COMMENTARY: The comic relief afforded by these two cantos is rooted in the nature of the sin of swindlers or grafters, whose dirty work must be done under cover of darkness. The lake of boiling pitch in which they now wallow and from which they are not permitted to emerge, reflects the dark yet seething atmosphere in which they must operate, while the roguish demons represent evil cunningly turned upon itself. Their attempt to trap Dante and his guide, their graphically comic names (Evil Paws, Curly Bird, Dog Scratcher, etc.), their coarse language and behavior, and even the clever escape of their scheming prisoner afford an interesting commentary on the nature of the sin being punished and, more generally, on the spectacle of evil abandoned to itself.

Canto XXIII While following Virgil on the way suggested by the demons, Dante is suddenly struck by the thought that the two angry ones might give pursuit. Virgil, also aware of such a possibility, decides to carry Dante across the ravine when he hears the sound of the approaching devils. Fortunately, the demons cannot proceed beyond their own ditch and so the two wayfarers safely reach the sixth ditch, where they observe a silent throng of cloaked, weeping figures walking about extremely slowly. The cloaks remind Dante of monks' habits, but he notes that while they appear to be gold on the outside, they are of heavy lead on the inside. It is their weight which makes walking so difficult, and this is the punishment of the hypocrites who are relegated to this ditch.

As Dante asks Virgil to try to identify some of them, two come forward, eager to talk with Dante. They are recent men of great authority, both well known to Dante, who is almost prompted to pity were it not for the most unusual sight of another shade crucified to the ground by means of three stakes. He is identified by one of the speakers as Caiaphas, the high priest who favored the sacrifice of Christ. Dante also learns that the other false counselors involved in the Passion of Christ suffer a similar punishment of being trampled by the walking shades. Virgil views these hypocrites with marvel and surprise since they were not here on his first journey through Hell. Upon asking for further directions, Virgil learns that the demons of the preceding ditch had lied in saying that the embankment over which they were to cross was destroyed. Virgil appears unusually disturbed at having been deceived.

COMMENTARY: The erring soul must once again depend on Reason to avoid the clutches of uncontrolled evil with its wiles and cunning. In point of fact, Reason itself almost falls prey to such wiles, as indicated by Virgil's disturbance at having been misled by the demons of the preceding ditch. The essence of hypocrisy is depicted according to Matthew 23: 27, in which is written: "Woe unto you, scribes and Pharisees, hypocrites! for ye are like unto whited sepulchres, which indeed appear beautiful outward, but are within full of dead men's bones, and of all uncleanness." The seemingly handsome cloaks worn by the hypocrites, their deliberate pace, their exaggerated decorum, and their generally pious attitude are all in keeping with the basic nature of hypocrisy. Their very pose now weights them down eternally. The arch-hypocrite Caiaphas, as well as the other false counselors involved in the crucifixion of Christ, are themselves now crucified and bear the burden of all subsequent hypocrisy. The marvel experienced by Virgil at the sight of these arch-hypocrites indicates how such crimes are even beyond the grasp of Reason.

Canto XXIV   After finding the alternate bridge broken, Dante and his guide have difficulty in reaching the seventh ditch. The ascent up from the sixth is so arduous that Virgil must once again carry and assist Dante laboriously over the ruins, and the exhausted pilgrim must rest awhile. Finally, at Virgil's urging, he makes one last effort to reach the next embankment, and is confronted with perhaps the most horrifying spectacle in Lower Hell.

     The seventh ditch is littered with serpents of all shapes and sizes, among which run naked and terrified shades. Their hands are tied with snakes whose heads and tails penetrate their bodies and are tied in front. Suddenly one shade is pierced at the neck by a serpent and thereupon burns to ashes, only just as suddenly to be restored to a human shape, like the legendary Phoenix being reborn from its ashes. In answer to Virgil's question the shade identifies himself as Vanni Fucci of Pistoia, apparently well known to Dante who expresses surprise at not having seen him among the violent. Vanni, somewhat embarrassed, confesses that his true sin is theft from a church sacristy. He then foretells the misfortunes that will befall Florence and Dante's party in the hope that it will upset Dante who now knows the truth about him.

Canto XXV   Having ended his account, Vanni boldly blasphemes against God by directing an obscene gesture to the heavens. This prompts Dante to applaud two serpents which attack Vanni, one winding itself about his neck, the other binding his hands together. Dante directs an apostrophe against Pistoia for having given birth to such scum. As Vanni runs off, a frightening Centaur with a mane of serpents and a fire-belching dragon on his back comes looking for Vanni. Virgil identifies him as a monster of antiquity, Cacus, who was guilty of theft against Hercules and whom Dante makes a Centaur.

The canto describes further horrifying scenes beheld in this ditch of thieves: one shade is completely entwined in the grasp of an ugly serpent that clutches him so tightly that, in a horrendous metamorphosis, both snake and shade become a kind of third unidentifiable being; another shade is attacked by a small snake at its navel, with the result that the shade is slowly transfigured into a serpent and the serpent into a shade, all within a dense and mysterious smoke. The detailed descriptions of the transmutations are among the most vivid in the *Comedy*. During the episode, Dante recognizes a number of acquaintances whom he openly identifies by name.

COMMENTARY: Just as Cantos XXI and XXII afforded comic relief to the horrors of Lower Hell, so do Cantos XXIV and XXV accentuate to what extreme degree a human creature can lose identity as a result of sin. The gruesome details found in these two cantos dramatize how much a thief resembles the sly creeping serpent as he plies his trade. The dreadful implications of yielding to sin are thus forcefully brought home to the learning soul. Vanni Fucci exemplifies all that is degrading in human nature.

The sustained realism found in both cantos provides a measure of Dante's remarkable power of imagination. His lengthy descriptions of the metamorphoses in Canto XXV suggest the eye of a child naively relishing inconceivable transfigurations ordinarily associated with nightmares. The thief's possession of things not his is reflected even in the assumption of a form not his own. We are further reminded of the serpent responsible for the very first sin (Genesis 3).

Canto XXVI   This canto opens with a sharp invective against Florence full of sarcasm and bitterness, reminding the poet's beloved city that it was well represented among the thieves and predicting that the day of reckoning is near. The two travelers then climb the ridge overlooking the eighth ditch where Dante once again beholds an incredible scene: the entire hollow appears full of individual flames as far as the eye can see. Virgil explains that each flame encloses a sinner guilty of having used his mind in giving evil counsel.

Attracted by an unusually calm double-flame, Dante asks Virgil who might be enclosed therein. Virgil reveals that it is Ulysses and Diomed, two prominent heroes of the Trojan War, who are relegated to this ditch for three reasons: (1) they had instigated the treacherous overthrow of Troy by use of the Trojan horse, (2) they inveigled their comrade Achilles into breaking troth with his beloved Deidamia, and (3) they had perpetrated the theft of the famed Palladium, the image of the goddess Pallas, on which Troy's fate depended. At Dante's eager request to speak with the two shades, Virgil suggests that he do the talking since he had written about them, and they would perhaps be more responsive to him.

In answer to Virgil's questioning, Ulysses narrates a long journey he undertook after departing from the temptress Circe. In his search for knowledge and experience, he had encouraged his band of followers to probe together the unknown region beyond the pillars of Hercules (Strait of Gibraltar). In this undertaking, he completely overlooked his other responsibilities as a father, husband, and ruler. Nevertheless, he urged his men on into the unexplored waters beyond the pillars until, after five months, they sighted a dark lofty mountain. However, before they could reach the mountain a whirlwind rose which sank the ship after spinning it about three times.

COMMENTARY: This is perhaps one of the most intriguing and most
                 debated cantos of Dante's entire poem. The poet's
handling of the Ulysses theme focuses sharply on the inexorability of Divine Justice by taking the greatest of heroes and
showing how even the greatest achievement cannot com-
pensate for moments of injustice. Ulysses, like all the evil
counselors, now burns eternally for having cunningly hidden
his thought in the flaming speech with which he had given evil
counsel. This misuse of mental power runs against the will of
God Who had endowed man with such powers for doing good.
        It is easy to overlook the real reasons for Ulysses'
presence here if one comes away from the canto confusing
Ulysses' death and the reason for his perdition. While he did
meet destruction for having attempted to go too far in his quest
for knowledge, this is not why he is relegated to the eighth circle. Virgil clearly indicates the three reasons for both Ulysses
and Diomed being among the evil counselors. Yet Ulysses'
story is so pregnant with pathos (deriving in part from his ignorance of why he has been damned) that a casual reader
might conclude that Ulysses' quest for greater knowledge had
led to his perdition. In Ulysses' exhortation to his band of men
to push onward with him, we have a moment highly suggestive
of the spirit of the Renaissance that is yet to come. In the image of the mountain, with Ulysses' failure to reach it and the
threefold spin of his shipwreck, we have clear indications of
the medieval sense of divinely ordained limits.

Canto XXVII   As Ulysses ends his account, Dante notices another flame
               nearby which, in contrast to Ulysses', flickers violently
and emits a confused sound like the bellowing of an ox. Dante inter-
prets the indistinct words of the shade enclosed to mean he too would
like to talk with him, out of eagerness for news of his native Romagna.
Dante informs him that the entire region continues to be wracked by
factional dissension and then asks for the shade's identity. It is Guido
da Montefeltro, perhaps the greatest Ghibelline general of the 13th century.
        Guido recounts how in his old age, having joined the Francis-
can order to make amends for his life of violence and warfare, he was

one day summoned by Pope Boniface VIII for advice pertaining to a battle that the pope was waging at the time against an enemy faction in Rome. Since the battle had reached a stalemate, the Pope needed a stratagem for resolving it. At Guido's hesitation, the Pope absolved him in advance of any sin he might incur as a result of giving his advice. Whereupon Guido suggested that the best strategy would be to make false pledges with the enemy and thereby trap them. When Saint Francis came for Guido's soul at the moment of death, a "black Cherubim" convinced the Saint by logic that the soul belonged to Hell, not Heaven, for Guido had never truly repented for his action, hence the pope's absolution was invalid. He was thereupon delivered to Minos who assigned him to the ditch of evil counselors. As the flame ends the account, it takes its departure flickering as violently as ever.

COMMENTARY: The wild flickering of Guido's flame, as well as his bellowing speech, contrasts sharply with the calm and peaceful flame of Ulysses and Diomed. While the pagan Ulysses has no awareness of why he was damned, Guido, a Christian, does, and the knowledge of it constitutes part of his punishment. A doctrine is involved here which will emerge more clearly in Purgatory: only personal and sincere repentance before death can assure salvation. No earthly means, be it absolution by the pope himself or a religious life, can serve as substitute. By the example of a foremost Italian of the 13th century noted for his dedication to the civic welfare, Dante lends emphasis to the import of the doctrine.

Canto XXVIII   This canto, in which wayfarer and guide enter the ninth ditch which imprisons the sowers of discord, opens with an elaborate simile whereby Dante would have us envision a massing together of the countless thousands of mangled bodies from the many wars fought in southern Italy through the centuries. Such a scene of carnage now meets the poet's eyes.

Among the first he sees is Mahomet whose body is cleft straight down the middle so that all of his innards hang out in ghastly fashion. Dante and his contemporaries considered Mahomet responsible for a great schism in the Christian Church. Mahomet tells Dante that this is the fate of all the sowers of discord or creators of strife.

Inferno XXVIII. The Sowers of Discord.

Each is hacked by the sword of a demon before whom each must con-
tinually pass. As the wounds heal, they are reopened once again by the
demon each time a shade retraces his steps. They are rent asunder in
retribution for their "sundering" on earth. To Mahomet's question regarding Dante's journey Virgil replies that it is necessary in order to
provide him with "full experience."

Other mutilated shades gather around Dante and identify themselves. Among them is one Mosca who had been responsible for the
first conflict between Guelphs and Ghibellines in Florence. There is
also the Provençal poet, Bertram de Born, who had fomented quarrels
between Henry II of England and his two elder sons. His punishment
consists in carrying his severed head in his hand like a lantern. The
appropriateness of the punishment undergone by these sinners requires
no comment.

Canto XXIX   Dante appears almost inebriated as he contemplates the
             fate of the sowers of discord. He is rebuked by Virgil for
such dallying, which he weakly justifies in terms of having sought the
shade of a relative whom he expected to be in this ninth ditch. Virgil
warns him that it is about noon and they must move on. Whereupon
they enter the tenth and last ditch of Malebolge whose laments and
stench remind Dante of overcrowded hospitals in the heat of summer.
We are told that this is the ditch where infallible justice punishes falsifiers of all kinds. Graphically wracked with disfiguring disease, the
shades drag themselves about in painful silence. Dante's gaze falls on a
pair sitting back to back and covered with scabs and sores which they
scratch ceaselessly. Virgil asks the two shades whether they know of
any Italians located in this ditch. Hearing that they themselves are both
from Italy, Dante asks about them and learns they have been damned
for practicing alchemy.

Canto XXX   In this canto we learn that other kinds of falsifiers include
            impersonators, counterfeiters, and liars. The canto opens
with an extended simile in which Dante cites classic acts of madness
which pale by comparison with the far more incredible savageness of
two shades whom he sees madly chasing and biting one another in their
rage. They are identified as the recent mimic Gianni Schicchi, whose
acts of impersonation were legendary, and the classical Myrrha of Cy-

prus, who in her desire to sin with her father had impersonated someone else.

Dante then sees a huge shade completely disfigured by dropsy,
Maestro Adamo, a famed counterfeiter of Dante's day whose un-
quenchable thirst now makes him caress images of water in his speech.
The shade gives vent to one of the most powerful expressions of hatred
in the *Comedy* when he states that he would forego all water and crawl
the entire circumference of this ditch if it were possible to get his hands
on the Counts of Romena who induced him into counterfeiting.

Close by Maestro Adamo's bloated form sit two famed liars,
Sinon the Greek, who had persuaded the Trojans to accept the Trojan
horse, and Potiphar's wife, who had falsely accused Joseph (Genesis
39). Sinon suffers from such high fever that he emits an unbearable
stench. Angry at disclosure of his identity, he argues with Maestro
Adamo over the relative guilt of each. Dante becomes absorbed in the
argument and merits another reproof from Virgil for lingering over
such unworthy things.

COMMENTARY: As we continue through the eighth circle together with
                Dante, we see in the tenth ditch the human creature
mutilated rather than transformed. The sins punished here are
such that they disform a person both physically and mentally
even as he retains his former identity. As usual the retribution
reflects the nature of the sins themselves. Thus the sowers of
discord have their bodies mangled while the falsifiers have
their bodies disfigured by atrocious diseases. The implication
emerges that the sins here are far more deadly than those previously encountered.

Canto XXXI   Recovered from his embarrassment, Dante follows Virgil
               onto a plain which separates the tenth ditch of the eighth
circle from the ninth circle. Lofty shapes rising in the gloom ahead and
the sudden blast of a horn breaking the silence give Dante the impression he is approaching the walls of a city. Virgil informs him that what
appear to be towers are really giants whose upper bodies emerge here
but whose feet rest on a ledge of the pit below. Thus they seem to be
guardians of the last circle. As Dante's sight gains better focus, he is
deeply shaken by the enormous size and terrifying aspect of the giants.

He is moved to cry out that nature had done well to eliminate such
creatures from the face of the earth, while continuing to produce only
such other giants as elephants and whales.

The first giant approached by the travelers is Nimrod who had
designed the Tower of Babel and therefore caused the confusion of
tongues. Of all the giants, he speaks a language understood by no one
and can give vent to his feelings only by blowing upon a horn which
hangs from his neck. The other three giants mentioned were involved
in the classical account of the giants' attempt to scale Heaven at Phle-
gra. Of these, only Antaeus is not bound by huge chains, since he did
not participate in the actual fighting. Virgil bids Antaeus deliver them
down into the next circle. This he does in a surprisingly gentle fashion
despite his huge proportions.

COMMENTARY: In the last few cantos we observed that the sowers of
               discord and the falsifiers were punished by having their
very bodies tortured in some fashion. Here in this canto we see
the giants tortured by having their powerful bodies, as well as
their minds, rendered immobile and helpless either by being
enchained or by being implanted in the ground. The sound of
the horn reminiscent of Roland's attempt to save Charle-
magne's forces at Roncesvalle, the reference to the thunder-
bolts of Jove, the mysterious language of Nimrod, all recall
great instances of pride and treachery. Dante's outcry that nature did well to do away with such creatures is based on the
idea that the addition of enormous size and strength to an evil
will and an evil mind can only lead to greater iniquity and deg-
radation among the human species. The appropriateness of
Nimrod's language and horn as his punishment for his role in
the building of Babel emerges without difficulty. As we shall
see shortly in the case of Satan himself, the symbolism of the
giants being firmly implanted into the ground conveys a profound message.

Canto XXXII   Upon entering the ninth and last circle of Hell, Dante ap-
               peals to the Muses to help him find words adequate to
describe the incredible scene now confronting him. It is a circular lake
of ice containing shades frozen fast in it at different levels. As the

scene unfurls, we learn that the entire icescape consists of four concentric divisions: (1) Caïna, with traitors to their kindred; (2) Antenora, with traitors to country or party; (3) Tolomea, with traitors to guests; (4) Giudecca, with traitors to benefactors. All forms of treachery punished here involve murder. To match expression to his subject, the poet now fittingly employs words, rhymes, and imagery associated with extreme cold, harshness, brittleness, and pressure. The very opening verses of the canto emphasize the fact that all the weight of the Universe presses down upon this ninth circle, the ultimate pit of Hell.

In the first division of the circle, Dante notes that the shades are embedded in ice up to their faces which they hold in a lowered position. As Dante speaks to a number of shades and these identify themselves, reference is made to the fact that, because of their heinous crimes, the spirits addressed would rather not be remembered in the world. In Antenora we find two supreme examples of the "embodiment" of Dante's vision when we see him in one instance stubbing his foot on a protruding head and in another actually tearing chunks of hair from a traitor's scalp to make him give his name.

Canto XXXIII   While in Antenora, Dante sees a pair of shades, one holding fast to the other and gnawing savagely on his head. As bidden, the first identifies himself as Count Ugolino and recounts the pathetic story of how his victim, Archbishop Ruggieri, had confined him together with two sons and two grandsons in a prison tower to starve slowly to death. The moments preceding the death of each are described with stark vividness and pathos, accentuated by the sons' even offering themselves as food to their father. (Several commentators have inferred a suggestion of cannibalism as Ugolino's pangs of hunger reached the breaking point!) The episode is followed by a bitter apostrophe against Pisa for permitting such tragedies. However, the reader must not forget that Ugolino is damned for an act of treachery which led to his imprisonment in the first place.

In Tolomea the heads of the shades are thrown back, thus exposing their faces to the frigid air, which causes thick layers of ice to form within their eyelids. When Dante asks the source of the chill wind that keeps sweeping their way, Virgil assures him that he will soon see for himself. A shade cries out to have the ice removed from his eyes in order to shed some tears and have some relief from the excruciating pressure. Dante leads him to believe he will do so in exchange for his identity. It is the shade of Friar Alberigo who had murdered two of his immediate family at a banquet. Surprised that he has already died, Dante learns further from Friar Alberigo that his crime was so heinous that his soul went immediately to Hell, while his body remained on earth occupied by a hellish demon. This is apparently the case for all souls in Tolomea. Righteously and proudly, Dante refuses to keep his implied promise to remove the ice from Alberigo's eyes, for to be rude to these sinners was considered part of true courtesy — actually a way of participating in the divine punishment. The canto closes with an apostrophe against Genoa for having begotten such sinners.

COMMENTARY: In this and the preceding canto the wayfaring soul has seen representations of the lowest form of fraud, or malice, punished in Hell. The simply fraudulent are not so culpable as the treacherous, since in Dante's scheme the first are guilty of deceiving persons not bound to them in any special way. But the act of deceiving those who are closest to one, or where there obtains some relationship of trust, represents the worst possible sin that can be committed by a human being. Such people patently have the coldest, hardest hearts, from which all warmth of human feeling has vanished. The appropriateness of ice as a punishment for traitors requires little comment.

The cold cruel spirit of treachery seems to permeate the atmosphere of the ninth circle, where the shades are even seen betraying each other. Indeed the same spirit seems to have infected Dante himself as he deliberately breaks his word to Friar Alberigo. The very names of the four divisions define the atmosphere by recalling Cain, Judas, and Ptolemy from Scripture, and Antenor from classical-antiquity. The story of Ugolino, like that of Paolo and Francesca, is deeply touching, but for this very reason it defines more clearly and poignantly the inexorableness of Divine Justice.

Canto XXXIV   Entering the fourth division of this last circle called Giudecca, Dante notes that the souls are completely imbedded in random positions within the ice. He also senses an increase in the cold wind which causes him to snuggle close to Virgil who promises to show him the source of the wintry blast. Suddenly they behold Satan himself in all his ugliness and horror. Caught fast in the ice, he is visible only from the waist up, but his proportions are truly gigantic and his ugliness is incomparable. He has three faces, red, yellow, and black, and six huge, bat-like wings whose constant beating creates the winds that cause the water of this circle, Cocytus, to freeze over. His eyes emit tears while his three mouths drool constantly, each with a sinner hanging from it. The sinner in the front or red face has his head inside the demon's mouth, while his body is rent constantly by Satan's claws. The other two hang downward from the black and yellow faces. These arch-sinners are Judas, Brutus and Cassius, respectively.

Following his brief account of them, Virgil abruptly suggests they move on, for they have seen all there was to see. He asks Dante to hang on to him and, carefully avoiding Satan's wings, he carries him downward along Satan's shaggy flanks to which he clings for support. At Satan's waist, Virgil laboriously turns upside down and proceeds to climb until they reach a rocky ledge, where he deposits his burden. Dante looks back at Satan and is surprised to see him now with his legs upward. Once again Virgil prevents the pilgrim from lingering and they move on into a cave-like aperture devoid of all light. To satisfy Dante's curiosity about what happened to the ice and to Satan, Virgil informs him that they just passed the center of the universe and are now in the opposite hemisphere of the earth. The long cavern through which the wayfarers climb, led by the sound of a stream, had resulted from Satan's headlong fall from Heaven. Finally, through a small opening they sight the stars, and, shortly after, emerge to the light of day.

COMMENTARY: The soul is now ready to see sin stripped of all semblance of good. Treachery to one's benefactors being the epitome of evil, it is appropriate that the arch-traitor Lucifer, once the fairest of angels, now Satan, be the ultimate symbol of sin. Every detail in his description reflects this. With parodic overtones, the devil's red face signifies the love of evil, the black symbolizes ignorance, and the yellow impotence. Judas' position of "honor" and indeed the name of this division, Giudecca, recall the betrayal of Christ, founder of the

Church; while the fate of Brutus and Cassius is merited by their betrayal of Caesar, founder of the Empire. Since for Dante both Church and Empire were divinely ordained, their founders were sacred.

The winds produced by the flapping of Satan's wings represent the inspirations of sin which cause the human heart to freeze over. Presumably the three sets of wings correspond to the three major divisions of Hell, since love of evil begets fraud or malice, ignorance begets violence or bestiality, and impotence begets incontinence. The allegorical significance of Satan goes even further. As the negative counterpart of God, he too comprises three "persons." But where the Father, Son, and Holy Spirit signify power, wisdom, and love, the three faces of Satan stand for the opposite. Finally, Satan's very immobility and helplessness suggest the essential negativeness of evil. The more he flaps his wings, the more he remains stuck fast in the ice. The turning at Satan's waist is needed to comply with the shift in center of gravity.

The soul that understands the true nature of evil recognizes its foolishness, just as Dante is struck by the silliness of Satan's huge body being eternally stuck fast upside down in cold matter, forever helpless and impotent. With the aid of Reason Dante willingly and laboriously frees himself from the attraction of sin. The sound of the streamlet which now begins to lead the soul upward signifies the necessary tears of repentance that form part of the whole process. The wayfarer's soul, having now full cognizance of evil, has freed itself from the clutches of evil. It must now cleanse itself of any disposition to sin.

Purgatorio

Canto I   From the opening verses of this first canto of the second canticle the poet strikes a refreshing note of optimism and hope as he employs the image of a sailboat entering calmer waters, in keeping with the nature of this new realm where the human spirit cleanses itself for the ascent to Heaven. Following an appeal to the Muses to restore sweetness to his poetry, Dante paints a landscape which contrasts significantly with the heavy, close environment of Hell. Inherently pleasing words and concepts, like "sweet," "beautiful," "delight," "love," "laughter," along with gentle, restful colors, predominate. In contrast to the dark, subterranean hollow of Hell, Dante's Purgatory is set in the open air and sunshine of a mountain isle located in the southern hemisphere. Where the journey into Hell began in the evening, here it is now just before dawn.

Off to his right Dante notes four bright stars which are never visible from the northern hemisphere. A venerable old man with a white beard stands nearby, bathed in the light of the four stars. He asks the wayfarers how they gained entry to this realm. Out of deference, they kneel before him, and Virgil gives a detailed account of how and why he has guided Dante to this place. He emphasizes that his ward is on a journey which assures ultimate liberty, the very ideal for which the elder, whom he identifies as Cato the Younger, has died. Cato promptly grants them admission, but first bids them descend to the lower reaches of the shore, where Virgil must gird Dante with a rush that grows there and also cleanse his face with pure dew, for one must be unsoiled to enter. After giving further directions to the wayfarers, Cato disappears and Virgil directs Dante to the shore just as the first rays of the sun appear. Like people rediscovering a lost road, they traverse a solitary plain. With dew from the grass Virgil washes Dante's face of the stain of tears and infernal fume. By the sea, which no man alive had ever navigated successfully, he girds the pilgrim with a rush that immediately renews itself as it is plucked.

COMMENTARY: The descent into Hell began on the evening of Good Friday, while the arrival on the shores of Purgatory takes place just before sunrise on Easter Sunday of the year 1300. While the tone of the initial canto of Hell was sombre and threatening, here the tone is exactly the opposite. The constellation of four stars invented by Dante represents, as we shall learn, the four cardinal virtues of Prudence, Temperance, Fortitude, and Justice. The isle of Purgatory in Dante's cosmology is located in the southern hemisphere, opposite the northern hemisphere inhabited by man. Before the Fall, Adam and Eve were able to behold the four stars, but fallen man is not.

The constellation illuminates with sun-like clearness the face of Cato who is presumably the guardian of Purgatory. Cato the Younger had taken his own life rather than submit to the tyranny of Caesar. This heroic act in the name of freedom was apparently considered by Dante not as a revolt against God's law but as an assertion of man's right to true individual liberty whose Christian definition we will subsequently learn. Cato thus represents the freedom which the souls in Purgatory are attempting to regain through purification and penance. We also learn that Cato had originally been condemned to Limbo, then was freed during Christ's harrowing of Hell, which marked the creation of Purgatory.

Cato's request that Virgil wash Dante and gird him with a rush at the bottommost shore underscores the requirement of purity and humility for further progress. Such cleansing and girding just as day breaks, along with the solitude of the setting, emphasize the strictly personal character of the symbolic acts, while the tears on Dante's face evince the humble repentance of a soul willingly removing the stain of sin. The reference to Easter Sunday recalls the rebirth of the crucified Christ after His humbling descent into Hell. Furthermore, the many references to the sea, to the shore, and to the land untouched by human feet, recall the misguided and unsuccessful journey of Ulysses, with which Dante's offers poignant contrast.

Canto II   As the brilliant dawn breaks, the two pilgrims see an unusually bright light on the horizon speedily crossing the water toward them. As soon as Virgil recognizes it to be the heavenly angel who transports souls to Purgatory, he bids Dante to kneel. The swift boat, propelled by the angel's wings, contains a large number of souls singing a hymn of deliverance. At the shore, the souls debark and the boat once again disappears over the horizon. Like our wayfarers, the new arrivals are unfamiliar with the place and look about them in bewilderment. Seeing Virgil and Dante, they inquire after the fastest way up the mountain. Virgil answers that they too are but newly arrived, adding that Dante is actually still alive.

The souls crowd around Dante with incredulous stares, and one steps forward to embrace him. Dante tries to return the embrace, but in vain, for three times his arms close on nothing but air. It is the soul of Casella, a musician of Florence. Dante relates the purpose of his trip and asks why Casella's arrival in Purgatory was delayed, since he had died some time before. Casella explains that he was a beneficiary of the plenary indulgence granted by Boniface VIII for those pilgrims who attended the great jubilee of 1300 in Rome. Thus, only now did he board the heavenly ferryboat on the Tiber to come here. Dante thereupon asks him to sing a song in pleasant reminiscence and refreshment. Casella complies by singing one of Dante's own love poems he had set to music, with the result that all of the other shades stop to listen with undivided attention. Suddenly, Cato appears and berates them for their negligence and hesitation, bidding them immediately to go and cleanse themselves of their remaining stains of sin. The repentant souls quickly disband and hasten to obey Cato.

COMMENTARY: The contrast between the approach of the angelic boatman in this canto and Charon at the beginning of the Inferno effectively reflects the distinction between Purgatory and Hell. Here Dante's sight is almost overcome with the brilliancy and speed of the angel and his boat. The ease with which the angel navigates and the lightness of the boat, added to the fact that the passengers are singing a song of liberation, emphasize the spirit of hopefulness and joy that will become more pronounced as the journey progresses. The sensitivity of the shades to the beautiful music of Casella is also indicative of the greater gentleness and refinement of these souls. The voice of Cato that interrupts the song, however, is a reminder that even artistic beauty, if considered for its own sake and unrelated to heavenly things, is inherently dangerous. The Christian soul must keep in mind that its primary and exclusive responsibility is the return to God's fold. Art for art's sake is, from the divine perspective, a form of truancy. Indeed, the reaction of the shades to Cato's voice evinces their own awareness of a serious lapse.

Canto III   As the shades disperse to do Cato's bidding, Dante turns to
             Virgil for guidance and notes that even he appears highly
embarrassed as he hurries off. When Virgil finally slows his pace,
Dante for the first time looks up to the summit of the mountain and
gets some measure of its size. He also notices for the first time the
shadow of his body caused by the rising sun. Seeing only a single
shadow he anxiously turns to determine whether Virgil still accompanies him. Virgil reassures him by explaining that he can no more cast a
shadow than can the heavenly spheres one upon the other. How a body
can exist without substance is, according to Virgil, one of those
mysteries the human mind cannot and should not try to fathom. Like
the Trinity, it is a mystery that must be accepted on Faith.

The travelers come to the foot of the mountain, where they
seek a way up the steep incline. As Virgil meditates on a possible solution, Dante notices a group of shades, and suggests that perhaps they
could indicate the way. At Virgil's request for directions, a few of the
shades come forward but suddenly stop upon seeing Dante's shadow.
Virgil quickly explains that Dante is still alive and is undertaking the
trip by special dispensation. Whereupon one of the shades comes forward and identifies itself as that of the great Manfred, son of Emperor
Frederick II, King of Sicily. He asks Dante to report to his daughter
that notwithstanding his excommunication by the pope, he has
achieved salvation by a last-minute repentance of his sins. He also reveals the location of his remains and the fact that he is now among the
excommunicated but saved, who must spend in this lowest section of
Purgatory thirty times the number of years they had been excommunicated. It is Manfred's hope that, through her prayers, his daughter will
shorten his term of exclusion from Purgatory proper.

COMMENTARY: Perhaps the most important thing to note in this canto
              is Virgil's behavior. Psychologically, his reactions sym-
bolize the role that Reason plays in a predicament such as
Dante's. First of all, we note that Dante's initial reaction to
Cato's outcry is to turn to his Reason in the form of Virgil who
in turn seems embarrassed for having dallied. In a moment of
confusion Virgil too hastens away, until he realizes that this is
undignified. This gives Dante occasion to look about him as
well as up at the mountain for the first time here in Purgatory.

His sudden awareness of his shadow implies the presence of both the sun (enlightenment) and his flesh (weakness and decay). Virgil's disquisition on the mystery of shades and shadows and his warning about certain mysteries forever closed to human reason bespeak Dante's conviction that Reason can achieve only limited levels of knowledge. His two points that, if man had been all-knowing, there would have been no sin, and if human knowledge had sufficed, the vain longing of the ancient sages would have been satisfied, imply the pathos not only of Virgil himself but of the human condition in general.

Similarly, Virgil's pondering how next to proceed reflects Reason's habit of seeking knowledge within itself, while Dante's discovery of the shades suggests the human tendency to look without. The comparison of the group of shades to a flock of sheep contrasts with the fact that in life these shades had refused to join the flock of the Lord.

We also learn in this canto that the lower parts of the Mountain of Purgatory are occupied by classes of the "negligent" who must postpone their entrance into Purgatory proper until they have made amends. In the first class are the excommunicated. Dante here adopts the doctrine that the ultimate fate of a soul depends exclusively upon its actual state at the moment of death. While excommunicated souls must atone for their rebellion against the Vicar of God by humbly waiting for a specified term at the foot of Purgatory, their salvation is a matter of divine discretion. The image of the great Manfred requesting prayers of his daughter to shorten his wait is deeply touching.

Canto IV   Following a long description of the psychological process whereby a person focuses attention, Dante explains how he had been so absorbed in Manfred's words as not to notice that more than three hours had elapsed since sunrise. The shades lead Dante and Virgil to a cleft in the rock leading to a ledge above. Despite the difficult ascent, the travelers' desire to hasten their climb causes them to proceed with surprising speed toward the open slope. At a certain point, however, Dante expresses his weariness after falling some distance behind Virgil. He quickly recovers at Virgil's urging and they

soon reach the slope, whence they can examine the surrounding landscape. Dante's puzzlement at seeing the sun in an unaccustomed position in the heavens also disappears with Virgil's explanation of the
earth's geography.

To Dante's question as to how much distance still remains,
Virgil answers that the higher up the mountain they proceed, the less
difficulty they will experience. Their conversation is interrupted by a
voice and they note a group of shades lying by a huge boulder. Dante
recognizes the speaker as Belacqua, presumably a past acquaintance.
Dante asks Belacqua why he sits here and is informed that the latter is
one of the negligent souls of the second class: those guilty of late repentance as a result of their laziness. These must wait outside of Purgatory for a period equal to their life on earth. Belacqua's mocking hu-
mor is accepted good-naturedly by Dante. As noon approaches, Virgil
urges that they continue their climb.

COMMENTARY: The indications in this canto of the travelers' willing-
               ness to proceed as rapidly as possible despite the diffi-
cult climb contrasts sharply with the spirit and pace of the Inferno. The relative ease with which Virgil outdistances Dante
reflects the ability of Reason to proceed faster than the body or
flesh. Virgil's urging that they reach the slope in order to enjoy
a clearer view implies the presence of conscious progress.
Moreover, in the poem's first instance of good-natured amuse-
ment, the acceptance by Dante of Belacqua's mocking words
reflects an awareness that individual differences persist even
among the elect. It is important to note the positive nature of
whatever the soul learns on the journey through Purgatory. In
this canto, we also note an edifying contrast between Belacqua's indolence and the wayfarers' sense of urgency.

Canto V   As Dante follows Virgil up the slope, he hears an outcry
           from one of the shades amazed by his shadow. Virgil re-
bukes Dante for allowing the incident to slow his pace. Embarrassed,
Dante resumes his original pace behind Virgil, but shortly their progress is slowed by another group of shades that approaches while singing. Dante's body continues to be spotlighted as the shades interrupt
their singing upon seeing its shadow. Virgil reassures them by explain-

ing that, though a live man, Dante is worthy of their respect. The few shades who have come forward thereupon return to the group which now approaches the travelers and begins to make inquiries of Dante. Voices emerge from the group as it moves along with the travelers who do not arrest their climb. They explain that they are among those who had repented at the very last moment as a result of a violent death.

When Dante agrees to answer their questions, one Jacopo del Cassero, a former mayor of Bologna murdered through political intrigue, asks to be remembered to his townspeople and explains how he had come to a violent death.

A second shade, Buonconte da Montefeltro, a renowned Ghibelline leader and son of Guido da Montefeltro whom we met in *Inferno* XXVII, explains both his violent end and the mysterious disappearance of his body. Having appealed to Mary with his very last breath, his soul, like Guido's, was also contested by a heavenly emissary and a devil. This time the devil had failed to claim the soul and so in anger had conjured up a violent storm whose raging flood had swept Buonconte's body to a distant shore.

A third soul, identifying herself only as La Pia, gives a brief but poignant account of her death at the hands of her husband.

COMMENTARY: The reactions of both the second and third classes of the negligent to the presence of Dante's body reveal their excessive concern for things of the flesh, which had essentially caused them to delay repentance on earth. Virgil's rebuke of Dante's dallying and his assurance to the shades that even as a living man Dante can assist their progress reflect an awareness of the worth and importance of this life. The fact that the shades must walk along with the travelers indicates that the soul's progress at this point is virtually continuous and can hardly be interrupted.

All three examples representing this class of negligence provide focus for the doctrine that everlasting salvation or perdition depends upon the actual state of the soul at the very moment of death. Of the three, Buonconte has justifiably attracted most attention since his outcome contrasts so significantly with that of his father, Guido, in the *Inferno*. The deliberate contrast is enhanced by the fact that Guido, though a great Ghibelline, joined the Franciscan order and actually gave aid to Pope Boniface VIII and the Church cause in his old age, while Buonconte was a Ghibelline and supporter of the Empire to the end. Nevertheless, according to the judgment of Dante's poem, Guido was damned and Buonconte saved, the point being that political differences matter little where ultimate values are at stake.

The meteorological conditions resulting from the wrath of the foiled devil reflect the medieval belief that such devils were among the Intelligences exerting control over the elements. Often cited as a prime example of Dante's incomparable artistry with words are the few rapid strokes with which Dante paints the whole tragedy of La Pia, whom her husband murdered in order to marry another woman.

Canto VI   Dante finds it difficult to free himself from the press of shades seeking to win his attention in order to be remembered back on earth. Several of Dante's countrymen are identified by name among the crowd. This prompts Dante to inquire of Virgil whether it is indeed true that the souls' progress in Purgatory is hastened by the prayers of those on earth. He refers to a passage in the *Aeneid* where Virgil seems to deny this. Virgil, however, explains that in that passage the prayers of those on earth were not directed to the true God since they were uttered by a pagan not living in Grace. He reminds Dante that at the very summit of Purgatory the matter will be settled by Beatrice whom he defines as "the light between the Truth and the Intellect." This makes Dante more eager than ever to proceed, but he learns from Virgil it will take at least another day to attain the summit.

Virgil points to a shade who stands apart regarding them, and suggests they ask him for further directions. The attitude of the shade is one of dignified haughtiness as he waits for Dante and Virgil to address him. Instead of answering Virgil's specific request, he asks about their place of origin and their lives. No sooner does Virgil mention Mantua as his fatherland than the shade rushes forth to embrace him and identifies itself as the shade of Sordello, a roving Italian poet from Mantua, famed as a critic of corrupt and incompetent government.

Sordello's reaction leads to what is perhaps the most bitter invective against Italy and its corrupt rulers to be found anywhere in the

Comedy. The scathing attack spares no one, from Church leaders to the German Emperor and to Florence especially, whose unstable state of affairs is attacked with unmitigated sarcasm and irony.

COMMENTARY: The stress upon the value of human life on earth con-
                  tinues at the beginning of this canto as the shades anx-
iously crowd around Dante in their desire to be remembered in
the prayers of those they had left behind. Dante's questioning
of Virgil on the basis of a passage from the *Aeneid* which
seemed expressly to deny the power of such prayers, once
again brings to the fore what we have called the pathos of
Virgil, who must now retract something in his poem that was
stated in spiritual ignorance. In point of fact, he can only refer
Dante to Beatrice who as Revelation can deal with such mysteries which transcend the power of Reason. The unusual pains
taken by Dante to describe the impressive appearance of Sordello remind us of the episode of Farinata in the Inferno. The
deliberate contrast between Sordello's detachment and his reaction to meeting a fellow citizen of Mantua provides Dante
with an opportunity to attack the shameful political conditions
then existing in Italy. The references to the usurping of temporal power by the Church and the apostrophe against the Emperor Albert for having deserted Dante's beloved Italy, "the
garden of the Empire," when added to the invective against
Florence, clearly manifest Dante's concern for and involvement in the political scene of the time.

Canto VII   Upon learning the identity of Virgil, Sordello's reaction is
               one of delight and humility as he tries to embrace Virgil's
feet. In answer to his query, Virgil informs him of his location in Hell
and touchingly explains that he has been relegated to Limbo, among
innocent children, not for anything he did but for what he did *not* (indeed could not) do — profess faith in Christ. He is among those who
knew the four cardinal but not the three theological virtues.

    When Virgil asks Sordello for directions, Sordello suggests
that they stop for the oncoming night, since no progress is possible after dark. The pilgrims learn that the will simply becomes inoperative

once the sun has set. It is possible to travel back toward the lower shores, but not upward toward the mountain.

Virgil accepts Sordello's invitation to accompany them to a valley where they may enjoy conversation with other shades. Approaching the so-called Valley of the Princes, the pilgrims notice an abundance of color, fragrance, and song. From a ridge overlooking the valley, Sordello points out the shades of several famous rulers of the time whose wordly cares caused them to postpone until the last moment their reconciliation with God. As in actual life, Sordello here serves as a judge of kings.

COMMENTARY: The pathos of Virgil again echoes touchingly in this canto as he explains to Sordello why he is located in Limbo. At the same time we see once more a poet of renown paying homage to the great Virgil. When we recall, however, that Virgil also symbolizes Reason and ponder that pure Reason untouched by Grace is equated to the innocent babe, we sense more deeply than ever the complexity and precariousness of the human condition. This point receives even greater emphasis when we learn that true progress can be made only in the light of the sun. Without the sun of spiritual enlightenment, no ascent is possible for the soul.

Thus we see Dante and Virgil preparing to spend their first night on the island of Purgatory. As they look out over the Valley of the Princes with Sordello, we are reminded not only of the Noble Castle of *Inferno* IV, but also of Virgil's depiction of the Elysian fields in the *Aeneid* VI, 637 ff.

Canto VIII   As dusk descends upon the valley, the shades join in singing a hymn requesting divine protection against the evils of darkness. Having warned the reader to look beneath the allegorical veil of what is about to happen, Dante describes the appearance of two heavenly angels who take their stations on either side of the valley to protect the shades against the serpent, a regular nightly visitor.

Dante and Virgil follow Sordello down into the valley where Dante is approached by two shades. One is Nino Visconti, a judge or governor of a Pisan province. Dante presumably had a hand in one of Nino's campaigns against the Ghibellines and is delighted to see that his friend is not among the damned. Nino asks that Dante remember him to his wife and sadly foretells some of the misfortunes awaiting her.

As Nino's words come to an end, Dante is attracted by three bright stars in the heavens. Virgil explains that these three stars replace the four they had seen during the day. A dramatic interlude ensues in which the two guardian angels drive away a slimy serpent attempting to enter the valley.

A shade beckoned by Nino approaches Dante and identifies himself as Conrad Malaspina, a ruler of northern Italy whose family was famous for its liberality. Conrad asks about his possessions and his family and is assured by Dante that respect and fame still mark the Malaspina name. Conrad predicts that within seven years Dante will indeed appreciate the Malaspina family for what it will do for him.

COMMENTARY: The nostalgic opening verses with which Dante describes the approach of evening are full of earthly reminiscences which remind us that Dante, the pilgrim, is still influenced by earthly pulls. The chorus of shades intone a hymn which is often sung by the Church at eventide, and which here effectively introduces Dante's words to the reader preparing him to interpret allegorically the impending scene.

The arrival of the two angels and their role in warding off the serpent are indicative of the condition characterizing penitent souls that barely managed to escape damnation. Unlike the souls we shall meet in Purgatory, these just outside the gate require heavenly assistance, because they are still subject to the forces of evil and temptation.

The reference to the three stars completes the panoply surrounding the isle of Purgatory. During the day, the mount is under the influence of the four stars which represent the cardinal virtues, while at night it undergoes the beneficent influence of the three theological virtues.

Dante's kind words for the Malaspina family reflect his gratitude for the way they had befriended him during his exile.

Canto IX   In a lengthy introduction replete with allusions to myth and
            dreams, Dante describes how he fell asleep between the
shades of Virgil and Sordello and how before dawn he dreamt of being
snatched up to the sphere of fire by a golden eagle. He then proceeds to
describe, in a passage still marked by classical allusion, how he awakened just as he and the eagle were about to be burned in the hot flames.
As he opens his eyes, he sees Virgil on one side of him, the sun on the
other, and the sea at a distance. Virgil reassures him stating that he is
now at the gate of Purgatory and explains that in the early dawn he had
been carried aloft by Saint Lucy. The dazed Dante joyfully rises to his
feet and follows Virgil toward the gate, whose approach is marked by
three stone steps of different color and is guarded by an angel with a
shining sword. The latter blocks their advance until Virgil explains
their journey. At the angel's bidding, the two wayfarers climb the three
steps, the first of which is of shining white marble, the second of
scorched purple stone cracked along its length, and the third of bright,
blood-red porphyry.

        Reaching the threshold where the angel stands and prompted
by Virgil, Dante humbly kneels to request admission. The angel first
engraves seven P's on Dante's forehead and bids him cleanse them
each away as he progresses in Purgatory. He next takes two keys, one
of gold and one of silver, with which he unlocks the gate and invites
the pilgrims to enter, warning that once within they must not look back.
As he enters, Dante hears the notes of a *Te deum* sung with uncommon
sweetness.

COMMENTARY: With this canto, the allegorical nature of Dante's poem
               further asserts itself. The mysterious allusions to pagan
myth and legend found throughout the extensive introduction
have led at least one contemporary commentator to analyze the
passage in terms of a complex psychology of learning entailing
a return to the childhood of the race itself. The subtle allusions
to earthly temptations in the opening reference to the moon,
together with the dream sequence referring to the golden eagle
and to Ganymede, have been interpreted as moments of profound intuition into mysterious truths having to do with the purification of the soul. Virgil's revelation that it is Saint Lucy
who bore Dante to the gate climaxes the entire scene, since

Saint Lucy (Illuminating Grace) has traditionally been considered the patroness of sight.

Also highly significant is the moment of awakening, where the pilgrim finds himself comfortably cradled between his trusted guide Virgil (Reason) and the warmth of the rising sun (God).

The meaning thus emerges that souls sincerely desirous of reaching God can count on His assisting grace which mysteriously transports them to otherwise unachievable heights.

The three steps of innocence, sin, and redemption (or atonement), leading to the angelic guardian, who represents ecclesiastical authority, likewise epitomize the drama of man's return to Eden. The two keys used by the angel to open the gate are those entrusted by Christ to Peter and his successors as His vicars. The golden key of power (to pardon) and the silver key of discernment (to guide) reflect the two responsibilities borne by God's representatives of setting the just and deserving on the path of salvation. The seven P's are emblems of the seven capital vices of which Dante's soul is to be cleansed by the penitential climb up the mountain. The essence of Purgatory, reverent gratitude for God's mercy, emerges in the hymn accompanying Dante's entrance through the gate.

Canto X   Once inside the gate, the pilgrims proceed along a narrow crack that snakes through the cliff and eventually come to a solitary ledge flanking the mountain. Dante notes that the wall of white marble along the ledge is carved with extraordinarily realistic bas-reliefs that tell stories. The first depicts the Annunciation, as Mary is informed by the angel of her role in the Divine Birth. The second bas-relief depicts David humbling himself before the Ark as he leaps and dances in a manner unbefitting a king. A third scene relates a story current in the Middle Ages in which the Emperor Trajan acknowledges the justice of a poor widow's claim. The three bas-reliefs are so artistically perfect that Dante refers to them as "visible speech."

As Dante is admiring the three scenes, Virgil alerts him to a group of souls approaching. Dante cannot at first recognize them, for each is bent double under the weight of a huge stone which he bears on his shoulders. The scene prompts Dante to cry out against the pride of sinners who are incapable of recognizing they are merely worms born to become angelic butterflies. The approaching souls bear stones of varying weight which causes the knees of each almost to touch the chest.

COMMENTARY: Dante has now reached the first terrace of Purgatory proper, on which souls do penance for the capital vice of pride, the worst of evil dispositions. We later learn that all souls must suffer in this first circle, since pride is involved in every transgression.

The beautiful carvings on the upright wall of the mountain are part of a system whereby all souls are exposed in some fashion to examples of their particular sin and of the opposite virtue. The virtues, or "goads," generally appear to Dante as he enters each terrace; the sin, or "check," appears to him as he departs. In subsequent terraces they will take different forms, but here they appear as bas-reliefs.

The illustrations are drawn from Christian and pagan lore, but the first example of each of the seven virtues is taken from the life of the Virgin. The Creator of all the illustrations is of course the Master Artist, God Himself. The examples witnessed by Dante on this first terrace represent instances of humility, while the souls assigned here expiate their disposition to pride in a manner consistent with Dante's system of punishment. Although the sufferings constitute torments rather than punishments, they indicate the forms of discipline necessary to counteract the vice involved. Thus the heavy stones carried by the souls in this circle are images of self-imposed humiliation. The lesson inherent in the scene is poignantly brought home to the pilgrim.

Canto XI   This canto opens with an expanded paraphrase of the Lord's Prayer recited in unison by the souls of this first terrace. The prayer appropriately ends on a note of selflessness as the souls declare that their petition is in behalf of those left behind on earth. The great anguish the souls undergo in order to recite the prayer beneath their heavy weights is vividly depicted by the poet.

Virgil's request for directions to facilitate their climb is answered by a soul who identifies himself as belonging to the famed Aldobrandesco family and who frankly confesses to the excessive pride he had displayed on earth. As Dante sadly lowers his head, he is recognized by the soul of Oderisi of Gubbio, a famed illuminator of the period, who had been guilty of excessive pride in his artistic endeavors. He now expounds on the vanity of earthly glory, pointing out how quickly artists succeed one another in popularity. He in turn identifies a third soul, Provenzan Salvani, whose pride had spurred his quest for political power. It was only by a supreme act of humility that he had avoided being relegated among the negligent outside the gate of Purgatory.

COMMENTARY: Dante singles out three types of pride represented on this first ledge of Purgatory: arrogance of noble birth, vanity of artistic achievement, and haughtiness of power. Serving as effective contrast to such pride are the paraphrase of the Lord's prayer which opens the canto and the great difficulty and humiliation experienced by the souls in recounting their personal stories. By lowering his head as he hears the account of the first soul, Dante shows that symbolically he too is participating in the penance. It is ironic that Dante subtly incorporates an act of personal pride in this very episode by having Oderisi state that perhaps Dante himself has already become the leading poet of the time. But the dominant theme here is the fleeting nature of earthly fame and the pervading tone is one of present humility and selflessness.

Canto XII   Dante is so taken with the souls of this circle that he continues to walk along with them in a stooped position. It is only when Virgil reminds him they must move along that Dante straightens up.

As they resume their path, Virgil suggests that Dante observe the pavement on which they are walking. There our pilgrim sees another series of incredibly realistic illustrations, this time depicting scenes of pride. Here too the illustrations are arranged symmetrically so that pagan and Christian examples succeed one another. The poet's very stanzas partake of the symmetry.

Purgatorio XII. The Prideful.

Virgil's voice eventually draws Dante's attention from the pavement, informing him that an angel approaches to help them on their way. Looking up, Dante does indeed see the heavenly emissary who, after indicating the path, brushes against Dante's forehead. Soon the pilgrims hear voices sweetly singing, and Dante underscores the difference between the entrance he makes to the various levels of Purgatory and the passage through Hell, where screeching cries met the pilgrims at each circle. He also notes that he feels much lighter than previously and is having less difficulty in climbing. Virgil explains that one of the P's on his forehead was removed by the angel and that when the rest are removed, his feet will move quite effortlessly. Upon touching his forehead, Dante discovers that indeed only six P's remain.

COMMENTARY: Dante's propensity to continue walking in a stooped position reflects his own need for expiating an excess of pride. Virgil's subsequently calling attention to the life-like carvings on the pavement in turn suggests another essential element in the process of purgation. It is not sufficient to undergo self-imposed humiliation. The soul must also actively desire to shun the attendant vice by consciously focusing on its presence.

The architectural symmetry with which Dante depicts the realistic illustrations, incorporating it within the very structure of the Italian stanzas, once again bears witness to the artistic nature of God's handiwork. Just as the series of bas-reliefs exemplifying humility at the entrance to this ledge passed from divine humility before God to human humility before God and finally human humility before man, so do these illustrations of the opposing vice move from superhuman pride against God to human pride against God to human pride against man. The symmetry reaches a climax in the original Italian where, following three groups of four stanzas, the first of which has each stanza beginning with the letter V, the second with the letter O and the third with M, we are given a summarizing stanza which repeats these letters at the beginning of each verse, thereby spelling out the word *UOM* (Man) and producing an echo effect. (U and V were interchangeable.)

It is only after Dante has fully absorbed the significance of the illustrations that the angel appears to indicate the
way to the next ledge and to lighten Dante's mortal burden by
removing one of the seven P's engraved on his forehead.

Canto XIII   Not knowing in what direction to turn as he leads Dante
              onto the second terrace, Virgil decides to turn to the right
and to proceed in the direction of the sun in whose light and warmth he
expresses complete faith. Before long Dante hears mysterious voices
echoing about him, "graciously extending invitations to the table of
Love." Upon inquiring about the voices, Dante learns from Virgil that
they are now on the second terrace of Purgatory where envy is purged
and the souls are blinded. The phrases spoken by the voices refer to
famous examples of loving care, i.e., the opposite of envy.

Virgil invites Dante to focus on the path ahead. There Dante
sees a great number of souls sitting in a row and drably dressed in the
fashion of beggars. They seem to be repeating in unison the Litany of
Saints. Drawing closer, Dante notices that their eyes are sewn shut with
iron wire. Their plight so overwhelms him that he feels a pang of conscience at being able to see without himself being seen. Having asked
Virgil's permission to speak to them, he inquires if any of the souls are
from Italy. One of them identifies itself as the soul of a certain Sapia of
Siena who confesses to a consuming envy of her fellow townsmen and
describes how divine mercy alone enabled her to achieve salvation.
When she asks Dante to identify himself, he does so in terms of not
being a victim of envy but rather of pride. He also explains that he has
been led here in the flesh by Virgil and offers to inform Sapia's family
of her fate.

COMMENTARY: Dante's use of bright light imagery in this canto pro-
               vides vivid contrast with the darkness in which the
souls guilty of envy must now expiate their vice. Virgil's hymn
to the sun sets the stage for the contrast. Again, the examples
of the opposite virtue called out by the mysterious voices follow the established pattern of symmetry, with the first instance
of kindness drawn from the life of Mary, the second from pagan antiquity, and the third from Scripture.

That the souls once guilty of envy should in penance suffer blindness by having their eyes sewn shut is attributable to the very nature of envy, which is essentially a sin of the eyes. One ought in fact to close one's eyes to all beguiling temptations that may lead to such sinfulness. Although Dante momentarily seems again to share in the penance, he explains shortly to Sapia that he is not so prone to this vice as he was to that of the preceding terrace. Sapia herself, once an important person who took pleasure in others' woe, now gratefully acknowledges the charitable intercession of a humble and saintly comb-seller, Pier Pettinaio, whose prayers hastened her entry into Purgatory.

It is also important to note that, in response to Dante's question whether among these souls there be a citizen of Italy, the immediate answer is that they are all citizens first and foremost of the one and only true city, the City of God.

Canto XIV   Two souls of the second ledge decide, after some discussion, to ask Dante who he is and where he is from. Dante modestly withholds specific information and indirectly indicates that he is from Florence. This results in three passages of twelve lines each which satirize the inhabitants of various cities located along the Arno River. The two blind spirits identify themselves as citizens of Romagna and participate in the satire against the times. In one of the apostrophes interspersed throughout the passages is an outcry by one of the souls against mankind's propensity to avoid sharing things with others. This will eventually lead to a central theme in the *Comedy*.

As Dante and Virgil prepare to move on, they once again hear voices, in this instance proclaiming classic examples of envy. The canto ends with Virgil berating mankind for being so much more easily attracted by the small earthly temptations of the devil than by the incomparable lures of the heavens above that ceaselessly and openly revolve about the earth.

COMMENTARY: The focus of this canto is on those human actions which involve the "exclusion of sharing." Mankind is everywhere fallen into picayune quarrels over ownership of earthly goods that distract from the primary goal of salvation.

The benign heavens which would uplift us with their eternal beauty are ignored, to our undoing, as we insist on keeping our eyes fixed on earthly concerns. The concept of sharing and that of the beckoning heavens will recur frequently in future cantos.

Canto XV   The opening verses of this canto inform us that it is mid-afternoon of the Monday after Easter. Dante suddenly feels the light of the sun toward which he is walking become unbearably bright. When he realizes it is not sunlight, he turns to Virgil who explains that another angel has come to welcome them to the third ledge of Purgatory. Although not specifically stated, it is clear that the dazzling but invisible angel removes the second P from Dante's forehead.

As the two pilgrims enter the third terrace, Dante asks a question that has been puzzling him since hearing the statement of the soul from Romagna in the last canto regarding "exclusion of sharing." Virgil points out that it refers to the distinction between possession of earthly goods and of heavenly ones. Earthly possessions, he explains, can belong only to one person at a time. Heavenly possessions, comprised primarily of knowledge and love, cannot only be possessed by everyone together but actually increase in proportion to the number of sharers. When Dante remains puzzled, Virgil offers an explanation in terms of reflected light: the more light shines upon a bright body, the more light is reflected. He adds however that perhaps Beatrice will be able to explain this mystery more fully.

Before Dante can continue with his questioning, he suddenly witnesses three visions portraying loving gentleness, the opposite of wrath, which is the vice punished on the third ledge. The visions constitute the goads that regularly appear at the entrance to each terrace. In keeping with the established pattern, they are taken from the life of Mary, from pagan, and from biblical sources, respectively.

Dante is so overwhelmed by the visions that he walks as in a daze until Virgil's words reassure him. The progress of the two pilgrims is unexpectedly impeded by a thick haze or smoke which obscures their sight.

COMMENTARY: The discussion on the difference between spiritual and temporal possessions and the allusion to the nature of celestial goods as comprising primarily shared love and knowledge is most effectively introduced at this point near the center of Dante's journey and consequently near the threshold between the earthly and the heavenly. The concept of sharing goods with one's fellow creatures, together with the infinite possibilities of such sharing in God's kingdom, prepares the progressing soul for the more complicated discussions that are to take place in the next few cantos, ushering in the second half of the poetic journey. Dante's reaction to the visions that appear to him at this point again implies a degree of personal participation in the punishment.

Canto XVI   The dense smoke of the third terrace makes it necessary for Dante to proceed by leaning on Virgil's shoulder. Through the smoke can be heard the voices of souls chanting the *Agnus Dei.* Virgil explains to Dante that these are the souls of the wrathful. A voice asks Dante who he is and if he is indeed alive, as he appears to be. Encouraged by Virgil to answer, Dante admits that he does travel with his body and asks the soul to identify itself.

It is the soul of a certain Marco Lombardo, about whom little is known. Declaring that on earth he had tried to lead a life of virtue which no longer appeared possible, Marco requests Dante's prayers. This prompts Dante to ask him to explain why virtue seems to have fled the world, thereby leaving it in the clutches of evil. Such a state of affairs has been puzzling our wayfarer, since many ascribe it to heaven, others to man himself.

In a lengthy analysis, Marco begins by showing how illogical it is to blame the heavens for the state of mankind inasmuch as it is clear that man possesses free will. While the stars do have an influence on human actions, man's free will is, with proper guidance, capable of combating wickedness. Men are free subjects of God and if conditions in the world are awry, man can only blame himself.

The soul at birth is an innocent creation, quick to accept as good and desirable whatever seems to provide joy and happiness. It will act indiscriminately without a guide or check to restrain it. This is why rulers are needed. The contemporary world is in chaos because, while laws exist, there is no one to administer them properly. At the heart of the situation is the absence of an emperor; moreover, the Church's attempt to fill the breach by assuming temporal power is fundamentally wrong. Emperor and Pope should rule side by side, the one in temporal, the other in spiritual matters. Until there is such harmony of rule, chaos will continue. Meanwhile, this is why in the whole of Lombardy there are but three senior citizens who can be called upright.

COMMENTARY: Midway in its journey back to God, the soul begins to cope in greater detail with the distinction between earthly and heavenly life. The blinding, suffocating cloud of smoke that envelops the penitents affords a kind of neutral zone within which angry passion is forcefully stifled. In the absence of such passion, Dante learns four essential lessons. First, the soul is endowed at creation with a joy for existence that causes it forever to be attracted by the promise of such joy. Secondly, inasmuch as part of its nature is freedom of choice, the soul must have the guidance of duly constituted laws and rulers. Thirdly, since the soul partakes of both the divine and the earthly, God ordains a spiritual and a temporal ruler. These two rulers, as Emperor and Pope, are to enjoy mutual respect, having been assigned by God the responsibility of leading the soul to the joys inherent in earthly and heavenly life. Fourthly, it is precisely because such dual leadership is lacking that the world of Dante's day seems to have forgotten the meaning of virtue.

Very little is known of Marco Lombardo except that he enjoyed an excellent reputation, as did also the three Lombards mentioned at the end of the canto.

Canto XVII   As the setting sun breaks through the thick mist, Dante is again presented with ecstatic visions, this time of wrath. The examples are taken, as usual, from both biblical and classical sources.

With the close of the third vision, Dante is almost blinded by the intense light of an angel who leads the wayfarers to the next ledge and removes another P from Dante's forehead. Night is falling, so Dante feels his strength failing to the point of immobility. During their enforced halt Virgil, in answer to Dante's question, indicates they have reached the ledge where the slothful are disciplined. He takes the occasion to explain the entire structure of Purgatory.

Virgil begins by stating that no creature was ever created without capability for love, natural or elective. While natural love cannot err, elective love can easily be misdirected. The more a creature pursues a wrong object, the more he turns away from his Creator. Consequently, love can be called the seed of every virtue and of every evil. Such love always has as its object something outside the creature.

Since a soul cannot hate itself or its Creator, the object of its hate can only be one's neighbor. The man who hopes to excel through the abasement of his neighbor is guilty of pride and is punished on the first ledge of Purgatory. The man who fears to lose honor or fame through another's success is guilty of envy and must be disciplined on the second ledge. The man who seeks vengeance for another's success is guilty of wrath, or anger, which is purged on the third ledge.

There is, furthermore, disproportionate love for the good. If a soul seeks the good too slowly, he is guilty of sloth, which is punished on the fourth terrace. If on the other hand a man directs his love excessively to temporal goods, he is guilty of the three vices of avarice, gluttony, and lust, punished in the three upper ledges to come.

COMMENTARY: Just as halfway down the abyss (*Inferno* XI) Virgil took time to explain the structure of Hell, so here, halfway up the mountain, indeed at the very midpoint of the poetic journey itself, he explains the structure of Purgatory. The basic concept that love is the root of all good and all evil provides a key to a proper understanding of the *Comedy*.

God the Creator is all-loving, thus none of His creatures can be without love. This love, however, can be distinguished as instinctive or elective. Elective love reflects the essence of man's free will which enables him to direct his love to any and all objects. So long as it is directed to heavenly things or to good things of earthly life in due measure, man cannot go astray. But when his love for divine things is lukewarm or his desire for worldly goods is immoderate, or indeed when he favors evil, he opposes the will of his Creator and is guilty of turning away from Him.

We thus have three wrong courses open to man's love: the choice of a bad object, insufficient devotion to a heavenly object, excessive attachment to a temporal object which is not

evil in itself. The first results in sins of the spirit which constitute the three vices punished on the three lower ledges. The
second error results in the negative vice of sloth, which is expiated on the fourth ledge. The third leads to sins of the flesh
which produce the three vices of the three uppermost ledges.

Canto XVIII   After Virgil's explanation of the structure of Purgatory,
               Dante feels a thirst for further knowledge rise within him.
He asks Virgil to explain the workings of love.

According to Virgil, one's mind or intellect is attracted by
every pleasing object. Our perception conveys the image of such an
object to our mind which causes a turning toward the object. If in the
process the mind inclines toward the object, this is love. From that
moment the mind does not rest until it can enjoy the desired object.
The Epicureans are therefore wrong in believing that all objects of
love, indiscriminately, are good.

Dante is next perturbed at the thought that if the objects of love
come from without, the soul should be held responsible for the choice
of objects. Admonishing that Beatrice will have to elaborate later,
Virgil undertakes an explanation of the workings of the will. He starts
by reiterating the soul's inborn disposition to love which merits neither
praise nor blame. To assist us in making all our inclinations conform to
this natural instinct for the good, the Creator gave us judgment, "the
faculty that counsels." While our first impulses may be instinctive, our
decisions are subject to our own free will.

As Virgil concludes his explanation, Dante describes a vivid
night scene in which he portrays himself as sleepy. He is suddenly star-
tled by a group of souls running swiftly around the ledge in a manner
reminiscent of the Bacchic orgies. These are obviously the slothful
whose running symbolizes the now enforced spiritual activity they had
lacked in life. The throng of souls swiftly comes and goes, calling out
examples of celerity and of sloth. One soul identifies itself and omi-
nously forecasts what will befall certain members of the ruling family
of Milan. At the end of the canto the demanding intellectual activity he
has just undergone causes Dante to fall asleep and to have a strange
dream.

COMMENTARY: The soul has now actually crossed the midpoint, of its journey. Having learned the cause of evil in society and the kinds of love that motivate people, Dante is here informed about the operations of love in the individual. And so, at this threshold of salvation, we find him learning the secret of life and eternity in terms of one's responsibility for one's own destiny. The nocturnal setting and the startling haste of the souls on this ledge tend to dismay Dante who also seems to feel that Virgil's answers are no longer sufficient.

Canto XIX   In the prophetic early morning hours Dante has a dream in which an ugly witch turns into an alluring temptress. Before Dante can fall completely under her spell, a heavenly lady appears who bids Virgil reveal the inner ugliness of the witch by tearing away her outer wraps.

At this point Dante awakens to be told by Virgil that he had tried three times in vain to rouse him from his sleep. Continuing their journey, the two wayfarers are led to the entrance of the next ledge by an angel who appears unusually visible and whose wings brush another P from Dante's forehead.

When Dante expresses concern over the dream, which he cannot put from his mind, Virgil explains that it had to do with "the ancient witch" responsible for the sins of the flesh punished in the next three ledges. He also states that in his dream Dante has seen how man can free himself from the witch. Virgil then exhorts him rather to turn his eyes to the lure of the heavens which the Lord constantly dangles before us. Dante, like a falcon swooping for his food, presses on, to the fifth ledge, where he sees shades lying prone and uttering deep sighs and indistinct words.

While told to advance toward the right, the two pilgrims halt briefly in order to enable Dante to address a shade. It is Adrian V, who had held the papal office for slightly more than a month in 1276. The Pontiff confesses to his avarice in life which he now expiates. He also explains that his prostrate position is consistent with his sin inasmuch as avarice causes one's attention to be fixed on earthly things. Furthermore, since avarice leads to the cessation of good works, these shades lie bound and motionless. Dante's attempt to kneel reverentially is dis-

couraged by Adrian, who points out that such reverence has no place in
the afterlife where earthly distinctions no longer hold.

COMMENTARY: The soul has now reached beyond the midpoint in the
               journey to its Creator. The allegorical dream under-
gone by Dante in this canto demonstrates that the soul has
learned its lesson well. The entire dream is but an example of
the operation of love. The tempting advances of the witch held
in check by the use of judgment (the heavenly lady) and the final resistance resulting from Virgil's (i.e., Reason's) intervention illustrate dramatically how a mind can free itself of misdirected love. By the time the short scene is over, the soul is able
to view an example of evil stripped of all resemblance to the
good. Dante's subsequent outburst of energy expressed in the
image of a falcon swooping toward its food reflects the renewed strength that returns to a soul following a battle with
temptation. The fact that the angel appears so much more
clearly to Dante's sight is likewise an indication of spiritual
progress. The episode with Pope Adrian V recalls, by contrast,
the scene with another pope, Nicholas III, in the corresponding
canto of *Inferno* XIX.

Canto XX   At the close of the last canto Pope Adrian V urged Dante
            to proceed on his way since too much dallying was keep-
ing the Pontiff from shedding sufficient tears of penance. Moving on
with Virgil, Dante apostrophizes the "ancient wolf" of avarice, or im-
moderateness, and invokes the Savior or Champion that must inevita-
bly be sent by Heaven to destroy this "beast" once and for all.

He next observes that the prostrate souls cry out examples of
poverty and virtue which counterbalance their vice. Dante addresses
one of the shades and learns that it is Hugh Capet, King of France from
987 to 996 and founder of the famed Capetian line of rulers who
reigned in France for a number of centuries. Identifying himself, Hugh
traces his lineage down to 1300, indicating the progressive infamy that
has marked the family. As his account comes to an end and the pilgrims continue on their way, Dante feels the entire mount of Purgatory
tremble and hears all its souls shout in unison "Glory to God in the
highest." The two travelers are struck motionless like the shepherds

who first heard that shout when Christ was born. The need to hasten along makes Dante hesitate to seek an immediate explanation.

COMMENTARY: The soul, aware of the penance required to atone for the many vices and crimes that derive from avarice, cannot but decry this weakness or flaw in human nature, which presumably is correctable only by heavenly intervention. The lengthy account of Hugh Capet tracing the degeneracy of a royal line serves to emphasize the depth of the flaw. The account is also a clear example, notwithstanding certain historical errors, of Dante's incredible grasp of the contemporary scene.

The trembling of the mountain with the attendant outcry of its inhabitants and the temporary halt of the pilgrims is all the more dramatic because it remains unexplained despite Dante's strong curiosity. The casual reference to the night of Christ's birth likewise contributes to the effectiveness and suspense of the episode.

Canto XXI   Despite his curiosity to know why the mountain trembled, Dante faithfully follows Virgil's rapid pace. Suddenly, like Christ appearing to two strangers, a shade approaches them from behind and greets them. Again Virgil explains how and why Dante, a live man, is traveling through the netherworld. He then asks the shade whether he knows why the mountain trembled and why the souls cried out. The shade explains that no physical phenomenon was involved, since Purgatory proper lies beyond atmospheric conditions. The cause was spiritual, rather, for the tremors occur whenever a soul feels completely cleansed and is thus free to rise to a new level. Each such event prompts all inhabitants of Purgatory to cry out in joyful gratitude for the liberation of a fellow member. These miraculous occasions result quite naturally when a soul's conditioned will coincides with its absolute will which inclines only toward the good.

Virgil next inquires after the shade's identity and learns that it is Statius, a famous Latin poet of the first century A.D., whose two famous epics, the *Thebaid* and the *Achilleid* (the latter unfinished), were highly regarded in the Middle Ages as models of rhetorical elegance. Statius openly confesses that he had followed in the footsteps of Virgil upon whom he bestows highly flattering praise. Although signaled by Virgil not to reveal his (Virgil's) identity, Dante cannot help smiling. Pressed by Statius to explain his smile, Dante, with Virgil's consent, identifies Virgil, whereupon Statius tries in vain to embrace Virgil's feet.

COMMENTARY: The soul here comes to realize that the process of purgation and salvation is indeed a highly personal one. This lesson emerges from Statius' explanation of why the mountain trembled. When its inclination as expressed in its conditioned will follows firmly in the path of the infallible absolute will, the soul automatically rises toward heaven. Since every soul is but a member of the Mystical Body of Christ, all rejoice in the knowledge that one of their fellowship has completed its penance and is free to rise on toward its Creator.

    The appearance of Statius amidst the mysterious references to the Resurrection of Christ reinforces not only the theme of re-birth but also the motif of Virgil's pathos. Both were great Latin poets, but whereas Statius lived in the century following Christ's birth, Virgil lived in the century just before that birth. As a result, while one could know the fruits of salvation, the other could not.

Canto XXII   As Dante follows the two poets, Virgil reveals that he had learned about Statius in Limbo from another poet, Juvenal, and was puzzled as to why Statius was located in the fifth terrace of avarice. Statius reveals his real vice, prodigality, which he had fortunately been able to repent as a result of certain verses he had read in the *Aeneid*. Virgil next asks how Statius had achieved salvation, since he was still a pagan. Once again Statius reveals that it was Virgil's doing when, in his fourth eclogue, he had strangely predicted the birth of Christ. Like a man who bears a lantern behind him and lights the way for his followers and not for himself, Virgil had shown Statius the road to Christianity. Consequently, Statius owed all he was, both poet and Christian, to Virgil. He recounts how he had befriended Christian martyrs, and how out of fear he had hidden his own conversion from the authorities. As a result, after his death, he had been committed to the fourth circle of Purgatory for over four centuries before his penance of five hundred years and more in the circle of prodigality. Statius next asks about the location of other famous writers and heroes of antiquity only to learn from Virgil that the majority are with him in Limbo, while a good number also are scattered throughout Hell.

The three poets suddenly come upon a fruit-bearing tree standing upside-down at the foot of a waterfall. The tree emits sweet odors and strange voices that cry out famous examples of temperance.

COMMENTARY: In this canto the soul learns of the mysterious and wonderful ways in which God's grace reaches mortals. In a sense, Dante pays the highest homage to Virgil's knowledge and wisdom by the dramatic device of inventing the fiction of Statius' conversion. Allegorically, the meaning of Statius as Reason enlightened by Faith emerges clearly and unmistakably. Furthermore, Dante was here reflecting an old medieval tradition according to which Virgil, in his fourth eclogue, had predicted the coming of Christ. This tradition continued well into the sixteenth century.

It is also possible that for Dante a certain change of tone which occurs in the movement from Statius' *Thebaid* to his *Achilleid* invited an interpretation of his Achilles as a symbol of Christ. Why Dante chose to make Statius a spendthrift is also a mystery. There is some possibility, however, that Dante himself felt guilty of such a vice and employed this episode as an example of why it should be avoided.

The upside-down tree encountered by the poets at the end of the canto prepares us for the next ledge on which gluttony is expiated. The tree is symbolic of prohibition and abstinence.

Canto XXIII   Virgil's voice urging him to follow along rouses Dante from his rapt concentration on the mysterious tree. Proceeding behind the two poets, Dante next hears singing and observes a group of souls whose emaciated condition gives them a skeletal appearance. One of them recognizes Dante and is in turn recognized by him as Forese Donati whose brother was a famous leader of the Black Guelphs and to whom Dante's wife was related. He and Dante had evidently lived a worldly life in their youth.

In answer to Dante's request, Forese explains that he is among those penitents who were guilty of gluttony. These are constantly tormented with the thought of food and drink evoked by the odor from the tree and by the spray from the water flowing upon it. Dante wonders why Forese is not waiting outside of Purgatory, since presumably Forese had postponed his repentance until the end of life. Forese informs him that the prayers of his devoted wife Nella made it possible for him to be admitted into Purgatory proper.

The discussion of Forese's wife results in a bitter attack against contemporary Florentine women whose immodesty allegedly exceeded that of the barbarians. Finally Forese requests that Dante explain his condition and identify his friends. In complying, Dante emphasizes that Virgil's guidance has helped him turn away from a life of sin.

COMMENTARY: In the portrayal of Forese, Dante shows how both Divine Grace and the power of prayers can assist a soul that had enjoyed a highly questionable life on earth. Forese's assurance that the torment suffered by these shades ought rather to be called pleasure stresses once again the concept that, unlike Hell, Purgatory subjects the shades to disciplining torments rather than punishments. Finally the brief, rapid strokes with which Forese portrays the Florentine women of the time strikes a universal note which echoes throughout every century. The reference is particularly relevant at this point, since Dante and Forese had exchanged a series of coarse youthful sonnets reflecting a riotous life of pleasure.

Canto XXIV   Dante continues his discussion with Forese while following behind Virgil and Statius. In a human touch, he remarks it may take Statius a little longer to achieve salvation as a result of lingering with Virgil. He then inquires after Forese's sister, Piccarda, and whether there are other souls of note on this ledge of gluttony. Forese indicates that his sister has already achieved Paradise and then proceeds to identify a number of other souls.

Among these is a certain Bonagiunta from Lucca who seems particularly anxious to converse with Dante. After making a dim prophesy concerning Dante's exile, he asks whether Dante is the poet who had given love poetry a new direction. Dante defines himself as a poet who treats of love inspirationally by following the dictates of his heart. Whereupon Bonagiunta avers that he now realizes why he and so many other poets of his time had failed to achieve the "sweet new style" of Dante's generation. (The term *dolce stil novo,* appearing here for the first time, has subsequently come to be used for the kind of lyric poetry written by Dante and his followers.)

Dante sadly takes his departure from Forese, following another vague prophesy by the latter concerning the political future of his brother. Continuing his journey behind the two poets, Dante discerns another tree laden with fruit and surrounded by many souls with arms outstretched and vainly shouting requests toward the branches. As Dante approaches the tree, a voice commands them to proceed without lingering, for the essential tree is the one to appear later, the tree of Adam and Eve. The pilgrims depart from the tree, while other voices call out famous examples of gluttony drawn from antiquity and from Scripture.

Their silent way is unexpectedly interrupted by a voice counseling them where to turn in order to further their climb. The voice comes from a being whose brilliance reminds Dante of molten glass or metal. Turning to the two poets, and half-blinded from the brightness, Dante feels his forehead wafted as by a fragrant breeze in May. At the same time, he hears the words of a hymn blessing those who control their appetites with moderation.

COMMENTARY: The most significant part of this canto is the passage in which Bonagiunta learns from our pilgrim the difference between Dante's practice of poetry and that of his Italian predecessors. The basic difference lies in the distinction between convention and introspection. Dante's forerunners had considered poetry primarily a rhetorical or stylistic exercise in which old themes were rehashed with minor technical innovations. For Dante and his "school" of the "sweet new style" technique was subordinate to thought and feeling. More important perhaps was their view that *amore,* the most important subject of vernacular poetry, went beyond the traditional meaning of love and included the pursuit of knowledge.

The Bonagiunta of this canto was indeed a predecessor of Dante's poetic "school." The discussion centers quite natu-

rally on such a topic, since most of the onlookers are love poets. It also prepares us for the next canto.

    The episode of the tree, with its mysterious voices and
reference to the tree of Eden, is a fitting prelude to the beatitude on moderation recited at the end of the canto. Similarly,
the reference to the spring breezes, fragrances, and flowers
suggests the approaching rebirth of our pilgrim's soul as still
another P is removed from his forehead, this time by an angel
whose red brilliance symbolically reflects Charity or Love.

Canto XXV   It is early afternoon when Dante and his two poets depart
from the sixth terrace. Dante's curiosity has been aroused
to the point where Virgil must bid him to ask his question. Dante wants
to know why a shade, which no longer requires physical nourishment,
can exist in an emaciated condition or even desire food. Virgil first
cites two examples of equally wonderful phenomena, then asks Statius
to provide the answer to Dante's question. Replying first that Virgil
could also have answered the question, Statius begins with a detailed
explanation of the processes involved in the birth of both flesh and
spirit. The three moments in the development of the human fetus end
with the introduction of the incorruptible spirit into each child at the
very moment of birth. Every man therefore has but one soul which is
his alone, endowed with life, sense, and intellect.

    When death overcomes the physical body and a soul is rele-
gated to one of the three spiritual realms, it radiates its own formative
power upon the surrounding atmosphere, thereby producing the appearance of a body, much as the sun's rays form a rainbow when they
shine upon moisture-laden air. In this body-like image, the soul can
reflect its likes and dislikes even as it did in its original earthly body.

    As Statius' explanation draws to an end, the travelers come to a
ledge from whose inner bank hot flames shoot outward across the path-
way. From the flames emerge the notes of a hymn sung by souls who are
evidently engulfed in the fire. At the conclusion of the hymn the souls
cry out examples of chastity from biblical and classical sources.

COMMENTARY: Dante is now ready to grasp a mystery hovering on the
threshold between Reason and Faith. This is implied
by the manner in which Virgil refers to Statius Dante's ques-

tion on the relation of soul to body. The description of human generation derives primarily from St. Thomas but with echoes of some other Christian sources. The acquisition of an aerial body by the soul is clearly an invention of Dante's, designed to enhance the credibility of his vision. The entire discussion also reflects a process which Dante himself is undergoing — the process of being spiritually reborn, purified and worthy of admission into Heaven. There is but one vice left to purge: lust, to which the body with its senses is especially prone. The flames of passion must be replaced by the flame of Charity in order to achieve a true rebirth. In this canto Dante already feels the heat of the fire.

Canto XXVI   The souls within the hot flames enveloping the ledge of carnal vice, intrigued by Dante's body, call out to him asking for an explanation. As Dante observes them, he notes a second group of souls approach the first and exchange a kiss of brotherly affection. On parting, the two groups rebuke each other — the first shouting "Sodom and Gomorrah!" — the second recalling the bestial sin of Pasiphae, the human mother of the Minotaur. They then continue circling the ledge until they meet again and repeat the scene.

In addressing the shades Dante assures them that he is there with his real body, and that through grace procured for him by Beatrice he is thus privileged to view the world of the spirit before his time. At Dante's inquiry about the two groups, one of the souls explains that they are composed of the normally and the abnormally lecherous, and constantly remind one another of the prime historical examples of their vice.

The speaker then identifies himself as Guido Guinizelli, causing Dante to acknowledge his debt to him as the father of his poetic school. Guinizelli however assures Dante that another soul located nearby was really superior to himself and indeed superior to many of the poets to whom fame has been kinder. The new poet is the Provençal, Arnaut Daniel, who identifies himself to Dante in his native Provençal language.

COMMENTARY: It is perfectly appropriate that the poets of love should occupy a central place in this seventh terrace of carnal vice. The canto contains an interesting assessment by Dante of the contemporary poetic scene. By tracing his own type of love poetry back through Guinizelli to the Provençal poets, Dante records for us his personal view of the evolution of medieval love poetry. Of equal significance is the invariable consistency with which the artists thus far met in Purgatory disclaim any particular merit and humbly concede the superiority of fellow artists. By making Arnaut Daniel speak in his own tongue Dante in turn performs an act of humility as well as tribute.

Other interesting points developed in this canto include the apparent increase in the heat of the flames as a result of Dante's shadow; the care exercised by the souls to remain within the flames in their desire not to interrupt the process of purification; the statement by Dante that he is making this journey in order to overcome his blindness and to "die better"; and the comparison of Heaven to a cloister having Christ as its abbot.

Canto XXVII   As dusk begins to fall, the pilgrims meet an angel who sings a hymn to purity and informs them that further advance is impossible without entering the fire. Dante's reluctance to do so is met by an impassioned exhortation by Virgil who reminds him that the fire is now the only barrier that separates him from Beatrice. This provides Dante with new courage and the three pilgrims enter and pass through the flames.

Following this act of purification, the travelers who are about to enter Eden decide to sleep, since night has fallen. Like a sheep or goat watched over by shepherds, Dante feels comfortably protected as he falls into a deep slumber. In the early morning hours he has his third dream in Purgatory. He dreams of a young maiden by the name of Leah who gambols about lovely fields, plucking and adorning herself with flowers. She informs Dante that her sister Rachel is the opposite of herself and sits all day in contemplation before her mirror.

When Dante awakens, Virgil announces that the goal of the journey is now at hand. He further states that he has done all he could to lead Dante thus far and that what Dante has seen, heard, and learned as a result of the journey has now given his will the strength and ability to choose unerringly. Like a young man come of age, Dante is ready to venture forth on his own. Virgil urges him to proceed into the lovely landscape before them and to feel free to act without further advice from him. Dante's will is now not only free, but perfectly straightened to choose to do only what is right.

COMMENTARY: In this canto the soul is about to purge the last vestiges of potential vice. Dante has understood and shaken off six of the seven capital vices. There remains the least serious of all, the vice of carnal desire or lust.

The desire to possess another person can easily exceed the limits of moderation. When this happens, there is need for tempering such desire. The fiery path confronting the pilgrim in this canto signifies the quenching of carnal desire, fire having been recognized throughout history for its purifying action. Dante's reluctance to traverse the flames despite the angel's words that it is the only way to achieve the "music" of the other side, is finally overcome by Virgil when he refers to Beatrice who awaits them there. This moment is particularly significant on this ledge inasmuch as other poets like Dante are here being subjected to the torment of fire.

The fact that Dante undergoes this trial just at nightfall implies another moment of excessive stretching of the mind to a point where restful sleep is necessary. Again such sleep leads to a significant dream whose meaning, for the moment, is not perfectly clear to the soul that is about to rise freely upward. Comfortably ensconced between the Reason of humans and Reason enlightened by Faith, like a goat shepherded by its masters, Dante dreams of a lovely garden of joyful activity and quiet contemplation. Both activities are legitimate, both lead to happiness.

Upon awakening, the soul now realizes that it has understood all the essentials of spiritual life and death. It feels the confidence of its own self-determination. Virgil's words merely reinforce the idea that the journey thus far has been but a disciplining of the will, which has been perfected to the point of being in consonance with God's. Like a combination of

Pope and Emperor, the will's powers can now determine unfailingly the correct choices to be made on both the temporal
and the spiritual levels. Reason need no longer serve as a coun-
tercheck.

Canto XXVIII   The three pilgrims find themselves on the outskirts of a
               lovely "forest" full of the most attractive colors, sounds,
and fragrances. Dante enters eagerly into the "ancient forest," but his
path is soon blocked by a stream of the purest water. As the poet stands
enchantedly gazing about him, he suddenly notices a lovely lady walking about in the forest, happily singing and plucking flowers. Dante
calls out to her to come near and let him hear her sweet song. When the
lady approaches, the words of her song and particularly her eyes, full
of laughter and joy, have a most profound effect on Dante. Addressing
the three travelers, she suggests that, to understand her joy, they recall
the Psalm (Ps. 92; Vulgate 91) which proclaims the joy inherent in the
creations of the Lord.

      Still separated from the lady by the narrow stream, Dante man-
ages to inquire about the surprising presence of such elements as water
and gentle breezes. The lady explains that in this garden-like forest is
to be found every possible type of vegetation and that the breezes felt
are but the natural movement of the atmosphere. As for the water, it is
not ordinary water, but that which flows from a miraculous fount and
subsequently divides into two streams, one known as Lethe and the
other as Eunoe. She then reveals that the place in which they stand can
be compared to the Parnassus sung by poets of old, for in this garden
humankind had once lived in perfect innocence and happiness. Her
words bring smiles to the lips of Virgil and Statius.

COMMENTARY: The final purification by fire has led the soul to a vision
              of the Garden of Eden, or earthly paradise. It is interest-
ing that Dante alludes to the Garden as a forest, a forest, we
note, that contrasts sharply with the forest on which the poem
opens at the beginning of *Inferno*. That first dark, ominous
wood has given way to this most lovely and inviting garden at
the top of Purgatory.

      This golden-age setting is enhanced by the presence of
a beautiful maiden. As a reflection of the dream in the preced-

ing canto, this maiden too engages in the kinds of activity associated with the life of perfect innocence and bliss. Combining the qualities of both Leah and Rachel in the dream, she embodies the guardian spirit of the place. Her description and explanation of the Garden reflect a state of plenty and of perfect happiness.

The soul has now traveled back to its original home, the first abode of Adam and Eve. There remains, it will soon become clear, only the purification by water to remove the last vestiges of negative inclinations.

Canto XXIX Dante follows the lady along the stream to a point where she bids him observe and listen. A sudden flash of light rends the air, accompanied by an outburst of sweet music. The experience is so pleasant that Dante is prompted to reproach Eve for depriving mankind of such unparalleled pleasure.

The mysterious sights and sounds gradually assume distinctive form. First Dante notices what appear to be seven golden trees which he comes to recognize as candlesticks. The candles leave seven multicolored trails in the air above the evolving form of a procession. A quick look at Virgil shows that he, too, is puzzled.

At the lady's urging, Dante looks beyond the lights and notices people dressed in dazzling white. He slowly distinguishes twenty-four elders, then four strange animals, each with six wings and eyes on the wings. After them comes a two-wheeled chariot drawn by a griffin, half eagle and half lion, the former gold, the latter white and red. By the right wheel of the chariot can be seen three dancing maidens, one dressed in red, another in green, and a third in white. By the left wheel are four other maidens clad in purple. Following this group are two more elders identified as St. Luke and St. Paul. These in turn are followed by four additional elders of humble mien. Bringing up the rear, comes a sleepy old gentleman. These last seven elders are dressed, like the first twenty-four, all in white, but they are crowned with red instead of white flowers. The procession comes to a halt opposite Dante as a roll of thunder resounds in the distance.

COMMENTARY: The soul on the way to salvation has now progressed
                beyond the power of reason. As an individual soul, it is
about to be received into the arms of Mother Church which
now reveals herself in all her majesty. The procession observed
in this canto unfolds in the shape of a cross. At the central position is the chariot of the Church drawn by Christ, its founder,
whose two natures are symbolized by the griffin. The latter,
being half eagle and half lion, belongs to both heaven and
earth.

      As the procession unfolds, Dante sees ever more clear-
ly. He is able to identify the seven candlesticks as representing
the seven-fold gifts of the Holy Spirit (Wisdom, Understanding, Counsel, Might, Knowledge, Piety, and Fear of the Lord).
These are followed by twenty-four old men representing the
books of the Old Testament and clad in white to emphasize
that the Old Testament is the expression of faith in the Savior
to come.

      The four animals surrounding the chariot of the Church
are the four Gospels (Matthew, Mark, Luke, and John) whose
message has been winged throughout the earth. Around the
chariot dance the seven maidens, three representing the theological virtues of Faith, Hope, and Charity, the remaining four
representing the cardinal virtues of Prudence, Temperance,
Justice, and Fortitude.

      Next come St. Luke (of the Acts) and St. Paul fol-
lowed by Peter, James, John, and Jude. Finally there comes St.
John the Divine whose revelation represents the last book of
the New Testament. These seven old men are crowned in red,
the color of Charity, or Love, as compared to the white, the
color of Faith, which marked the dress of the first twenty-four
elders.

      In the vision before him, Dante is, in fact, viewing di-
vine history. Starting with the Old Testament and ending with
the last book of the New, the central focus falls upon the chariot and the griffin, around which everything seems to revolve.
In short, what we really have in this symbolic representation of
the history of the Church is universal history as God had ordained it from the beginning. The saved soul must now com-

prehend all the vicissitudes of this history before it can take its rightful place therein.

Canto XXX   Upon coming to a halt, all the participants in the procession turn their eyes to the chariot at the center, while a voice sings out verses from the Song of Solomon calling to a beloved to return from exile. The singing is echoed by choirs of angels who sing out "Blessed art Thou who comest!" And as the angels scatter flowers about the chariot, Dante glimpses within a cloud of blossoms, clad in white, green, and red, his beloved Beatrice.

Even before actually seeing her, Dante feels his old passion for his beloved surge back within him. Turning to his guide for counsel, he discovers that Virgil has departed. His tears are interrupted by Beatrice's stern voice from across the stream, calling him by name and suggesting he restrain his tears until he hears what she has to say. Having demanded his attention, she asks in the manner of a judge, how he dared approach this place where man is truly happy. Amidst further singing by the angels and their attempts to intercede in his behalf, Dante breaks into tears of sincere repentance as he hears Beatrice explain how he had willingly turned to images of evil and vice shortly after her death, notwithstanding her many attempts to influence him in dreams and visions. He had eventually fallen so low that it became necessary to show him the realm of the dead and she herself actually had to visit that realm in order to prevail on Virgil to serve as Dante's guide. His tears of contrition must now be proportionate to his sinfulness.

COMMENTARY: As all focus attention upon the chariot, it becomes clear that a judge of some kind is anticipated. The choral singing echoes as through a vast cathedral and culminates with the words "Benedictus qui venis!" which clearly call for the coming of Christ, the Saviour. The very last Latin verse sung by the chorus of angels is taken from Virgil's *Aeneid.* Thus, at the very moment of Virgil's departure, Dante pays him the highest homage by having angels sing one of his verses.

Despite the elaborate preparation for a kind of second coming of Christ, we instead behold Beatrice, on the chariot where we expected Christ. The multitude of flowers and colors

with a predominance of white, green, and red (Faith, Hope, and
Charity) surround Beatrice with the clear attributes of Revelation. Since Revelation is a highly individual experience, it
should not prove shocking that Dante employed his beloved
Beatrice to portray the manner in which he personally experienced the mystery. The sudden disappearance of Virgil at this
point marks the substitution of Divine Authority for Reason.
Furthermore the calling out of Dante's own name emphasizes
the fact that we are here witnessing a strictly personal moment
of redemption. In a kind of analogy with the Last Judgment,
this individual soul must now undergo a sincere confession and
repentance equal to the seriousness of his guilt. By rebuking
Dante for having neglected her simply because she was no
longer physically present, Beatrice accuses a sinner, just as
Christ might conceivably do at the Last Judgment. The infinite
patience of Divine Mercy is implied in Beatrice's account of
how it was necessary for her to go to Limbo itself to seek a
means of persuading Dante to change his evil ways.

Canto XXXI   Beatrice now asks Dante publicly to proclaim his inno-
              cence or guilt. In a profusion of tears, Dante confesses his
guilt, admitting that he had indeed led a wayward life of the senses.
Once again Beatrice orders Dante to look up at her directly. Her cutting
remarks, which imply he had behaved like a silly child, bring about a
sincere repentance. As he beholds Beatrice in all her glory, surrounded
by angels and with her eyes on the griffin, Dante becomes so overwhelmed that he faints away.

    When Dante regains consciousness, he finds himself in the arms
of the beautiful maiden of the forest. She first submerges him in the
waters of the river, then places him among the four dancing nymphs
who identify themselves as handmaidens of Beatrice. These, in turn,
lead him to the griffin and to Beatrice herself. Mirrored in the eyes of
Beatrice, which are fixed upon the griffin, Dante beholds the strange
animal assume first a human and then a divine nature. During this
strange and beautiful vision, the other three maidens approach, perform
a dance, and petition Beatrice to turn her eyes to her faithful companion so as to reveal her lovely mouth as well as her eyes. The intensified

vision that ensues is so overwhelming that Dante can only describe it in terms of the ineffable.

COMMENTARY: In the prolonged episode of Beatrice compelling Dante to confess his guilt are encompassed the formal steps involved in a sincere confession. To make amends for his past wrongs, Dante intensely undergoes each step, from contrition, to confession, and to satisfaction, leading to absolution. Beatrice's insistent harping on Dante's truancies following her death emphasizes the extent of Dante's foolish waywardness. When the process is completed, the new sight of Beatrice cannot be withstood by the soul until it has been submerged in Lethe, the river of forgetfulness, by the hand of innocence symbolized in the maiden of the Garden. Having forgotten all past evil, the soul can be introduced to the four cardinal virtues which enable it to view the eyes of Revelation and the mysterious fusion of the human and divine. The soul is then led by the three theological virtues to see the very mouth of Revelation, representing the higher Reason which empowers the will not only to know the way, but also to follow it to salvation.

Canto XXXII   Dante's entranced contemplation of Beatrice is interrupted by the seven maidens, who cry out that he is staring too fixedly. Upon turning his eyes back to the procession, he sees it begin to depart toward the East like an army. As the long column wheels slowly back in the direction whence it came, Dante walks with Statius, the lady guardian of the Garden, and the nymphs representing the theological virtues, alongside the chariot bearing Beatrice. Angelic singing accompanies the moving procession. Suddenly Beatrice descends from the chariot at the general cry of "Adam!" All now circle around a leafless tree of inordinate height and strength. They compliment the griffin for not despoiling the tree, whereupon the griffin ties his chariot to it. The tree immediately blossoms with wondrous colors and leaves, thereby prompting a mysterious hymn of peace to break forth on all sides. The scenes and the singing cause the weary Dante to fall into a peaceful sleep.

Rudely awakened, he finds the young maid of the Garden standing over him. In response to Dante's query, she points out Bea-

trice seated at the base of the tree with the seven Virtues surrounding
her. The maiden further informs Dante that all the other participants in
the procession have followed the griffin to Heaven.

From within her circle of Virtues Beatrice asks Dante to keep
his eye on the chariot and note carefully what transpires. There follows
a succession of violent visions as the tree undergoes a series of attacks.
First an eagle swift as lightning rends the bark of the tree and attacks
the chariot. A hungry fox then tries to board the chariot, but Beatrice
succeeds in driving it away. This action is followed by a return of the
eagle which leaves its feathers scattered throughout the chariot. A
frightful dragon, in turn, appears between the two wheels of the chariot
and encloses it within its tail. More feathers cover the rest of the chariot. Suddenly the chariot sprouts seven ugly faces of monsters, three on
the shaft and one at each corner. Just as suddenly there appears on the
chariot a prostitute sensually reveling with a giant who finally un-
hitches the chariot from the tree and drives it violently off into the forest.

COMMENTARY: By asking Dante not to stare too fixedly at Beatrice,
               the Virtues remind him that Revelation cannot be
grasped directly, but must be seen through its manifestation in
the Church. The procession now begins to march back toward
the East, from which it had come. Thus would the Church have
peacefully returned to its abode, were it not for the drama of
the Fall. The several tableaux following the outcry of Adam's
name seek to portray the ramifications of man's original sin.
The temporal tree of Law (or knowledge of good and evil)
provides the focus for all the tableaux. The bare tree does not
give signs of life until the chariot is securely fastened to it by
the griffin. Only in the alliance of Church and State can the human race enjoy perfect peace, symbolized by Dante's dropping
into a tranquil sleep.

When the sleeper awakens, Christ and the Scriptures
are no longer on earth, having left behind as official representative the Church, with Revelation as guide accompanied by
her handmaidens, the seven Virtues. The tableaux that follow
epitomize the vicissitudes of the Church, which Beatrice asks
Dante to record for the benefit of mankind. The attack upon the

tree and the chariot by the eagle represents the persecution of the Christians by the early Roman emperors. The repulsed attack by the fox symbolizes the attempts of heresy to undermine the Church from within and the role of Revelation in warding off such inroads. The eagle's subsequent return and covering of the chariot with its feathers recalls the Emperor Constantine's so-called donation to the Church, which for Dante marked the beginning of the Church's usurping temporal powers. The attack upon the chariot by the dragon stands for Satan's success in producing the great schism which divided the Church, East and West. With the assumption of temporal possessions by the Church, corruption followed, as symbolized by the further covering of feathers which finally engulfed the entire chariot. The seven monstrous heads that sprout at key points on the chariot represent the seven capital vices which infected the Church following its assumption of temporal powers. The closing scene of the unbridled harlot and the passionate giant dramatizes the illicit relations, in Dante's own day, between the Papacy and the House of France.

The soul on its way to salvation has thus been shown how seriously mankind has thwarted God's plan. Had man not been so proud, he could have enjoyed full membership in the original procession. Confusing temporal and spiritual values, he perversely chooses rather to test his own powers of self-reliance.

Canto XXXIII   The profanation of the Church is decried by the seven Virtues and by Beatrice who, as Revelation, now repeats and symbolically acts out the words of Christ prophesying the return of the Church in all its glory, notwithstanding the activities of heathens. Beatrice then invites Dante to walk by her side and explains that some day a mysterious leader (whose identity is couched in the Roman numerals "DVX" which also spell "leader" in Latin) will restore goodness to the Church and to the human condition. She commissions Dante to write down on his return to earth all that he has seen and heard, for all men must understand that Divine Justice will ultimately prevail.

During the conversation, Dante indicates that he no longer recalls the distance which had separated them after her death. She smil-

ingly reminds him that his forgetfulness results from his immersion in
the river Lethe. Indeed, the fact that he has forgotten is itself an indication of his guilt.

Meanwhile, Dante together with Beatrice, the seven Virtues,
and Statius come to a dark pool under the trees, the waters of which
divide to form two streams. For an explanation, Beatrice yields to the
maiden of the Garden whose name is now given as Matelda. Matelda
reveals that she had already informed Dante about the two streams. But
Beatrice points out that perhaps he had forgotten because of a greater
concern. She then requests Matelda to immerse Dante in the river
Eunoe. The effect of the immersion is such that Dante afterwards feels
truly reborn, pure and disposed to ascend to heaven.

COMMENTARY: The symbolic words and actions of Beatrice at the be-
                ginning of this canto define even more clearly her role
as Revelation. In the hands of sinners and heathens, the Church,
like Christ, may seem to depart for short periods of time, but it
is destined always to return in ever greater glory. Thus, even
while the Church is in the worst possible state, as was portrayed at the end of the previous canto, Revelation attended by
the seven Virtues is still capable of escorting a soul on the road
to salvation.

Beatrice's words of assurance to Dante as they walk
together with Statius prophesy the coming triumph of Justice
in mysterious terms which have been variously interpreted.
Whether referring to a political or a spiritual leader, the DVX
prophesied by Beatrice convinces the soul of the inexorable
and ultimate triumph of the good. The constant focus on the
tree of Law emphasizes the idea that Justice entails a proper
balance between spiritual and earthly values. The true Rome
must reflect both kingdoms, that of God as well as that of man.

Having been convinced of the inevitable triumph of
the good, Dante is now ready to have his innocence completely
restored. His immersion in Lethe removed all memory of sin.
A further immersion in the river Eunoe will revive his memory
of the good that is his due. The symbolic immersion is per-
formed by Matelda, who personifies perfect innocence, or justice (order) in the soul. After the symbolic act, the soul is like a

plant renewed by putting on new leaves. Free of all stain and therefore completely "weightless," the right-ordered soul is at last ready for the flight to Paradise.

Paradiso

Canto I   The poet's struggle to recollect his journey to the heavenly kingdom prompts him to open this first canto of *Paradiso* by humbly confessing his inadequacy for doing justice to the glory of the Lord which he saw glow forth everywhere in His creation. He apostrophizes Apollo and the Muses for help in his attempt to convey what he experienced. He then returns to his narrative, informing us that it was high noon of a spring day when he departed from our globe.

The heavenly journey begins as Dante fixes his eyes on Beatrice, who in turn fixes hers upon the Sun. It appears as an extremely bright point of light emitting sparks and heat like molten metal. And the pilgrim finds he can withstand its brilliance only by viewing it mirrored in Beatrice's eyes.

Dante's contemplation of this image through Beatrice's eyes causes him to undergo a sensation which he can only define as "transhumanizing." The mystic experience is such that he cannot even recall whether he was in or out of his body. The intense light is accompanied by sweet, ineffable sounds as of music. So entranced is the pilgrim that it is necessary for Beatrice to apprise him of his lightning-swift flight by her side. When he asks how this is possible, Beatrice explains it in terms of a return to one's natural home. All created things having any kind of intelligence are naturally inclined to return to their Creator who rules from the ultimate heaven, or Empyrean, where reign the perfect peace and happiness sought by all creatures. Since, however, these are endowed with free will, there are those who mistakenly turn elsewhere.

Having divested himself of all impediment, the pilgrim rises swiftly and unerringly toward his Creator. This is as natural for him now as it is for a river to flow downstream.

COMMENTARY: The positive note of this first canto is struck in the very
               first verse. It is a hymn to the glory of Him who moves
all things. Unlike the *Inferno* and the *Purgatorio,* there is nothing in this last *cantica* that cannot be called truly majestic.

The canto opens with a prologue consisting of a proem
and an invocation. Following this prologue, we are told that the
heavens were astronomically in an almost perfect position when
Dante began his flight. The image which subsequently monop-
olizes the canto is that of an unbearably hot, bright sun which
Dante can view only indirectly through the eyes of Beatrice.
This intense light is accompanied by incredibly sweet music
producing in the poet an experience of elation and joy which
makes him feel almost divine. Amidst such sweetness and
brightness it is Beatrice who must inform the poet that he has
now left the earth behind and is flying upward toward his natural abode. The flight is similar to a body being pulled by a new
center of gravity. In such wise do all created things possessing
intelligence instinctively strive to return to their Creator. While
free will causes some men to stray after false pleasures, Dante
here is like the soul which has crossed the threshold of salvation and now is drawn, as by a magnet, to the source of all
happiness and being.

Canto II   In an opening apostrophe, the poet warns his readers unaccus-
           tomed to sailing uncharted seas to turn back. Only those few
followers already accustomed to feeding upon "the bread of the angels"
can traverse the mysterious waters that he is now about to sail with
Minerva as breeze, Apollo as helmsman, and the nine Muses as pilots.

Dante's natural thirst for the divinity was causing him with
Beatrice to soar heavenward at an incredible rate of speed. As they
travel upward with the poet's eyes fixed on Beatrice, they suddenly
reach the first of the heavenly bodies, the moon. The sensation felt by
the poet is one of fusing with the new element rather than being apart
and detached from it. Indeed he once again cannot explain whether he
was in possession of his body or not. This sense of fusion makes the
poet ever more desirous to rise to Heaven in order to see and compre-
hend directly how the human and the divine are fused in Christ.

To Dante's question regarding the nature of "moon spots" Beatrice responds with a lengthy and complex explanation of the operations of Nature. The vital principle that derives from the Godhead is handed on to each of the nine spheres of the heavens in diverse fashion, imparting to each body varying portions or degrees of the illumining energy. This, rather than the ordinary explanation based on densities of the bodies, is, according to Beatrice, the correct explanation of such phenomena as "moon spots."

COMMENTARY: The uncharted sea mentioned by the poet at the beginning of this canto refers to the ultimate truths of the universe and of the spirit within the framework of the fundamental teachings of Christianity. This is why Dante must count on the help of Minerva (Wisdom), Apollo (Inspiration), and the nine Muses. No poem had previously undertaken such a theme. And this is why readers unaccustomed to "the bread of the angels," or sacred knowledge, are warned to turn back. The apparently naive question regarding "moon spots" is really but a device to introduce a general discussion of the workings of Nature. For the medieval mind Nature meant basically the operation of the heavenly bodies, which are controlled by the heavenly intelligences or angels. The passing on of the vital principle from God Himself through the various heavens down to the earth, as described by Beatrice, is the basic process whereby seeming imperfections of the works of Nature are explained. It is the function of the eighth sphere, or heaven of the fixed stars, to differentiate the degree of vital principle flowing from one sphere to the next. The brightness of heavenly bodies is likewise associated with the flow of this vital principle, for it is the joy inherent in God's creation that is the source of all light. The ultimate lesson deriving from the discussion is that there is a perfect correspondence between the world of matter and the world of spirit. Whence it follows that the world of matter is but a visible image of the world of God.

Canto III At the conclusion of Beatrice's exposition of the workings of Nature, Dante wants to ask further questions of his beloved, who now is compared to a sun. He is kept from doing so by a vision which he has difficulty describing. Like images reflected in glass or water, or like a pearl dangling before the whitest flesh, a group of souls appears. So indistinct are their images that Dante turns to see if they are but reflections. Beatrice assures him they are true substances before him, representing the souls relegated to the sphere of the moon for having been remiss in their vows. Encouraged by Beatrice to address them, Dante courteously asks one its identity. The soul willingly identifies itself as a certain Piccarda and explains that she is among the inconstant nuns whose goodness suffered an earthly stain.

Dante inquires whether the souls in this sphere desire to be located higher up. Piccarda assures him that they are all perfectly happy with what they have and that desiring more would make their wills be in disagreement with the Divine Will, a condition which is inconceivable in Heaven where only Charity reigns. Every blessed soul's happiness lies in the Divine Will which is like a sea toward which everything moves.

Having understood how Paradise can be won, although Divine Grace may differ in degree for each blessed soul, Dante then proceeds to ask about Piccarda's personal situation. Piccarda explains that she had taken vows as a young girl, but was kidnapped from the cloister by her brother and his followers who compelled her to marry. She then identifies her companion, the Empress Constance, who in 1186 had married Henry, son of Frederick I of Swabia.

As the two souls retreat and mysteriously vanish, Dante turns to Beatrice, whose brilliance now so overcomes him that he hesitates to ask his question.

COMMENTARY: Beatrice's brilliance at the beginning of this canto reminds us of her role as Divine Revelation. Similarly, the evanescent appearance of the blessed souls of Paradise reminds us that we are in the realm of the spirit, where one can scarcely expect to find visible forms. Dante is now in the first of the nine heavens, or spheres, of his *Paradiso*.

As we learned in the last canto, the power of Nature results from the influence of the various stars or heavenly bodies located in each sphere. Each of the nine heavens is presided over by God's ministers, the divine intelligences or angels. In the first heaven of the moon are located the inconstant nuns,

nuns who were compelled to break their vows. Presumably all weak and inconstant persons who win salvation belong to this lowest heavenly rank.

The most significant lesson learned by Dante in this first sphere is the hierarchical concept of the degrees of happiness. According to Church doctrine, every soul in Heaven receives all the happiness of which it is capable. But this capacity differs according to the mysterious ways in which each soul is endowed with Divine Grace. Such Grace provides each soul with a certain degree of spiritual sight which enables it to enjoy the vision of God according to its individual capacity. This doctrine, developed by St. Thomas, enabled Dante to retain the concept of individuality, even in Paradise.

Later we shall learn that the real abode of all blessed souls is in the Empyrean, the realm of pure spirit located beyond the nine spheres. In order to enable Dante's mind to apprehend the structure of the spiritual world, he is first made to grasp the correspondence between the latter and the material universe by seeing the souls of the blessed as they appear to him in the heavenly spheres that symbolize their spiritual state. It is interesting to note that by placing Piccarda and Constance side by side, Dante makes it clear that in the world of the spirit all souls are equal, regardless of their former earthly station.

Canto IV   As the two souls fade away, Dante's mind entertains new doubts which he hesitates to express. Beatrice, however, divines Dante's thought and identifies the two dilemmas that seem to be disturbing him. The first is how souls whose will remains intact but who are constrained by someone else to act improperly can be held responsible for such acts. The second dilemma has to do with the location of the souls on the planets which seems to reflect Plato's doctrine that souls return to their stars after death.

She resolves the second question first by pointing out that the souls they have encountered in the heaven of the moon are not really assigned to that heaven. Like all other blessed souls, they sit in the highest heaven, joyously contemplating their Creator. It was only to help Dante's understanding that they appeared to him here, for only in such fashion can he grasp the concept of degrees of blessedness. While this may seem in accord with Plato's ideas, it really is not, unless Plato too conceived of the planets as simply having their influence on human actions.

As for heavenly justice appearing unjust in such cases as those of the inconstant nuns, it is only because of the limitations of the human mind. Actually, the compulsion surrounding the cases of the inconstant nuns does not justify their act, because no outside power can really force the will. While it may be true that their "absolute will" preferred the veil, their "conditioned will" induced them to take the easier way out.

Dante expresses his gratitude to Beatrice for her explanations, which prove that the mind cannot refrain from doubt as long as answers are not forthcoming from a truly heavenly source. In fact, he is moved to ask another question. He would like to know whether a man can make amends for unfulfilled vows by means of what he calls "other goods."

COMMENTARY: It was in the *Timaeus* that Plato developed the concept that human souls were all created at once at the beginning of the world and that each waited in an appropriate heaven or star for the birth of a body to inhabit. The doctrine also held that after death the souls of those who had led a good life would return to their stars again. Here Beatrice explains that what appears to be similar to Plato's theory is really a means offered by God to man to assist his understanding. The contemplation of the Creator is an act of such infinite proportions that in order for a human mind to grasp the distance that separates even a blessed soul from the Godhead (even as it enjoys the beatific vision in the Empyrean) the only conceivable unit of measurement is the huge distance between planets. Therefore, although, as Dante will eventually discover, every soul he meets on his journey through Paradise actually sits in a kind of amphitheater in the last heaven enjoying the direct vision of God, selected souls of the blessed descend to the various planets to aid Dante's limited understanding. His intellectual vision can only gradually be conditioned for the final goal.

As for the guilt of the inconstant nuns, they could have refused to break their vows and suffer death or ill treatment.

Instead, even though their absolute will still preferred the convent, their conditioned will, shaped by given circumstances, caused them to yield. For this reason, they are considered souls least endowed with intellectual vision and therefore least capable of love and happiness in the realm of light. Nevertheless, despite their differing degrees of blessedness, all souls of the saved belong in the heavenly kingdom.

Canto V   As Dante awaits Beatrice's answer to his question, she appears brighter than ever. She explains that her brilliance is the result of the entire movement involved in grasping divine truths. Happiness depends on love, love depends on perfection of spiritual sight, such sight in turn depends on divine light, and consequently happiness itself is reflected as light. This is why the brightness of the soul is an indication of the amount of joy it has. Beatrice's intensified brilliance is therefore proportionate to the increasing acuity of Dante's insights into divine truths.

Dante's question regarding possible reparation for broken vows can only be answered in the negative. A vow is a covenant between God and man, and therefore cannot be taken lightly. When a vow, such as that of a nun, involves abdication of the will, which is the most precious of God's creations, no release is possible.

At the conclusion of Beatrice's explanation, Dante feels himself speed like an arrow into the second heaven. Here too they enter a strange element which Dante can only describe in terms of a water image. He sees strange figures coming forth like fish in a bowl attracted by some lure. Like the fish, these souls seem to be eager to come forward and they encourage Dante to interrogate them, implying that they are there for his edification. Since Dante can make out an indistinct form in the bright light which surrounds each shade, he directs a question to one of them asking who he is and why he is in the second heaven. This arouses such joy in the soul that the light surrounding it becomes so intense that Dante can no longer see the form itself.

COMMENTARY: Why Dante takes so much of the *Paradiso* to discuss the problem of broken vows has been a puzzling problem to commentators. Part of the answer no doubt lies in the very nature of the important problem of understanding the relationship between God and man. While pledges between men can often be taken lightly, pledges made with God cannot. This is especially so when the pledge involves an offering that one knows to be dearest on both a human and a divine level. Such is the free will, which can never be falsely pledged in God's sight.

The concept of equating joy and happiness to brilliant light represents a device that the reader must keep in mind throughout the *Paradiso*. Only in this fashion can one appreciate the incomparable artistic effects that will mark Dante's poetic journey henceforth. In this canto not only does Beatrice explain how such brilliance is to be equated to joy, but also Dante sees a clear example of this as he enters the second heaven, where the souls are barely discernible within the bright points of light. As we shall see, this is the last time Dante can see the souls themselves. After this canto they will be entirely concealed within the light they emanate.

Canto VI   The soul that now addresses Dante is that of Justinian, Emperor of the Eastern Roman Empire in the sixth century, who was responsible for the famous compilation of Roman law known as the Justinian Code. Having identified himself, Justinian feels moved to give a protracted answer to Dante's question, in order to indicate fully what it means to be a Roman citizen and why and how the political factions of Dante's own day, the Guelphs and the Ghibellines, were actually defiling the Roman name. To make his point, Justinian undertakes a long account of the history of the Roman Empire with all its ups and downs, casting it as a narrative about the vicissitudes undergone by the Roman Eagle.

He subsequently turns his attention to Dante's second question regarding the types of souls relegated to the second heaven of Mercury. On this planet are to be found the spirits of those who had engaged in the active life out of a craving for earthly honor and fame rather than out of love of God. While such activities properly directed can also lead to ultimate salvation, the path is much more indirect than in the case of those who devote their earthly lives exclusively to the service and love of God. Although the happiness of the souls on the planet

Mercury depends upon their innate merit, each feels duly rewarded for his individual desert.

Justinian then refers to a certain Romeo of Villeneuve who had been minister to a certain Provençal court in the first half of the 13th century. According to legend, Romeo arrived at the count's court as a poor pilgrim, proceeded to increase the wealth and stature of the count almost beyond measure, but then, because of the envy of the courtiers, he departed as poor as he had come.

COMMENTARY: The basic lesson learned by the pilgrim soul in this canto relates to the providential role of Rome in the progress of civilization. Roman sovereignty, symbolized by the eagle, deserves the respect of friend and foe, for it has divine sanction.

At this point, Dante also develops the concept that earthly activities directed to just causes are not detrimental to salvation, even though they may be motivated by ambition and desire for glory. While such activities may not be the most direct road to ultimate happiness, they are not necessarily an obstacle to its achievement. The joy of Heaven consists of various kinds of beatitude.

For their respective deeds and accomplishments Justinian and the humble Romeo fully participate in beatitude according to their individual portion.

Canto VII   On completing his account, Justinian fades into the overwhelming light of Mercury, joining the other souls that dance to a hymn honoring the glory of God. Beatrice again foresees a question aroused in Dante's mind by Justinian's words. In describing the vicissitudes of the Roman Eagle, Justinian made the crucifixion of Christ a culminating event in the chronicle of the Roman Empire. The event had been a kind of "vengeance" for Adam's sin. This vengeance had in turn been avenged when Titus overran Jerusalem. What puzzles Dante, therefore, is how a just punishment can itself be justly punished.

In order to answer this puzzle, Beatrice has to start with the creation of mankind and the fall of Adam and Eve. Original sin had caused the human species to suffer death, a condition to which man would not have been subjected were it not for Adam's sin. It was not until God decided to assume human form and to suffer death upon the cross that human nature was vindicated. But the Crucifixion was also an outrage to God's divinity. Because the Jews had exulted at this outrage and sacrilege, they were justly punished by the fall of Jerusalem.

Beatrice's explanation leads to another question in Dante's mind. Why did God choose to bring about man's redemption by means of His crucifixion? The essence of Beatrice's answer lies in the concept of God's infinite love. Being perfect, God chose to redeem his favorite creature by what might be called a perfect action. By choosing to be crucified, He exercised both mercy and justice, forgiving humanity while at the same time exacting satisfaction. Indeed only such an act could possibly have redeemed man, since his arrogant disobedience of God's command was of such a nature that no merely human act of humility could be sufficient to atone for the sin. Only God Himself could achieve the necessary depth of humility by assuming human flesh and undergoing the extreme self-abasement of a crucifixion. In this way, human nature was able to shake off the yoke of unredeemed death. This was as it should be, for all creation deriving directly from the hand of God can never die.

As for Dante's doubts concerning the creation and fate of the other elements, these are resolved by Beatrice's pointing out that they were not created directly by God's hand but through His agent, Nature. Only men and angels enjoy God's predilection.

COMMENTARY: Despite the seemingly pedantic nature of the subject matter covered in this canto, it marks a critical milestone in the enlightenment of the questing soul. It is significant that in the heaven in which earthly striving is depicted as a possible road to salvation, Beatrice, as Revelation, expounds on the meaning of the most glorious of earthly events. The significance of the Crucifixion in explaining not only the infinite love of God but the inherent dignity of man emerges most vividly. Man's horrendous sin in Eden is an example of the infinite depths to which he is capable of descending. God's willingness to assume the flesh and to suffer the humiliation of crucifixion in order to redeem man is an indication of what a lofty creature man truly is.

Canto VIII   As Dante enters the heaven of Venus, he cannot refrain
from recalling the attitude of the ancients towards this planet, which they held responsible for whatever "mad love" permeated the
Universe. The planet itself is composed of a bright substance which
Dante enters in company with Beatrice. Not only does Beatrice's loveliness increase markedly, but swift sparks of light dash forward to greet
the visitors. Dante resorts to a music image to describe the manner in
which each soul could be distinguished.

Upon a sign from Beatrice, Dante inquires after the identity of
one of the souls. We learn that it is Charles Martel of the famed Anjou
family which ruled in Naples, Provence, and Hungary at the time of
Dante. While Charles's remarks relating to the succession of rulers in
Naples are of some interest, it is the doctrine of heredity suggested in
his account that constitutes the basic lesson learned by the wayfaring
soul. To Dante's question as to how a bad seed could develop from a
good one, Charles responds that it is not a matter of family heredity,
but the workings of the stars which constitute "Nature," the handmaid
of God. An individual's character depends on these providential influences rather than on family lineage. It is essential, therefore, that in
preparing youth for a future career we must consider his inherent character rather than his family status.

COMMENTARY: Again we see Dante's art struggling to convey the poetic experience as he enters the third heaven where are
located those souls whose love and excellence is marked by
some taint of worldliness. To depict their individuality, Dante
uses the image of sparks and flames, or of notes and songs, or
of a bolt of lightning to convey both their appearance and
speed. Their brilliance and movement again reflect the degree
of their respective joy.

The conversation with Charles Martel likewise focuses
on the importance of individual traits in human beings. Many
of the world's ills result from leaders whose character was
judged by family heredity rather than by celestial influence.

It is apparent from this canto that Charles Martel must
have become acquainted with Dante personally during his visit
to Florence in 1294. The allusion by Charles to one of Dante's

longer poems attests to the popularity that it enjoyed in Florence at the time of the visit.

Canto IX   Following Charles Martel's dire predictions of what will result from the actions of his successors, another bright soul steps forward to identify itself. It is a certain Cunizza, the youngest of six sisters of a notorious tyrant of the period. She too foretells dire events in the course of her story.

Cunizza is in turn followed by the soul of Folquet de Marselha, an Italian turned love poet in southern France, who eventually repented for his worldly life, entered a religious order, and ultimately became Bishop of Toulouse. He tells his story and then introduces a third soul, that of the biblical harlot, Rahab, who was, according to Dante, one of the first souls to occupy the heaven of Venus following the harrowing of Hell by Christ. We also learn that Venus is the last heaven to be reached by the earth's conical shadow, as it is projected in space. The canto concludes with some bitter remarks about Florence and the Church, both of which, in Dante's opinion, seem to make financial gain their primary concern.

COMMENTARY: Particularly noteworthy about this canto is the manner in which Dante, as in the case of Pier delle Vigne in the *Inferno,* prepares us for our encounter with a Provençal poet. By addressing Folquet in the precious language of the Provençal school, Dante projects greater realism into his characterization. Also worthy of note is the reference to the earth's shadow whose most remote reaches strike Venus. We are now on the threshold of a purer realm of the universe where no traces of earthly concerns or effects are to be found.

Canto X   As Dante follows Beatrice beyond the earth's shadow, he prepares us for a new type of experience by reminding us of the ineffable quality of the Creation when the Love, Wisdom, and Power of God combined to produce the universe *ex mihilo.* He directs our attention to those portions of the heavens which are responsible for the seasons and for the infinite generation of being, recalling the incredible perfection of all the processes involved. He then goes on to explain the mysterious manner of his entry into the fourth heaven of the sun.

A sight that greets Dante in this heaven is that of souls whose brightness exceeds even that of the sun. At the suggestion of Beatrice, Dante renders thanks to God for the privilege of having reached this point. As his attention returns to the scene around him, he notes great numbers of moving lights forming a garland about him and Beatrice while uttering the sweetest of sounds, melodious beyond description. Like a dancing chorus of women, the lights circle three times before coming to a halt. Whereupon one of them comes forward and joyfully volunteers information, since it is clear that Dante himself must be among the elect, judging from his presence in this heaven. The soul then proceeds to identify the "flowers that compose the garland." First declaring itself to be St. Thomas Aquinas, it then goes on to identify the other members of the group, which comprises some of the greatest Christian theologians, including Albertus Magnus, Peter Lombard, Isidore, Bede, Richard of St. Victor, and even Solomon.

COMMENTARY: The heaven of the sun is a most suitable place for the theologians since it represents the image of enlightenment. Their brilliant appearance, their forming of a garland, and their sweet song reflect the joy of meditating on God. The symbolic revolution of the dance continues the opening image of the canto where the poet invites us to fix our minds on the intersection of the equator and the ecliptic, whose movements so control all of creation that we cannot doubt that a triune God produced "all that revolves through mind or through space." Each of the twelve great Doctors identified by St. Thomas represents the great capabilities of the human mind to contemplate and identify eternal truths. The immense distances cited throughout this canto reflect the journey that the mind must travel even to begin to shake off the shadow of Earth.

Canto XI This canto opens with an apostrophe condemning the petty concerns of mankind on earth, which can never compare with the eternal joys of the blessed encountered by Dante here in the *Paradiso.*

St. Thomas returns to his place in the circle of lights before acknowledging that he knew there was a question puzzling Dante concerning a remark made in the last canto. In speaking of St. Dominic as a shepherd leading a flock, St. Thomas had stated that if one followed the master's path faithfully, one would "fatten well." To clarify the point, St. Thomas undertakes a eulogy of St. Francis describing his life and actions in some detail.

He begins his account by asserting that Divine Providence had ordained the birth of two spiritual Princes who were to play crucial roles in the evolution of the Church on earth. One of these was St. Francis who personified the life devoted to heavenly love. The other was St. Dominic whose order was to foster the pursuit of celestial wisdom. St. Thomas, a Dominican, starts with St. Francis' birth in Assisi, whose very name (derived from Ascesi, meaning "I have risen") tells a great deal about the qualities of this unusual man. While still very young he took as consort Lady Poverty, despite his father's protestations. This was the first time that Lady Poverty had taken husband since she lost her first one, Christ. Before long he had a considerable group of followers which was shortly recognized as an official order by Pope Innocent III. The account goes on to relate how the order soon spread throughout the world, how St. Francis received the stigmata, and how he chose to die, unclothed, on the bare ground.

Similarly, St. Dominic possessed outstanding qualities, but his flock, like that of St. Francis, eventually strayed from the Master's path causing the Dominican Order to lose prestige. Those who do pursue the spirit of the Master do indeed "fatten well" at the table of the Lord. This is what was meant by the statement in Canto X.

COMMENTARY: We have seen that the first three heavens of Paradise are inhabited by souls whose goodness had suffered some earthly defect. In this and the next two heavens we meet the souls of those who had engaged in righteous activity on earth. In this fourth heaven of the sun, we have the great teachers of true wisdom, the essence of which is the understanding of God.

Upon joining the circle of lights, St. Thomas cites two of those teachers whose monastic orders had had such an impact on the world that they could be compared to the two wheels of the chariot of the Church. A Dominican himself, St. Thomas eulogizes the head of the opposite order, St. Francis. Through this account of the life of St. Francis, the pilgrim soul

perceives the mysterious ways in which God's charity permeates the entire world. The fact that a Dominican undertakes
the eulogy shows the type of harmony and courtesy intended
by God in human relations. Instead, members of each order
have strayed from the fold, causing strife and degeneracy. Ultimate happiness depends on the correct blending of the will and
of the intellect, of the good and of the true, as represented by
the Franciscan and Dominican Orders.

Canto XII   When the account of St. Thomas comes to a close, the
               circle of souls begins to revolve, singing as it moves. It is
joined by another circle which encircles it in turn, singing with equal
sweetness. Here again Dante's language and art are pushed to the extreme as he compares the sight to a double rainbow, while at the same
time enhancing the imagery with mythological allusions. He then compares the circling lights to garlands of roses revolving around him and
Beatrice. Finally he likens the entire scene to a pair of eyes sparkling
with joy and beauty.
      A singing voice can eventually be distinguished by Dante. At-
tracted to it like a compass needle, he hears it utter a eulogy of St.
Dominic which follows the same pattern of that in honor of St. Francis
by St. Thomas. The voice belongs to St. Bonaventure, a learned Franciscan of the 13th century. Declaring it is love that moves him to
speak, St. Bonaventure recounts the life of St. Dominic. He emphasizes
that both the latter and St. Francis were ordained by Christ to serve as
generals in leading the army of the Divine Empire. From his very birth
in Spain, St. Dominic showed signs of his religious zeal. In fact, even
before his birth his mother had dreamed of bringing forth a black and
white dog with a burning torch in its mouth. These became the colors
of the Dominican Order, with the torch signifying zeal and the very
name Dominican etymologically suggesting "dogs of the Lord." St.
Dominic too espoused Lady Poverty, but his talents were such that he
soon became a learned doctor of the Church. Having received official
sanction for his order, he struck hard at heretical beliefs. From his order sprang many others like little streams which serve to irrigate the
growing Christian faith. St. Dominic is for good reason, then, like the
second wheel of the chariot of the Church.

As for the followers of St. Francis, they have largely failed to pursue the track left by the chariot wheel. The order has split into two hostile factions, so that it is scarcely recognizable any more. Like the account of St. Thomas, this too concludes with the identification of the remaining members of the "wheel," including such names as St. Augustine, Hugh of St. Victor, St. Anselm, Rabanus Maurus, and Joachim of Flora.

COMMENTARY: Dante's attempt at the beginning of this canto to describe the double circle of lights turning one within the other is, we shall see, an initial prefiguration of the final vision. The revolving circles of bright light, of song, and of rose garlands are all images which contribute both to the final vision and to a grasp of the structure of the poet's *Paradiso*.

The account of St. Dominic's life by St. Bonaventure parallels the account of St. Francis' life given by St. Thomas in the preceding canto. In fact the parallels go so far as to cover like information in precisely the same numbered verses. Thus, the love of both St. Dominic and St. Francis for Lady Poverty is declared in lines 73 to 75 of each canto. Similarly, each canto ends with a series of verses whose exact meaning remains a puzzle. The resulting effect of mutual and equal recognition betokens the harmony that obtains between the religious orders here in the Heavenly Kingdom, where earthly differences and rivalries have no place.

We must bear in mind, however, that in this canto Dante has been standing in the midst of twenty-four Doctors of the Church who surround him in two concentric rings whose brilliance is the result of their complete dedication to Christianity and to the teachings of Christ. The symbolism of the scene encompasses the range of Christian philosophy of the time. The two circles represent two schools, the Platonic-Augustinian and the Aristotelian-Thomistic. The first proclaimed the primacy of the will and of the good over the intellect and the true. The second maintained the reverse.

Canto XIII   Again Dante must struggle to portray the encircling and
              dancing lights of the twenty-four doctors of the Church.
This time he makes use of heavenly constellations to convey the magnificent symmetry of the scene. The song being sung deals with the
triune God. When the singing ceases, St. Thomas' light once more
comes forward, moved by love, in order to explain another problem
which has been puzzling Dante.

In making reference to Solomon, St. Thomas had previously
stated that Solomon had no equal in understanding. Dante's mind was
not able to reconcile this with the roles of Adam and of Christ who presumably were the perfect specimens of God's creation. We are therefore led again to the perplexing problem of the imperfection of our
earth. According to St. Thomas, what we see about us is only a shadow
of the Divine Idea. The world is but the product of the nine heavens
which encircle it and, being the farthest away from the loftiest heaven,
it is the least perfect portion of creation. As we have previously learned,
the handiwork of nature is like that of the artist whose creativity is
spoiled by a trembling hand. Only where God creates directly is absolute perfection possible. Whence it does indeed follow that Adam and
Christ were perfect creations.

The perfection associated with Solomon was the perfection relating to kingly prudence. It was within this context that Solomon had
been referred to as having no superior. St. Thomas concludes by cau-
tioning Dante against the dangers of reaching rash conclusions through
failure to grasp essential distinctions. He gives various examples of
such thinking in the past which led to heretical conclusions.

COMMENTARY: This canto still opens with Dante standing at the center
               of two concentric rings which emit overwhelming light
and music. Having reached this lofty degree of heaven, the
soul is literally bombarded with joyful insights which now enable it to grasp more subtle distinctions between perfection and
imperfection. Human nature possesses the inevitable flaws resulting from the distance which it chose to place between itself
and its Creator by original sin. The direct results of God's creation, embodied in Adam and in Christ, exemplify the perfection of which human nature remains capable. Similarly, the
perfection of a Solomon reflects a kind of relativity which man

must also grasp in order to understand himself more clearly. So long as man recognizes he is subject to degrees of perfection and so long as his mind is clear on the examples that serve to embody such perfection, to that extent can he be called wise.

Canto XIV   This canto opens on the same concentric circles of moving lights. To describe the effect created as Beatrice now speaks from the center of the rings of souls right after St. Thomas' speech from one of the rings, the poet recalls the homely image of water rippling in a round container when struck alternately at the edge and at the center.

Beatrice's words express a question that Dante himself had yet to formulate in his own mind: will the brilliant light adorning these souls remain with them eternally, and, if so, how can their sight withstand the brilliance after they have reacquired their bodies? Following more sweet song, the voice of Solomon answers from the inner circle that the garment of light will certainly remain in eternity. Its brilliance will depend on the ardor of each soul's love which in turn will depend on the clarity of the soul's vision of God. This vision, finally, will depend upon the God-given degree of grace with which the soul has been divinely endowed at its creation. The souls indeed welcome the resumption of the body because it will increase their capacity for blessedness and therefore joy. There is no doubt of their being able to withstand the brilliance, inasmuch as the glorified body can suffer only through the spirit.

At this point, a third and brighter circle of dancing lights forms, like a gleaming horizon, around the first two rings of shining souls. Dante suddenly feels himself transferred to another planet, which he recognizes as Mars because of its ruddy glow. Upon rendering thanks to God for this new grace, Dante beholds two huge bands of light, each reminiscent of a milky way, traversing the planet in such a way as to form an immense cross, in the middle of which could be discerned an indistinct image of Christ. Bright lights move from one point to another of the cross like dust motes in a ray of light. The poet's image then assumes musical form to describe the ineffable harmony which emanates from the sparkling lights as from a viol or harp. So overwhelming is the vision for Dante that it seems momentarily to vie with the beauty of Beatrice's eyes.

COMMENTARY: Circularity continues to dominate Dante's imagery as
               he proceeds to the last lesson that he learns in the planet
of the sun. This lesson appropriately has to do with the identification of ultimate happiness with light and joy. Since the
Song of Solomon celebrates the union of the Divine with the
human, it is his voice that explains to Dante how the resurrection of the body will lead to a brilliancy in which the vision of
God will be as clear as the capacity of each soul will allow.
Upon grasping the full significance of this concept, Dante beholds a kind of triumph of the Holy Spirit which takes the form
of a third circle of lights surrounding the two rings of souls. It
is as though he has joined the host of those who are wise in the
things of the spirit.
               The image which greets Dante as he enters the planet
Mars is once again based on the concept of a circle. It is within
a circle that he defines the cross formed by the constellations
of light which seem to dominate the planet. By then having the
heavenly host sing out in unison, Dante succeeds in conveying
the immense sweetness and joy of Paradise.

Canto XV   The spectacle of the Cross of Mars with its incomparable
            colorfulness, sweet music, and infinite movement suddenly
becomes still, while one of the bright lights, like a falling star, quickly
moves from the right arm of the cross to the center and then down the
main strip in order to come as close as possible to Dante. Coming to a
halt, it addresses Dante in Latin in a manner recalling an episode from
the *Aeneid*. At first the soul's speech is beyond Dante's grasp, so that
he is momentarily bewildered. Slowly, however, the language does
descend to the level of human comprehension and Dante realizes once
again that these souls are capable of anticipating questions even before
they come to the mind of a mortal. Nevertheless, the soul wants him to
articulate his own questions.
            With a nod of approval from Beatrice, Dante requests that the
soul identify itself. Whereupon the "live topaz" reveals that it is the
soul of Dante's great-great-grandfather who had lived at a time when
Florence was a far more sober city than it presently is. He then goes on
to describe the peaceful, domestic life that was once enjoyed by the
Florentines. He finally identifies himself as Cacciaguida who had not

only sired Dante's ancestors but also, as a crusader, had been knighted by the Emperor.

The poet continues to make us sense the mystery and beauty of the vision which confronts him in the heaven of Mars through imagery based on astronomy, music, and color. As the singing of the souls in the Cross of Mars ceases, Dante compares the cross to a lyre. In describing the movement of his ancestor's soul, he compares it first to a falling meteor and quickly thereafter to a precious stone on a ribbon. The use of Latin, the obscure words of Cacciaguida, the inability of Dante's mortal mind to keep pace with the intuitions of the souls, all contribute to the effect of being present in the ineffable world of the spirit.

COMMENTARY: The motion of Cacciaguida's light as it performs a kind of front-and-center maneuver is in keeping not only with his military career on earth, but also with the general atmosphere of the heaven of Mars, which appropriately harbors soldiers of the faith. The pilgrim soul on its way to salvation now learns something of its earthly roots. It also is made to sense that somehow the golden age of mankind had its existence in the past. The Florence of old provided a much better form of life than the Florence of the early 14th century.

Cantos XVI and XVII   In Canto XVI Dante cannot resist a feeling of family pride in the presence of his noble ancestor Cacciaguida. Despite having written elsewhere of the insignificance of family lineage in determining the true worth of an individual, he opens this canto with a frank confession that he was the victim of such pride even in these reaches of Paradise. In fact, he makes conscious use of the polite "voi" form in addressing Cacciaguida. As he asks about his distinguished forebear's birth, family heritage, and the Florence of old, a smile of indulgence lights the face of Beatrice who stands aside to permit the interview.

After indicating its pleasure by glowing more brightly, like a live coal fanned by the wind, the soul of Cacciaguida undertakes an account of the family history. Starting with his birth, Cacciaguida moves on to a description of the Florence of his youth which he depicts in sharp contrast with the contemporary Florence overflowing with deceit and crime. The long list of family names that had inhabited the city two centuries earlier represents the old feudal aristocracy that had once prevailed.

In Canto XVII Dante's desire to learn of his future is manifest to the discerning eyes of Beatrice, who encourages him to ask Cacciaguida what destiny awaits him. After indicating that throughout his journey he has heard vague forecasts of a direful fate in store for him, Dante requests Cacciaguida to reveal his future. Cacciaguida does so clearly and without ambivalence. He predicts Dante's exile from Florence and the difficulties of his wanderings. He also predicts that his companions in exile will prove disloyal and that it will be necessary for Dante to stand alone. He further reveals the course of Dante's wanderings and his reception at the court of Verona, for whose rulers he has nothing but praise. Of one of these in particular, Can Grande della Scala, Cacciaguida predicts things so extraordinary that he asks Dante not to repeat them.

At the conclusion of Cacciaguida's prophecy, Dante asks whether it would be wise for him to reveal all he has heard and seen throughout his journey. Cacciaguida urges him to omit nothing, for while his message may at first prove distasteful, it will provide "vital nourishment" when digested. The fact that he has witnessed the fate of those of greatest renown will assure enduring fame to his work, since it is through illustrious example that one learns most.

COMMENTARY: In these two cantos, we have Dante passing judgment on his own times. The touch of justifiable pride in family heritage, with the implication that family cohesion extends from individual families to such social groups as the city, or indeed the nation, and that social justice must have its roots in the dignity of the individual family, seems to pervade the entire account. By looking back almost two centuries and forward several years as well, Dante sets in sharp focus the decadent social and political conditions of his day. The device of placing his journey back in 1300, though he was writing several years later, enables Dante in these cantos to make heaven itself appear to prophesy and pass judgment on forthcoming events. The political events of Florence during the first four years of the 14th century are used as examples of the extreme wickedness of man as a social animal. The enlightened rulers of Verona are depicted as alone capable of the kind of leadership necessary to effect the proper reforms. It has been long believed by some interpreters that Can Grande was the "hound" prophesied in Canto I of *Inferno* as the one who was to set the world straight again. Cacciaguida's prophecy of Dante's fate and his subsequent words of advice concerning the appropriateness of revealing the truths learned on the journey afford Dante the occasion to explain why he had peopled his poem with so many persons of renown. Only such examples could serve as significant lessons to all readers.

Canto XVIII   As Dante meditates upon Cacciaguida's words, Beatrice interrupts his wandering thoughts to remind him that only God enjoys the right to avenge wrongs. Her look is so full of love and loveliness that Dante finds his language inadequate to describe it. At Beatrice's bidding, he returns his gaze to the heavenly cross of souls, whose other members Cacciaguida now proceeds to identify. Following the identifications marked by each soul's shining forth like a flash of lightning, the voice of Cacciaguida rings loud and clear as he joins the singing which has continued throughout the episode.

Dante turns to Beatrice and realizes from her increased brilliance and beauty that they have entered another heaven. This is confirmed when he finds himself in an atmosphere of great whiteness, which contrasts with the redness of Mars. He is now in the sixth heaven of Jupiter sparkling with dancing and joyful souls who in their gaiety form letters that spell out, in Latin, the first verse of the Book of Wisdom: "Love righteousness, ye that be judges of the earth." Having reached the last letter of the verse, the letter M (of *terram*), the souls hold for a moment and then regroup in such a way that the M gradually takes on the figure of an eagle. In short order, certain souls who had hesitated to abandon the M formation now also join in the figure of the eagle. This prompts an outcry from Dante who berates the Church for its present corruption and misuse of power.

COMMENTARY: It is important to note in this canto that the surest sign of progress by Dante in the *Paradiso* is the increase in beauty of Beatrice. Having been warned by Beatrice that he must not harbor vengeance in his heart, Dante is made to note various champions of the Faith who compose the cross of Mars together with Cacciaguida.

The events which greet Dante in the heaven of Jupiter are intended to indicate the poet's belief that human justice is a product of this heaven. The first verse of the Book of Wisdom, as cited, stressed this point, since it urges judges to love righteousness (or justice). The thirty-five letters composing the Latin verse may reflect both the midpoint of human life by scriptural reckoning and the total books of the Old and New Testaments as revealed in the procession at the top of Purgatory. Similarly, the M formed by the souls of the just represents a number of things. It symbolizes the harmonious fusion or union of Church and State, body and soul, the earthly and the spiritual. The two downstrokes of the M recall the two horns of the Bishop's miter (signifying the Old and New Testaments). In addition to the heraldic form of the eagle, which stands for Empire, the M also recalls the name of Mary, ideal monarchy, and the Roman numeral for 1000, which is the outer limit of the ancient number system and a symbol of ultimate perfection. Thus the justice represented by the eagle signifies many ideals, as well as harmonizing earthly dualities.

Canto XIX   The astounding spectacle of the eagle composed of an infinite number of souls, each splendorous as a ruby, prompts Dante to reiterate the insufficiency of mortal language for describing such visions. This sense of ineffability is compounded when the eagle begins to speak a language of utter selflessness. As a symbol of justice it proclaims its merited glory which everyone exalts but few follow. Dante compares the unified speech of the many souls that compose the eagle to the steady heat that emerges from a number of burning coals. He addresses the souls as "perpetual flowers of eternal happiness," and asks their aid in resolving a problem that has perplexed him for sometime. The problem that seems to trouble Dante is the justice of damning virtuous pagans who had no opportunity to know Christ. Without waiting for Dante to put his question, the eagle undertakes a lengthy disquisition on the unfathomableness of God and the inability of creatures to grasp His infinite wisdom. Satan is cited as an example of what happens to a creature that is too impatient and eager to grasp mysteries beyond his portion. The arrogance of man is manifest in that even with a guide like the Bible he persists in his skepticism.

The eagle shows its displeasure by making a circling movement above Dante and then proceeds to expound in the clearest terms that without faith in Christ no one can be saved. On the other hand, many who profess such faith hypocritically will likewise not know salvation. Indeed these may find themselves in the netherworld more remote from the Godhead than the virtuous pagans. At the end of the canto, the eagle delivers a harsh condemnation of the chief sovereigns of the time who ruled without justice.

COMMENTARY: By stressing the unity of the souls composing the eagle here in the heaven of Jupiter, Dante points to the inherent unity of justice and the harmony of the righteous. This unity contrasts sharply with the many, divided, and unjust rulers of the time, and the implication is that human justice can be achieved only under a universal monarchy.

To question Divine Justice in human terms merits a rebuke, for it implies that man is capable of grasping the infinite wisdom of God. Without faith in Christ no person can aspire to heaven. However, such faith depends on the light of grace rather than historical accident. Many are the self-styled Christians who after the Final Judgment will occupy a lower place in God's universe than virtuous pagans.

Thus does Dante in this heaven of Jupiter learn the nature of justice, even as in the heaven of the sun he learned the nature of prudence and in the heaven of Mars the nature of fortitude.

Canto XX   Dante compares the image of the eagle become silent to that of the sky at sundown when it appears suddenly covered with glittering stars. The shining souls composing the eagle lift their voices again in heavenly song. When the singing ends, a murmuring sound, from the very depths of the eagle, slowly winds its way to the beak whence it emerges in words addressed to Dante.

Dante is asked to concentrate his attention on the eagle's eye which, the eagle explains, is formed of the souls of six foremost champions of justice, two Hebrews, three from classical antiquity, and one modern. David is the pupil of the eye and the other five, forming the eyebrow, are Trajan, Hezekiah, Constantine, William II, and Ripheus. This latter together with Cato, whom we met at the beginning of Purgatory, are the two examples in the *Comedy* illustrating the possibility of salvation for virtuous pagans.

A very minor character in the *Aeneid,* the Trojan prince Ripheus was called by Virgil "the most righteous of all, and the strictest observer of justice." The Emperor Trajan, though he died a pagan in Christian times, was, according to legend, permitted through the intercession by prayer of St. Gregory the Great to resume his body and return to earth in order to embrace the faith and die a Christian. King Hezekiah and William II were likewise upholders of justice. Dante's curiosity centers on the destiny of Trajan and Ripheus, whose location in heaven puzzles him. The eagle's explanation of each case proves satisfactory, and the canto ends with the two souls under discussion flashing together like strings plucked by a lute player.

COMMENTARY: The doctrine expounded in this canto is in accord with the teachings of St. Thomas who held that presumably unenlightened people could be blessed with the necessary grace for them to believe in salvation through Christ. The six examples cited as forming the eye of the eagle are presented in a structured manner reminiscent, for instance, of the symmetrical verses of *Purg.* XII, 25–63. Each example fills six verses of which the second tercet opens with the same two words. The number six thus receives emphasis in this sixth heaven of Jupiter where Dante fully grasps the power and inscrutability of divine justice.

Canto XXI   Dante turns to Beatrice who warns him that she can no longer smile because his human sight could not withstand her beauty. She also reveals that they have now reached the seventh heaven of Saturn and asks him to fix his sights carefully on a vision that is about to appear. Dante gladly complies, and as he contemplates the transparent atmosphere of the planet he beholds a golden ladder that extends upward as far as the eye can see. The ladder appears covered with an infinite number of glittering lights.

One of the closest lights glows with such brightness that Dante recognizes its over-abundance of love. Encouraged by Beatrice, he inquires of the light why it has come so close and why there is such silence among the souls here in Saturn. The soul informs him that there is no singing here for the same reason that there is no smile on Beatrice's face. He has come forward to greet Dante simply out of love for all of God's creatures. Dante, however, is curious as to why this particular soul and not another was predestined to perform this office. The soul swiftly spins about and then answers that it is simply because the light of Divine Love so penetrates him that he joyously performs whatever God's luminous desire indicates. Furthermore the Seraphim themselves, the order of angels closest to God, could not give Dante a satisfactory answer to this question on predestination. Indeed he should warn mortals to desist from searching the answer, since the heavenly host themselves are incapable of providing it.

This cutting answer prompts Dante to limit himself humbly to inquire after the identity of the soul, which reveals itself to be that of Peter Damian. Following a brief biographical sketch that reaches a point which describes how he had reluctantly assumed the office of Cardinal, Damian directs a bitter invective against the successors of Peter for their increasing corruption. As the bitter attack comes to an end, the lights constituting the ladder spin and glitter in a spectacle of incomparable beauty. They all gather around the light of Damian and suddenly utter a thunderous outcry whose significance Dante cannot grasp.

COMMENTARY: The cold planet of Saturn represents for Dante the spiritual condition of contemplative minds. Unlike the souls encountered in the preceding spheres who had been directly involved in the active life, these souls, though more exalted, reflect the subdued atmosphere of monastic discipline. There is no song here, because the highest form of contemplation resides in absolute silence. The same spirit is reflected in the seriousness of Beatrice.

The ladder, like Jacob's ladder, is also a symbol of contemplation. The kind but stern answer to Dante's question regarding predestination is a similar indication of monastic discipline. It is interesting to follow the metaphor, appearing early in the canto, of God sitting on the throne of an eternal court like a feudal lord to whom all subjects have vowed absolute obedience.

Peter Damian, a famous Doctor of the Church of the eleventh century, withdrew to a Benedictine monastery after a secular life of considerable success. As a Benedictine he preached and practiced a life of asceticism and wrote a number of works dealing with the reform of Church discipline. This, together with his brief career as a cardinal, made him an appropriate figure of the lieutenant of the Lord around whom loyal troops rally, as occurs at the end of the canto.

Canto XXII   The deafening cry of the souls causes Dante to turn to Beatrice like a small child seeking comfort. Beatrice, in motherly fashion, reassures Dante, explaining that being in heaven he should realize that all things are done for the good. Had Dante understood what the outcry signified, he would know that it referred to the vengeance which sooner or later the corrupt clergy must suffer. She encourages Dante to turn back to the souls if he wants further enlightenment.

As Dante gazes again upon the souls, he sees great numbers of them like little globes of light resembling pearls. His reticence to direct a question to them is dispelled when one comes forward to volunteer his services. The soul identifies itself as St. Benedict and gives a short account of his life. He also proceeds to identify other inhabitants of this heaven. To Dante's question as to whether it would be possible to see Benedict more clearly, it is answered that such sight will be possible only in the very last heaven where ultimate perfection is to be found. Although geographically unchartable, this last heaven is the heaven to which St. Benedict hoped his order would climb by means of a ladder such as Jacob's. Instead, there is no one to undertake such a climb and the hallowed halls of his beloved monastery now ring with scandal and vice. Benedict then joins the other souls and together they depart in the form of a whirlwind.

Beatrice next leads Dante swiftly up the ladder which carries them to the next celestial sphere. It is the heaven of the Fixed Stars, where Dante now finds himself in the constellation of the Gemini, under whose sign he was born. The poet calls upon the powers of the constellation to assist him in crossing over the threshold of Paradise. Beatrice informs him they are so close to that threshold that he will have to sharpen his sights more than ever. She therefore recommends that at this point he look back for one last time on the distances they have traversed thus far. Upon doing so, Dante sees all of the seven celestial spheres below him and, at the bottom of all, the earth whose smallness and ugliness bring a smile to his lips. In fact, compared to the celestial spheres, the tiny earth appears like a mere threshing floor over which mankind is foolishly and constantly wrangling. With such a perspective Dante now turns away for the last time from the earth and fixes his eyes steadfastly upon those of Beatrice.

COMMENTARY: This canto brings us to the threshold of Dante's Paradise proper. The shape taken by the souls when Dante turns once more to address them begins to reflect the increasing roundness of everything. They appear in the form of globes, of pearls, and brilliant swirlings of light. Dante's question regarding the possibility of seeing souls more clearly leads to Benedict's observation that such perfection can be expected only in Heaven itself, which is the last sphere. Its location cannot be physically defined, but the ladder of these contemplatives does lead to it, and it is upon this same ladder that Beatrice takes Dante to the next sphere.

The return to his native star is symbolically significant in that Dante is returning home by way of a classical route. Plato and Cicero among the ancients had developed the theory of how a soul returns to its particular star after death.

Beatrice's suggestion that before crossing the threshold to Heaven Dante look back at their progress so far implies that he is about to acquire a new perspective. And indeed he does when he looks down past all the spheres and recognizes for the first time how truly insignificant the earth appears in relation to the universe. Dante has now had his "immortal sight unfolded" and is viewing things from the top down. In a sense, he is beginning to see as God sees.

Dante's act of turning away from what lies below and focusing on Beatrice is here symbolic of his willingness to pursue his search for the divinity through revelation or faith. He is now firmly committed to the City of God rather than to the City of Man.

Canto XXIII   Like a mother bird tending her young and awaiting the arrival of the dawn in order to continue her search for food does Beatrice appear to Dante as he enters the eighth sphere in her company. Before long the entire sky begins to light up, and Beatrice cries out that they are about to behold the triumph of Christ and to enjoy the ultimate fruits of creation. In order to describe the vision, Dante has recourse to the image of a bright night illuminated by the full moon which seems to tower above an infinite number of stars. In this preliminary vision of Christ, Dante cannot withstand the brilliance of His appearance. Beatrice tries to reassure him by explaining that no human mind could withstand the vision which encompasses the Wisdom and Power of God Himself. At this point Dante feels his mind exploding as he hears Christ's own welcome informing him that he is indeed ready to behold the heavenly vision directly. Here Dante's language fails him, but by that very fact he conveys to the reader a sense of the ineffability of the experience.

Beatrice urges Dante not to concentrate on her but to turn to the "beautiful garden that flowers under the rays of Christ." There, she says, he may see the rose in which the Divine Word became flesh. Slowly Dante turns again to the resplendent star-like figures which he compares to an endless field of flowers and lights. He notes that Christ has now moved beyond his field of vision in order to enable him to withstand the brilliance. Focusing on the scene, he beholds Mary in all her glory as she is crowned by a torch borne by a messenger who circles her head amidst the sweetest melodies ever heard. As the heavenly messenger proclaims Mary's divinity in what Dante calls a "circular melody," the other countless souls join in the singing. The triumph of Mary, like that of Christ, disappears upward toward the Empyrean, and Dante's sight is again incapable of following the "crowned flame" of Mary. The other flames that participated in the triumphs now seem to extend themselves in the direction whence Christ and Mary had disappeared like countless little children reaching out towards their parents. They burst into the hymn, *Regina Coeli* (Queen of Heaven), as Dante undergoes the indescribable beatitude experienced by the souls in this sphere where not only Christ and Mary but also St. Peter triumphs.

COMMENTARY: As the purified soul approaches the threshold of Heaven proper, it is met by God's personal emissaries to humankind, Christ and Mary. Images such as the rising sun, the protective mother, together with the meditative and contemplative mood of the opening verses, provide both the dramatic factors and the symbolic signs indicating how the soul, endowed with grace and willing to pursue Reason and Faith, can expect a heavenly welcome in Paradise. Beatrice's cry that they are about to enjoy the true harvest of the heavenly revolutions and the subsequent descriptions of the triumphs of Christ and Mary clearly reveal the centrality of the mystery of Christ in Dante's conception of salvation. The two triumphs which he witnesses contain the basic secrets which his mind has been trying to grasp throughout the journey. In this ecstatic experience of looking at the mysteries directly, his mind seems to explode and go beyond itself, just as fire bursts forth from a swollen cloud as lightning. Thus the human mind, even at this stage, is not yet fully ready to view the mystery of mysteries.

Dante does, however, succeed in undergoing, as it were, an audio-visual preview for which his language proves insufficient. Beatrice's suggestion that he persist in contemplating the vision in order to view it in its entirety prompts Dante to return his attention to it. The constant use of agricultural terms such as "the beautiful garden which blossoms under the rays of Christ," or the mention of roses and lilies and fields of flowers implies the sustenance that can be gained from the vision.

Christ fades away in order to enable Dante to view Mary whose triumph, perhaps better than any other moment in the *Comedy,* makes most effective use of images reflecting circularity and movement around a fixed point. As we shall eventually discover, this is another prefiguration of the final vision. Here we note that even the singing has a circular quality.

As Mary follows Christ upward, the canto returns to the mother-child image with the infinite lights around Mary in the act of stretching toward her like children reaching for their mother. The canto ends with Dante's tasting deeply of the rich harvest of this preliminary experience of Paradise.

Canto XXIV   Beatrice supplicates the souls of the eighth sphere to have
              Dante partake of their banquet of knowledge. The joyful
souls express their willingness by forming wheels of fire resembling
the works inside a clock. Their boundless joy is reflected in their
dance-like movement. A soul detaches itself from the group and gaily
performs a song and dance three times around Beatrice. Beatrice requests that this soul, which is the soul of St. Peter, test Dante's knowledge of his Faith, not because of any doubt, but because in this celestial
sphere it is most appropriate to glorify the Faith by talking about it.

       After Dante compares himself to a doctoral candidate about to
undergo his qualifying examination, St. Peter asks him for a definition
of Faith. There follow a series of questions and answers that analyze
the nature of Faith in considerable detail. Dante's ready answers lead to
a successful termination of the examination, at which moment the other
souls join in applause by singing a triumphant hymn. Having successfully passed his formal examination, Dante is asked by St. Peter to express his personal Faith. Dante thereupon paraphrases the Christian
Credo which he delivers so convincingly and well that St. Peter encircles him in a joyful dance three times, as he had done with Beatrice.

COMMENTARY: The triumph of the proceeding canto now resolves it-
               self into a kind of banquet where the Lamb forms the
       main course. This image of the infinite banquet in which the
       souls of Paradise participate will recur often. The flaming
       wheels and the circling dances of the souls, as well as the im-
       age of the clock-wheels transmitting motion from one to an-
       other, represent Dante's constant attempt to define the harmo-
       nious realm of the spirit in concrete terms.

              Dante has thus far seen God revealed through His
       works. Before he can contemplate Him directly, he must see
       Him revealed in Christian doctrine. The examination on Faith
       in this canto and on Hope and Charity in the following ones are
       staged exclusively for the benefit of Dante who is to return
       back to earth. These virtues apply only to the living, since for
       the heavenly souls Faith has become knowledge and Hope has
       become fulfillment. Furthermore, the three theological virtues
       come to man from above and not naturally. It is fitting there-
       fore that St. Peter, Christ's successor on earth, conduct the ex-

amination on the first of the three virtues, Faith. Dante's ready answers indicate the extent to which he understands the Faith, while his personal profession of faith reflects the extent to which it has truly become a part of him.

Toward the end of the canto, Dante compares St. Peter first to a baron, then to a lord welcoming a servant into the household. This, along with other instances to come, echoes the principle of hierarchy and contributes to the evolving image of Heaven as a divine court.

Canto XXV   Dante's symbolic crowning upon the successful completion of his examination on Faith prompts him to express the hope of some day being crowned poet laureate back in his native Florence. A new flaming soul now comes forward and is identified by Beatrice as another "baron of the Faith," St. James. Following an exchange of joyous girations between this new soul and that of St. Peter, St. James approaches Dante directly. Beatrice requests that St. James talk to Dante about the second great theological virtue, Hope, of which St. James is a perfect exemplar.

St. James asks Dante who had lowered his eyes at the brilliance of these souls, to raise his head to them. He then asks Dante for his definition and conception of Hope. After Beatrice points out that Dante has come from "Egypt" to "Jerusalem" to see God directly, Dante undertakes a definition of Hope and an explanation of how and why he possesses it. Once more the entire group of souls sings out, thereby proclaiming their satisfaction with Dante's answers.

A new light now detaches itself from the group, approaches the the souls of St. Peter and St. James, and together with them participates in singing and dancing while rotating together. Beatrice identifies the new light as that of St. John, who stands for Love, or Charity. The latter notes Dante's stare and, realizing that he believes the legend about St. John being taken up to Heaven in the flesh, hastens to explain that his body is back on earth; only Christ and Mary were privileged to ascend to Heaven with their bodies. Suddenly the entire sphere becomes quiet as at a signal, and all eyes focus on St. John and Dante.

COMMENTARY: At the opening of this canto on Hope Dante fittingly
                discloses his dearest human hope. As an exile from
Florence, he had constantly dreamed of the day when he might
return to be crowned poet laureate.

             The fact that St. James had proclaimed his "certain
expectation" of Heaven makes him a fitting exponent of Hope.
The singing, brightness, and movements of the souls continue
to symbolize the approaching ultimate vision. Beatrice's revelation that Dante has now advanced from "Egypt to Jerusalem"
indicates that the poet is nearing the end of his journey. The
appearance of St. John in the form of an unbearably bright
light which joins in dance with the other two apostles gives
hint of the greater brilliance that awaits Dante. This blinding
effect prepares the stage for Dante's examination on Love
whose blinding power is clearly suggested here.

Canto XXVI   St. John assures Dante that his blindness is temporary and
              that his sight will eventually be restored. He asks Dante to
reveal the end goal of his life, which Dante defines as the ultimate
Good whose other name is Love. In answer to a second question put to
him by St. John, Dante reveals that he had set his sights upon such a
goal as a result of his studies and of doctrinal teachings. As bidden, he
goes into greater detail to show the many influences that helped him
escape from "the sea of crooked love." As the souls rejoice once again
in ringing song, Dante feels his sight regain focus and notices a fourth
light joining the group. Beatrice identifies this new soul as that of
Adam who, having guessed a number of questions that are on Dante's
mind, is glad to provide answers. These relate to a number of details
concerning Adam's stay in the Garden of Eden.

COMMENTARY: Contrary to the pattern of the two preceding examina-
                tions, Dante is not asked for a definition of Love by St.
                John. Rather, he is asked to identify the object and reason for
his love. It may be well to point out the learned nature of
Dante's previous definitions and also of his answer to the questions in this canto. References to classical thinkers as well as to
Church Fathers and other ecclesiastical authorities abound everywhere in his answers.

Of particular note, also, are the kinds of metaphors
used by Dante to describe the nature and direction of his Love.
We have the images of the bow and arrow, of the partaking of
food, of the mariner on a lost ship, of God as gardener and as
mirror. Such images will increase in frequency as the poet
struggles to give substance to the invisible and ineffable.

While perhaps surprising, Adam's appearance here is
justified by the fact that the entire episode is a commentary on
the triumphs of Christ and Mary, in whose drama Adam certainly played a central role. Had it not been for Adam and the
Fall there would have been no Christ or Mary. Of particular interest is Adam's explanation of the nature of language which
occurs at the very end of the canto.

The soul now has a deep understanding of Faith, Hope,
and Charity and has here achieved full awareness of the moment when God created man in His own image.

Canto XXVII   With the conclusion of Adam's words all the souls in the
eighth heaven join in a hymn to the Trinity. The joyful-
ness is such that Dante compares it to a "smile of the universe." As
Dante observes the four souls before him (St. Peter, St. James, St. John,
and Adam), the brightness of St. Peter begins to turn to a reddish hue.
At this, all the souls become still, and St. Peter undertakes a bitter invective against his successors and the present state of the Church on
earth. He concludes by prophesying a sweeping reform and instructing
Dante to reveal all that he has heard.

The hosts of souls in the eighth sphere now begin to depart like
snowflakes falling upward. Dante beholds the spectacle in amazement,
but very shortly the voice of Beatrice beckons him to look downward
in order to realize how far they have traveled.

As Dante turns astonished to Beatrice he is suddenly and mysteriously transported to the ninth heaven. This is the Primum Mobile
whose nature and function Beatrice now undertakes to explain briefly.
This highest sphere before Heaven proper is the source of all of Nature's powers. It is this sphere that imparts movement and thus power
to all the other spheres. Beyond it lies only the light and love of God
Himself, by which this ninth sphere is directly surrounded. Beatrice's
description of the powers of the Primum Mobile terminates in an apos-

trophe against man's greed which renders him incapable of appreciating eternal truths. This is the cause for the Monarchy's failure to rule mankind as was intended. And this is why there will be a violent reformation of the social structure.

COMMENTARY: Dante has now reached a point in the spiritual realm which can be compared to the moment when he and Virgil were turning at Satan's waist. Once again he is on the threshold of a new world, the world of pure spirit. He has traversed all of the heavens and is about to enter the very highest sphere from which all earthly events take form. We are about to observe another shift in center of gravity. It is most appropriate, therefore, that as Dante leaves the eighth heaven St. Peter directs an apostrophe against the state of the Church, and that as he enters the ninth sphere Beatrice directs an invective against the Monarchy.

Particularly interesting is Beatrice's metaphor of the tree having its roots in the ninth sphere and its branches representing the various other spheres below. The upside-down tree is not a new metaphor, but here it helps prepare us for the shift in center of gravity.

Canto XXVIII   Upon reaching the confines of the world of matter, Dante has his first truly symbolic vision of God in His relation to the physical universe. He first undergoes this experience as he gazes in Beatrice's eyes. Turning to see if what is reflected there is real, he observes a microscopic point whose brilliance forces him to close his eyes. This minute point is surrounded by nine concentric circles that spin about it with varying speeds and brilliance. The one closest to the point revolves the fastest and is the brightest. Beatrice explains that the point of light is the source of all creation and that the vision is but an image of God's universe.

Dante is puzzled by the fact that in the vision or "example" of the heavenly spheres the innermost circle travels fastest, whereas in actuality it is the outermost sphere, or Primum Mobile, that revolves with the greatest speed. Beatrice's explanation is based on the concept that God is the spaceless center of the universe even as He is the all-embracer. Thus just as in the order of the heavens it is the Primum Mobile that is closest to God and revolves with the greatest speed, in the same manner, when God is viewed as the center of all things, the circle closest to this center must represent the Primum Mobile. In the spiritual world space is meaningless and only proximity to God matters.

As Beatrice concludes her explanation and Dante grasps its significance, the nine circles begin to emit a series of sparks whose brightness reminds the poet of molten metal. Sweet song issues from the sparks and Beatrice explains that these are the nine orders of angels which rule over the nine heavens. She even cites her authority in describing the names, orders, and functions of the angels.

COMMENTARY: Having received what amounts to divine insight not only into the spiritual mysteries of the theological virtues but also into the human condition as symbolized by the Church and the Empire, the soul on the way to salvation now has its first insight into the nature of God, not in His essence but in His relation to the orders of angels that govern the spheres. The vision first reaches Dante through Beatrice's eyes, indicating that his first perception of the Truth comes from Revelation. He is soon able to turn to the vision directly. Its form is that of a brilliant point of light surrounded by nine concentric wheels of fire spinning about it. Through his questions directed to Beatrice, Dante learns that God must ultimately be viewed as the center of all things as well as the embracer of all things. In the material universe, the center is most distant from God. In the spiritual universe, the center is God. Consequently, what Dante is now viewing is the material universe turned, as it were, inside out.

In his attempt to understand the orders of angels responsible for the operation of the heavens, Dante realizes how such understanding depends upon the soul's state of Grace and corresponding merit. This in turn leads to an intellectual vision and finally to Love, the ultimate goal of the entire process.

It is interesting to note the presence of the number three in the angelic hierarchy, which is represented in three triads, each in turn composed of three distinct orders. Also noteworthy is the manner in which the recurrent figures of revolving wheels of light now form the basis of this preliminary image of God. The clock figure comes readily to mind, as we see with Dante how the nine spheres and the respective angelic intelligences work together in unison.

Canto XXIX   At the beginning of this canto Beatrice explains that the act of creation was but an outward reflection of God's eternal and infinite love. Her detailed description of how God created the heavens, the angels, and brute matter on the first day, and how subsequently all of these beings or levels of creation were arranged in due order, is based on St. Thomas. Beatrice's discussion eventually focuses on the angels and touches upon a number of moot questions concerning them. From an explanation of how, where, and when they were created she moves on to the nature of their acts by which they were damned or saved shortly after creation. She also dwells on the qualities possessed by those that Dante now sees in his preliminary vision of God. She then proceeds to take surprisingly sharp issue with the scholastic quibbling of philosophers and churchmen back on earth, who apparently have lost sight of the fact that the ultimate authority on all such matters is Scripture itself.

The canto closes with a reference to the infinite number of these perfect beings — the angels — and the beauty of the love which is everywhere reflected in them as in so many mirrors projecting an infinite source of light.

COMMENTARY: It is only fitting that as Dante begins to cross the threshold between the physical and the spiritual universe he should receive insight into the nature of the earliest inhabitants of this new realm, the angels. Despite the apparent tediousness of the speculations involved, the fact that the poet projects them within the framework of God's infinite love, whose very perfection demanded the existence of such creatures, provides the canto with some poetic dimension. The further strategy of having Beatrice presumably correct some current misinterpretations of doctrinal points having roots in Scripture contributes to the general movement we have been noting of a soul returning to its source and learning to see with purified spiritual sight.

We must bear in mind that throughout this canto Dante is still contemplating his first vision of God and, with the help of Beatrice, is learning to understand the nature of the nine concentric circles that surround the bright point of light. The moment has now come when he may focus upon the Light itself.

Canto XXX   Dante's preliminary vision of God now begins to fade away as the sparkling flames of the concentric circles disappear within the overpowering brilliance of the Point. The poet turns to Beatrice for enlightenment and finds her beauty more dazzling than ever. There is some implication that Beatrice, too, is about to fade away.

She does, however, explain to the poet that they have now entered Heaven proper. They have indeed entered pure light, a light leading to infinite love and joy. She alerts Dante that now he will see the ultimate triumph, that of the angels and the souls of the Elect, whom she refers to as the "two militias" of Paradise.

Suddenly Dante is immersed in blinding light. He senses that he has gone beyond his mere human powers and struggles to describe the new vision to which he is now exposed. First he sees a river of light flowing between banks laden with colorful spring flowers. "Living sparks" seem to emerge from the river and nestle in the flowers. They then seem to return to immerse themselves in the flowing stream.

Beatrice reveals to Dante that before he can grasp what he has seen he must first drink of this river. She further explains that the vision appears to Dante in this present form because of the inability of his sight to perceive its true form as yet. Having stooped over the bank and let his lashes touch the water, Dante suddenly sees the vision assume a new form. The river takes on the appearance of a round sea of light while its banks are transformed into tiers of seats forming an amphitheater occupied by the Elect in their glorified bodies.

As Dante contemplates the scene, he cannot help comparing it also to an immense rose. In addition, he experiences a sensation of spacelessness. His vision is immediate and all-encompassing, for spatial distinctions of near and far do not obtain here.

Leading Dante to the center of the "rose," Beatrice tries to convey to him the size of the "City of God," which she also refers to as the

the Lord's "convent." She indicates that most of the seats are already occupied and draws Dante's attention to a particular one resembling a throne. She predicts that this seat will soon be occupied by the Emperor Henry VII who will attempt to "straighten out" Italy. She also predicts that Henry will fail because of Pope Clement V who will oppose him and who will be damned among the simonists in Hell.

COMMENTARY: This canto recalls Canto XXX of Purgatory where Beatrice also appeared in a new light and where Virgil withdrew from the action. Here it is Dante who enters the "light" and prepares the way for the exit of Beatrice, since he no longer needs an intermediary between the "light and the intellect," which was one of the definitions of Beatrice. The canto is full of signs that the end of the poem itself is very close.

Throughout the canto we meet images that have recurred again and again, but now for the first time we begin to grasp them fully. As Beatrice points out, they had been but "shadowy prefaces of the reality."

The basic meaning of the canto is that Dante has moved into the timeless and spaceless spiritual world. The River of Light represents the River of Grace from which he must first drink in order to perfect his sight. The straight lines before him now give way to circles, implying a movement from time to eternity. By its form, the amphitheater proclaims the unity of all participants. Finally, the image of the rose ties all meanings together into the all-encompassing one of Love, or Charity. Beatrice's surprising last words are directed against a Pontiff who presumably was impeding the spread of such Love on earth. The fact that all of this emerges in the third canto of the poem bearing the number 30 is also significant, reflecting, as it does, the clear presence of the Trinity.

Canto XXXI   As Dante views the lily white rose of light, he sees hosts of angels which like bees travel back and forth between the center of the rose and the outer portions where the Blessed sit row on row. These angels possess flaming faces, golden wings, and bodies of extraordinary whiteness. Plying back and forth, they seem to leave everywhere peace and love. Nor does their presence seem to interfere with Dante's view of the whole, for like transparent bees they permit the divine light to penetrate everywhere in just measure. Both "militias" seem intent on contemplating the light in the center.

Dante compares his amazement first to that of a pagan observing Rome for the first time, and then to the reaction of a devout pilgrim who has reached the final goal of his journey. The awareness that he is viewing "the general form of Paradise" prompts him to turn to Beatrice. Where he expected to see Beatrice he sees instead a venerable elder whose features seem to partake of the general joy. When Dante asks where Beatrice is the elder replies that she has sent him to take her place. She in turn has returned to her seat reserved next to Rachel, three rows from the top tier of the rose amphitheater. Despite the immense distance separating Dante from Beatrice's seat, he can see her clearly as she smiles to him. Whereupon he addresses a touching final prayer to her, expressing his gratitude to the Lady who has led him from "slavery to liberty."

The elder identifies himself as St. Bernard and invites Dante to raise his eyes to the Virgin Mary who will assist him to see the Godhead Itself. Looking more closely at St. Bernard, Dante is struck by the peace and serenity of his appearance. But St. Bernard urges him to look up to the Queen of this realm. Slowly raising his eyes, he discerns, in the midst of an infinite host of joyful angels, Mary herself, bathed in a light of ineffable beauty and love.

COMMENTARY: The bee-like activity of the angels described at the beginning of this canto powerfully epitomizes an essential function of heaven, namely, endless generation of joyous love of which all partake. Dante's perfected vision can now clearly distinguish this activity which in the preceding canto had appeared like a movement of sparks darting between the river and the flowers.

The image of the pagan first beholding the center of Christian Rome and then of the pilgrim reaching the holy place he had set out to visit enhance the theme of the soul returning to its spiritual home. The disappearance of Beatrice reflects achievement of spiritual maturity. Dante no longer needs an intermediary between the Truth and "the light of the intellect."

Paradiso XXXI. The Empyrean.

Dante's final apostrophe to Beatrice is indeed a memorable expression of gratitude. Once again the reader requires double vision as the poet fuses the real and the symbolic Beatrice. Most interesting in this regard is Dante's use of the second person singular, or familiar "tu" form, in addressing Beatrice. Previously, the poet always used the plural, or deferential "voi" form.

The substitution of St. Bernard for Beatrice, on the other hand, implies the need for another guide. Nowhere along this arduous journey can a soul depend exclusively on its own powers. Just as Virgil and Beatrice symbolized ways in which man can attain knowledge of God, the same is true of St. Bernard. From divine knowledge attained through Reason and Revelation, the soul now proceeds to knowledge through Intuition.

St. Bernard, as this third type of knowledge of God, gives Dante's sight one final adjustment. By gently urging him to look higher he succeeds in enabling Dante's sight to withstand the view of the Virgin Mary in all her glory.

In this canto we begin to appreciate what one critic says of the last four cantos of the *Comedy:* "(Dante) here achieves what no other poet, before or since, has attempted with so much as a shadow of success: the presentation of a world beyond the perceptions of sense."

Canto XXXII   St. Bernard now proceeds to describe to Dante the deliberate distribution of the souls in the rose-amphitheater of heaven. The general symmetry of their location is based upon faith in Christ to come or Christ already come. These two major divisions also include souls whose salvation depended not on their own merit but on the merit of others. Among these are the souls of children whose parents possessed the Faith. Nothing is left to chance. The actual degree of beatitude depends on the Grace with which each soul was originally endowed.

Having outlined the general form of Paradise, St. Bernard urges Dante once more to concentrate on Mary through whom alone the ultimate vision can be achieved. Again the sight of her is overwhelming. Dante notes that she is watched over by an angel who leads the entire assembly in a ringing hymn starting *Ave Maria*. To Dante's question regarding the identity of this angel, St. Bernard answers that it is Gabriel. Starting with Mary, St. Bernard then describes the horizontal and vertical divisions of the amphitheater leading to the location of St. Lucy who originally helped set the entire drama of the *Comedy* in motion. The canto ends with St. Bernard indicating that the moment has arrived for Dante to view the ultimate vision directly. All that remains is a supplication to the Virgin for the necessary visual power.

COMMENTARY: The mysterious role that Dante assigns to predestination in determining the location of souls in the Empyrean makes it difficult to attempt any clear classification. St. Bernard's implication of symmetry and clarity in the disposition of the souls seems to reflect only that proximity to Mary on the one side and John the Baptist on the other carries a degree of honor. Yet he also points out that actual merit and, consequently, power of vision depend on the degree of Grace with which each soul is endowed. This makes any attempt at classification rather futile. On the other hand, it does indicate that individuality is retained even in God's court, inasmuch as every soul possesses a specific degree of Grace.

We must also bear in mind that Dante is now viewing the souls as they would appear after the Final Judgment when they will assume their glorified bodies. This is a rare privilege indeed, and can be achieved only by a soul possessing the special Grace that accrues from sincere prayer and supplication to the Virgin. The brief allusion to St. Lucy and her role in the opening moments of the poem remind us that we are about to come full circle.

Canto XXXIII   The final canto begins with a moving prayer to Mary by St. Bernard. In the prayer are listed the many virtues of the Virgin in her role as direct intermediary between God and man. The purpose of the prayer is to request that she provide Dante with the necessary power of vision to grasp the very essence of God. The prayer also asks that Dante's human qualities not be adversely affected following such an experience. At prayer's end, St. Bernard assures the Virgin that Beatrice also joins him in his supplication.

Mary's eyes reflect her pleasure as they turn upward to contemplate the Eternal Light. With St. Bernard's encouragement, Dante also directs his sight upward and begins to distinguish the essential characteristics of the Godhead. First, however, he struggles to convince us of the inadequacy of human language to describe what he saw. Then slowly but surely he brings the vision into increasingly clear focus.

The description starts with an indication of how the Almighty contains within Itself the entire multiform world while yet remaining indivisible and undiversified. The basic unity of the Godhead is compared to "a book bound with love." The essential characteristic of the vision, however, remains the single brilliant point of light.

The next experience described by the poet is that of the impossibility of turning away from such a vision once its true nature is discerned, since it contains all that gives life value. As a source of all Good it is the ultimate positive attraction for the human mind.

As Dante's sight gains power, he finally sees the vision in its clearest form. He describes it as three circles of three different colors occupying exactly the same space, of the same dimension and yet distinguishable. In its self-containment, this triune Eternal Light slowly reflects a human figure which fits perfectly within the rings. As Dante struggles to understand how such a figure could conform so perfectly to the roundness of the basic image, he undergoes a sudden, climactic moment of deep intuition where he succeeds in grasping the relationship between the Human and the Divine. The soul feels its deepest longing satisfied in the awareness that its individual will is merged in the World-Will of that "Love that moves the sun and the other stars."

COMMENTARY: Dante's story of repentance, reform, and regeneration comes to an end in this canto as he achieves ultimate insight into the nature of God and of all creation. We note that the canto opens with a prayer to Mary and ends with a profound understanding of the nature of Christ. The vision thus recaptures the basic progress of the journey of the *Comedy* that moves from the essentially Human to the essentially Divine. St. Bernard's supplication that Dante be permitted to retain his human powers after the privileged vision reflects the poet's conviction that the individual human personality is one of the great wonders of creation and also prepares for the poet-wayfarer's "return."

One of the greatest moments in the poet's struggle with words is found in this canto where he first convinces us of the ineffability of his vision and then manages to convey it in a surprisingly persuasive manner. When the vision assumes the form of three concentric circles of different colors and of equal proportions, a storm of images returns to mind as we recall the many moments encountered throughout the poem where such circularity struggled to take on specific form. We suddenly realize that along the whole way of the journey the soul has been grappling with this final image and we understand why the vision could not take on final form until this moment. The soul had to travel back to its Creator and had to understand clearly what had caused the apparent distance that separated it from Him. It has indeed evolved from a worm to an angelic butterfly by struggling free of the constraining cocoon. When it understands why and how the Divine partakes of the Human and the Human partakes of the Divine, it has achieved ultimate knowledge and is once again in the fold of that "Love that moves the sun and the other stars."

NOTE. While the Holy Trinity permeates the entire *Comedy* with the symbolic number three, as we reach the ultimate goal of the poem with the dual figure of Christ, human and divine, flashing within the circle of divine light, it becomes clear at last that the poem is more specifically Christo-centric, as shown by C.S. Singleton's interpretation in his brilliant essay "the Vistas in Retrospect" (see BIBLIOGRAPHY). This obtains all along the way of the poem's emerging form, with distinct pivotal points at the end of the *Inferno* and the beginning of the *Purgatorio*. The descent into humility on the pattern of Christ on earth is the ultimate significance of the *Inferno*. This is later defined by the symbol of humility (the river rush) at the end of *Purgatorio* I. It is also at this pivotal point in *Purgatorio* I at the foot of the mountain (a flashback to the sun-topped mountain in *Inferno* I) that the pilgrim's ascent in "justification," defined by Singleton as the restoration of justice (order) in the soul, begins, and suggestively traces a pattern of redemption through Christ.

LEVELS OF MEANING The Basic Dual Sense of the *Divine Comedy*		
Main Action	Literal Level	Allegorical Level
INFERNO	The damned after death, fixed in their respective states of sinfulness and suffering retribution in eternal exile from God.	Figures the depths of sin to which the soul can sink in this life. Man's creation of his own hell in sin.
PURGATORIO	The redeemed after death as they purge away various stains of vice before ascending to Heaven.	Figures the repentive way of achieving order in the soul in this life. Perfection of man as man here on earth.
PARADISO	The beatified souls in Heaven, enjoying the direct vision of God.	Figures the soul in a state of grace and the process of rising to the mystical vision of God. Perfection of man beyond man.
Main Characters	Literal Level	Allegorical Level
DANTE	Florentine citizen and poet of the *Commedia* whose beloved was Beatrice.	Whoever would turn from sinfulness to God's way.
VIRGIL	Poet of the *Aeneid* and celebrator of Rome.	Symbol of Reason. The highest achievement of man as man in virtue and knowledge.
BEATRICE	Florentine citizen loved by Dante.	Functional analogue of Christ. Variously assumes attributes of Revelation, Grace, Wisdom.
ST. BERNARD	Medieval theologian.	A perfectly fulfilled Christian with intuitive knowledge of God.

CRITICAL ANALYSIS

I. The Medieval Perspective

A MAJOR REASON why many modern readers have trouble with the *Divine Comedy* lies in their inability to focus on more than one level of meaning at a time when reading a work of literature. The idea of searching for underlying meaning which has been carefully hidden by an author has lost favor since the Renaissance, and may actually be repugnant to modern readers.

In the Middle Ages, however, the opposite was true. The more a writer succeeded in making his public dig and reach for meaning, the greater his work was considered to be. The reason is quite simple. It was believed that this was the way in which God, the Creator and greatest of authors, had fashioned the "book of the world" and had inspired His other book — the Bible. Just as the Bible, for example, requires great concentration of thought and deep interpretation to extract its complex meaning, in the same manner were the truly serious works of literature expected to be demanding on their readers. Furthermore, as with the Bible, the ultimate end of such works was an understanding of God's ways in order to achieve salvation and happiness. St. Augustine had really meant the same thing when he said that the primary purpose of all great literature was the promotion of Charity. To state this in modern terms, we would say that, according to medieval tastes, the basic function of literature and, indeed, of all art, is to commune or communicate with God. Dante's *Divine Comedy* represents man's most impressive attempt to achieve this in a literary work of art. In both form and content, moreover, it is a supremely successful endeavor to imitate God's creation as conceived by the medieval mind.

II. Dante's Perspective

Everyone will readily agree that the *Comedy* is great both in its whole and in its parts. But since it is difficult to speak of the whole, most of what is said about the poem concentrates on the parts. This would have made Dante very sad, for, after all, his ultimate purpose in writing the poem was, in his own words, "to remove those who live in this life from the state of misery and direct them to the state of happiness." These words would certainly seem to imply the importance of grasping the whole. But somehow the modern aesthetic discourages treatment of this important dimension of total vision, as a result of its worship of form as purely literary technique. And yet, there is a way to treat the whole in a manner that would at least not clash with modern methodologies. It is simply to focus upon the setting or backdrop that Dante deliberately chose for the unfurling of his poetic journey, i.e., the world of the hereafter, or better, the world of the spirit, and see how it relates and contributes to the artistic structure of the whole.

If there is general agreement that in the *Comedy* we have one of the relatively few instances in the history of mankind when human creativity approached its zenith, then it appears logically incorrect to maintain that the framework of the poem, because of its religious and spiritual nature, contributes minimally to those qualities that make Dante's poem great. It might indeed be said that it is precisely the framework that constitutes the basic originality of the *Comedy*, for unlike Homer and Virgil who depicted man's journey on the frontiers of life, and unlike Chaucer or Boccaccio who were later to set their journeys squarely in this life, Dante elected to depict his in the hereafter. Why? Was it simply because he was just a religious man? Judging from the finished product, this remains doubtful. Was it not, rather, because as a great poet and artist he felt that such a setting would provide him with the desired perspective? What was this perspective? It was the perspective of both ultimate universality and ultimate infallibility, yielding a view of Man at his worst and at his best, not as seen by Man himself, but as seen through the eyes of God. For what do we have in Dante's setting if not a depiction of the baseness and grandeur of Man when viewed as a potential citizen of the City of God?

III. The Evolution of the *Comedy*

As Dante developed intellectually and spiritually, he wrote several works on various problems besetting mankind. Among these were a number of poems dealing with his love for an inspiringly beautiful lady called Beatrice. This love eventually served as a catalyst that helped "unbind his immortal sight," as he says in Canto XXI of the *Purgatorio*. In any event, around 1307, following a number of years of prolonged studies, he thought he found the answer to man's plight. While human history is unquestionably subject to periodic chaos, there is nevertheless an order that governs the physical world, just as there is one that governs the moral world. Everything, from angels to animals, proceeds originally from God; and everything instinctively aspires to return to God with a distinct and harmonious movement. This universal aspiration and movement gives to the universe its life; this determines its form and accounts for the essential circularity of its intricate movement. Everything in the world is in flux because of its impetus to pattern itself on the spiritual world of God. In other words, the City of Man instinctively strives to become the City of God. All social and political problems, moreover, can be solved through a revelation of the heavenly, therefore ideal, order of things. Dante undertook a poem that seeks to view the human condition precisely from that perspective, through the eye of the Christian God.

This brings us to the basic problem facing Dante as a poet: how to depict most effectively the cosmic harmony to which mankind is unconsciously trying to conform in order to achieve ultimate fulfillment.

What Dante wanted to express was not new. It had to do with the problem of human destiny, or man's place in the universe. But his solution became much more comprehensive and ambitious than previous ones, for he was moved to portray through the art of poetry not only the entire spiritual evolution of Man from the lowly worm to the angelic butterfly (to use his own phrase), but to do so on what he considered infallible grounds revealed by God Himself in the Scriptures. At the same time, he wanted to preserve the inherent dignity and freedom instinctively felt by Man as a creature in God's image even in this life. It thus became Dante's ultimate goal to depict as vividly as possible how man can achieve eternal salvation through the use of his free will. This is why the *Comedy* is a supreme hymn both to human dignity and potentiality and to divine mercy and perfection, as well as the supreme example of the fusion of poetry, philosophy, and theology. It is of course essential for the reader who wishes fully to understand and appreciate the poem to suspend disbelief and constantly bear in mind that at the heart of the poem is the full acceptance of the meaning and mystery of the advent of Christ in all its wonder and beauty.

To achieve his goal Dante had to undertake an artistic re-creation of the entire universe — of matter, of the senses, and of the spirit. Furthermore, he had to create an impression of infallibility, which in his day meant simply abiding by the teachings of the Church and of the Church Fathers. By using these teachings as a basis for portraying the universe as presumably seen through the eyes of God, Dante sincerely hoped to guide Mankind from the miseries of this world to salvation and true happiness. It was this movement from grief to joy that in part prompted Dante to call his work a "comedy" as distinct from "tragedy."

Dante's main problem, then, was to make *us* see as God sees. How does God see? Only God's own book, Scripture, provides the answer, since it projects complete history, past, present, and *future,* from Genesis to Judgment Day. There we learn that God sees in a way quite different from that of Man. In Scripture we find that God speaks with events rather than with words. In fact, things and events seem to be, for God, what words are for men. In short, God sees consequences and finalities, not as through a glass darkly, but face to face, timelessly. So Dante decided to model his approach on that of the Bible. That is, people, things, events indicated by his words must reveal an ultimate human and divine meaning.

There still remained the problem of what God sees. Here too the Scriptures have an answer. They teach us that God essentially sees from the standpoint of the world and life of the supernatural where there is no intrusion of time or space. The true life is there, in His abode. This is God's perspective. So Dante's poem too is centered on that other life and reproduces it so convincingly within the Christian framework that a reader of his day must certainly have come away with the conviction that Man must be blind to believe that the life he sees around him, on this earth, is the true life.

Such considerations made Dante conceive of a poem whose subject matter on the literal level is the life of the hereafter, the life after death, the life of the spirit. Now, God Himself teaches in Scripture that there is a connection between that life and life on earth. So any complete picture of the hereafter had also to teach Man a great deal about this life. How to achieve this was another problem faced by Dante.

To resolve this problem Dante had recourse to three ingenious devices. First, he takes a live man, not yet dead but about to give up, and makes him of his own will take a mysterious journey in that other life. This device enabled him really to portray the entire universe, i.e., both the natural and the supernatural, the now and the then, the imperfect and the perfect, evil and good.

The second device was to project the earthly personalities of the souls encountered in the afterworld against a background that reflects God's infallible judgment with respect to ultimate perfection or imperfection. We thus are made to feel that in such cases as Paolo and Francesca, Farinata, or Ulysses earthly fulfillment is indeed a far cry from ultimate fulfillment.

A third device employed by Dante to achieve the desired bridge or connection between that life and this was his use of Beatrice as an example of how thin a line may divide human from divine love. As everyone knows, the *Comedy* is essentially a hymn to love in all its manifestations. Consequently, Beatrice is but a sign of how divine love penetrates the entire universe, even down to particular individuals.

We have, then, in the *Divine Comedy,* the curious situation in which the afterlife is the true life or literal level of meaning while this, our life, is in large part a reflection of that life. As a result, each sinful soul of Hell, repented soul of Purgatory, or blessed soul of Paradise, in order to be seen in their fullest meaning, must also be viewed within the framework of this life.

But God's world meshes with our world in very mysterious ways, which are usually revealed to men through signs or symbols found everywhere throughout Creation. Since the *Comedy* is basically an imitation of God's Creation, it too must contain such hidden signs. Dante himself, the hero of the poem, is a sign or symbol just as are all the people, things, and events that make up the poem. In other words, they all bear more than one level of meaning. Furthermore, in order to give the impression of God's Creation since the beginning of time, there had to be a great number of people, things and events, just as in the Bible, which is God's account of Creation. But just as in the Bible, there also had to be certain leading actors or signposts along the way of the willing pilgrim's journey. All too often we forget that the real "protagonist" of the *Comedy* is God Himself, the Light toward which the pilgrim moves from the very beginning of the poem. As for the supporting cast, it is very large indeed; but the chief roles are certainly played by Dante himself, Virgil, Beatrice, and St. Bernard. These last three, as we know, are Dante's principal guides on his journey. Therefore, they represent three means offered by God to Man to help him achieve the Light. It is now generally conceded that Reason, Revelation, and Intuition are the most appropriate terms, repectively, for defining these three means.

There are innumerable such signs or symbols scattered throughout the poem that indicate either God's presence or His handiwork. For example, the very structure of the poem reflecting everywhere the numbers 3, 7, or 10 provides eloquent testimony of this, as does the setting of Eastertide, and even the numerically suggestive year 1300.

In sum, the poem truly reflects a perspective that can be defined as "divine" rather than "human," or, to put it another way, as the view from God's eye.

IV. Dante's Objectivity, or Seeing with God

Repeated experience of Dante's masterpiece yields inexhaustible rewards. Each new reading uncovers ever deeper insights of evocative imagery and aesthetic enjoyment, as well as edifying substance. In their frescoes, manuscript illuminations, sculptures, even whole cathedrals, medieval artists generally sought to capture the eye in order to capture the mind and heart. Likewise, in his own medium of the written word, Dante has succeeded to an extraordinary degree. But there remain two major features of the *Comedy* that command special attention: Dante's quite remarkable objectivity and his divine perspective.

We have noted throughout this guide-book how Dante builds into his poetic creation all manner of elements, allusions, and imagery suggestive of the Divine presence. Reflecting the Holy Trinity, there is the poem's obvious triune division of *Inferno, Purgatorio, Paradiso*; there is the very rhyme-scheme of *terza rima* as a constant reminder of the same Divine presence; and there are innumerable Scriptural echoes throughout the poem. We have also noted a major feature in the gradually emerging Christocentric figure from the Inferno to its final fulfillment in the image of the Trinity with which the wayfarer's journey concludes. Such elements serve as so many "fingerprints" of God along the way of Dante's striving to reify the ineffable, to "see" and to cause the reader "to see," the world of the Afterlife in the most graphically tangible terms. The reification is accompanied and controlled by Dante's own remarkable objectivity and unwavering "judgment," in keeping with the divine perspective of his Christian faith.

We have clearly discerned a three-fold figure of Dante in the *Comedy* — the poet (who occasionally even steps out on stage in the course of the narrative), the pilgrim wayfarer (who journeys beyond the grave), and everyman, or any man (who is invited to identify with the wayfarer protagonist by the term "*our* life" in the very opening verse of the poem). But a case can also be made for a *fourth* Dante in the many instances of apostrophe wherein he suddenly steps out of the narrative to assume the posture of an Old Testament prophet. These pronouncements effectively serve to enhance further Dante's objectivity as poet and narrator.

Dante has, of course, his occasional outbursts against certain contemporary persons and events, undoubtedly prompted, at times, by bitter personal experience. But it is also true that such instances are adequately rationalized by historical fact. Moreover, Dante's stern objectivity ensures that he place, as we have seen, even the dearest of his friends as well as the most honorable personages — honorable by earthly standards — among the damned of Hell, according as he determined to be their ultimate spiritual condition. Nor does Dante hesitate to place persons of questionable character according to human opinion, along with acquaintances of no particular favor or privilege, among the saved, again as the poet may have judged in light of his understanding of Christian doctrine. Artistic genius though he was, we are reminded that Dante was not God, but a mortal, subject to mortal fallibility in determining the fate of saints and sinners. But that does not matter in the myth of the poem. And in the myth of the poem, moreover, there is no denying that he succeeded remarkably well in maintaining his objectivity as a Christian poet, thanks to his divinely inspired perspective.[*]

---

[*] For an elaboration of the poet's divine perspective, the reader is referred to the article, "Dante's *Divine Comedy:* The View from God's Eye," by Aldo S. Bernardo, in De Sua and Rizzo, eds., *A Dante Symposium . . .* (see BIBLIOGRAPHY).

V. Some Matters of Style

Style, like artistic technique, is not easily definable with respect to a given author or work. We are quite aware of the resulting
effect, and this in turn prompts us to probe into the mechanism involved, although exact analysis, where the great poets are concerned,
usually proves to be an elusive thing indeed. There are, however, certain obvious elements which go into the outward form and structure of
a work of art. Just as the artist's painting is composed of canvas, paint,
colors, and elements of light and dark, so a poet's work is composed of
words and their syntactical combination, their distribution according to
a metrical pattern, and the ideas the words evoke and represent. While
each single element in itself does not make a poem, for the sake of
analysis and discussion, we are in a sense forced to do violence to the
work of art in order to focus on one element at a time. Some of a
poem's major component elements are metrical form, diction and suggestive quality of words, and, of course, imagery.

Because the users of this study guide are, for the most part,
limited to reading Dante's *Comedy* in translation, it is virtually useless
to discuss the metrical side of the poem. Some translators, for example,
Dorothy L. Sayers, have done English versions of the *Comedy* in the
original rhyme scheme, which is *terza rima,* or "triple rhyme" (aba bcb
cdc ded, etc.) with its ingenious linking feature. But the combination of
rhyme scheme and rhythmic line of the original poem can never be
recreated in another language. Even in Italy, later poets have sought
without success to imitate the verse of Dante: the particular quality of
tone and timbre are simply his and his alone.

Let us move on to the matter of diction. Dante was well aware
of the distinction between high and low styles observed by the great
classical writers of tragedy and comedy, and he explains his use of the
title "Comedy" in part by his use of a "lax and humble style." In other
words, his poem represents a mixture of genres, and his language
therefore is not exclusively the lofty, choice language reserved for high
tragedy, but more frequently on the low or humble side, such as that
for comedy. Actually, his diction represents a highly varied mixture,
including many "unrefined" or, as he puts it in the *De vulgari eloquentia,* "uncombed" words.

From the finished work, we see that the poet actually fitted the diction to the particular character, situation, or mood to be expressed. In the case of Pier delle Vigne (*Inf.* XIII), for example, Dante has the character speak in his own flossy style, characteristic of his own poetry. In presenting Arnaut Daniel at the end of *Purg.* XXVI, he goes to the extreme of having the 'shade' speak in his native Provençal language. When among the coarse devils of *Inf.* XXI–XXII, Dante again fits the verse in diction and tone to their own coarse behavior and speech. He names the devils with such suggestive denominations as Malacoda (Badtail), Barbariccia (Curlybeard), Graffiacane (Dog-scratcher), Cagnazzo (Mean dog), and Rubicante (Ruddy). On the other hand, when he has a former courtly lady like Francesca speak in *Inf.* V, her diction and manner are matched to her social station and to her own personal sensitivity of temperament. The same is true of La Pia at the end of *Purg.* V: her exquisite gentleness and modesty of speech and manner are subtly recaptured by the poet's mode of expression.

Let us also note that there is a significant difference in Dante's choice of words in the key position of end-rhymes among the three *cantiche* of the *Comedy.* The incidence of crisp, harsh, or outright ugly words, usually involving consonantal clusters or unusual phonetic combinations as well as conceptual unpleasantness of meaning, is particularly high in the *Inferno,* in keeping with the nature of the place and subject. There is a greater incidence of more pleasing words in the rhyme position throughout the *Purgatorio.* And of course the *Paradiso* contains the greatest proportion by far of the most beautiful and pleasing diction, in meaning and sound, of all three *cantiche.* In short, as the most conscious of artists, Dante effectively and consistently matched his diction to the matter to be expressed.

Turning to another major stylistic element, imagery, we must first note that Dante wrote in an age of symbolism of a particular kind. Much of this we can accept in terms of association. For example, it is easy for us to accept darkness and dark tones as signs of sin, evil, wickedness, and the like, as in the dark wood of *Inf.* I, or indeed the general atmosphere of gloom and fume of Hell as a whole. The airy brightness of Purgatory is, again, stylistically, in keeping with the place. Moreover, there was a whole metaphysics surrounding the concept of light and its symbolical appropriateness for the Godhead. Beyond the figurative significance of darkness and light and such colors as white, green, red, blue, and gold, there is of course the mystique of numbers discussed under BACKGROUND, in the introductory pages above.

In considering imagery as such, we must remember that Dante's whole literary mode is metaphorical. For example, in the journey metaphor, we can hardly speak of metaphor in our terms, understanding it as a mere stylistic element. It is too much a conceptual mode, an essential way of thinking, for that. Regarding metaphor and simile as figures of speech as we understand them, Dante favored the simile, or better, the extended simile, introduced by "like," "as," or "just as ... so ..." A good example is found at the beginning of *Inf.* XXI, where the poet recalls the feverish activity of the great marine arsenal of Venice in order to communicate vividly an image of the devils' busy activity about the pool of boiling pitch to which are condemned the souls of swindlers.

There is also the device of the evocative image of a familiar scene in one context employed to create a mood or enhance an atmosphere of a different scene. This device, not unrelated to imagery, generally speaking, is frequently used by Dante. A beautiful example is that at the very beginning of *Purg.* VIII, a part of which Thomas Gray in the eighteenth century confessed to imitating in his famous elegy ("The curfew tolls the knell of parting day ..."). Here the poet invokes the moment at twilight when sailors far from home are overcome with melancholy and homesickness to express the moment and the mood in which the pilgrim finds himself the first evening on Mount Purgatory. The passage goes even beyond the immediate context in its poignant expression of nostalgia, since nostalgia for their "true home" up there in Heaven is one of the leit-motifs of the Purgatorio, in which the souls know where they belong and are headed and cannot wait to get there.

There are of course many other devices employed by Dante in his poem. Apostrophe is frequent, as well as antithesis, personification, synecdoche, hyperbole, metonymy, and histeron proteron. The alert reader who is familiar with, or will take the trouble to familiarize himself, with these terms and more will be rewarded by the discovery of a wealth of examples in Dante's *Comedy,* which will significantly enhance his understanding and appreciation of the poet's artistry.

As a final note, it should be observed that imagery and other stylistic elements in Dante's poem are never strictly ornamental, or better, they are never there merely to serve as beautiful ornaments. The slogan of "art for art's sake" or variations thereof had no place in Dante's world. The poet's figures of speech and imagery are, rather, invariably put to hard work, often to the point of doing "double duty," such as in the example just cited from the beginning of *Purg.* VIII. The important thing to keep in mind is that Dante is concerned with *seeing,* seeing beyond this life. His whole poem is a supreme attempt to body forth in the most graphic terms that which is essentially non-physical, invisible, spiritual, and therefore ineffable.

We note especially in the course of the *Paradiso* the poet's increasing lament over the inadequacy of language generally and of his own human powers, to express what he encountered on his extraordinary journey. It is to help us see, feel, and hear every possible detail of his experience that he employs every available stylistic device in his poetic narration. As a tribute to his success stands the incredible fact that we do *see* with him, all the way!

CHARACTER ANALYSES

A S FAR AS THE POETIC JOURNEY narrated by the *Comedy* is concerned, there are very few main characters. They are of course, in
order of appearance, the protagonist or wayfarer (or pilgrim), Virgil,
Beatrice, and Saint Bernard. Satan is not really characterized in so
many words, but is an evil presence permeating the entire realm of
Hell. Along the course of the journey, the wayfarer encounters, in addition, hundreds of other characters, representing every conceivable human type of every possible moral stamp from every walk of life, some
major, some minor, some elaborately presented, some sketched in with
but a few brush strokes. On the whole, however, they are persons of
some prominence and therefore most effectively exemplify God's inexorable justice, as Dante states in the Cacciaguida episode *(Par.*
XVII, end). The most important of these are touched upon in their appropriate place in the COMPREHENSIVE SUMMARY and may be located
by means of the GLOSSARY-INDEX.

In general, Dante employs two techniques of characterization.
There are the main characters whose personalities are almost lost under
the burden of their allegorical meaning. In depicting these the poet
never loses sight of a third dimension which consists of projecting their
human nature against a background of ultimate spiritual meaning. Thus
the historical Virgil and Dante's guide is never permitted to abandon
entirely his identification with Reason.

Then there are the truly human types whose characterization
extends backward and forward, but not upward. Thus, a Francesca or a
Ulysses is depicted in brief, bold strokes which simply extend human
frailty on the plane of infinity. They may appear to be heroic figures in
earthly terms, but in divine terms, they are damnable. How can we
avoid sympathizing with Francesca in Canto V of the *Inferno* as she
undertakes her noble defense of her love for Paolo in the memorable
verses that go as follows:

> Love which flames quickly in noble hearts
> was kindled in this soul by the fair body
> taken from me: the manner still offends.

> Love that exempts no one beloved from loving
> caught me so strongly with his charm
> that, as you see, it still does not leave me.
>
> Love led us to one death together.
> Caina waits for him who quenched our lives.
>
> (Huse trans.)

How, we ask, can an all merciful God not forgive such a basic and noble human passion? The answer for Dante is simple. Both Paolo and Francesca *knew* the rules of the game. Adultery is a sin unless sincerely repented. But let us note that Paolo and Francesca are at the very top of Hell, while their murderer wallows in the lowest depths. All three, however, are equally doomed eternally, and they are incapable of entirely understanding why.

The same applies to Ulysses in Canto XXVI of the *Inferno*. Who can ever forget his inspiring speech to his men as they sailed uncharted waters:

> O Brothers, I said, you who
> through a thousand perils have come to the west,
> to the brief vigil of our senses
>
> which is left, do not deny
> experience of the unpeopled world
> to be discovered by following the sun.
>
> Consider what origin you had:
> you were not created to live like brutes,
> but to seek virtue and knowledge.
>
> (Huse trans.)

Poor Ulysses seems to think that he is in lower Hell because of his voyage. He seems incapable of recognizing the evil, among other transgressions, of his monstrously treacherous role in the Trojan Horse episode. And yet this is precisely what makes Dante's characters loom extraordinarily large. The fact that earthly life has ceased for them, so that they cannot change or grow, when combined with the fact that the passions and inclinations which had animated them still persist without ever being released in action, produces an intensified image of the essence of their being, fixed for all eternity in dimensions larger than life.

Considerably different is the characterization of the main figures, who are discussed briefly below.

Dante

Since the narrative is related in the first person, we immediately associate the wayfarer with Dante himself as poet of the *Comedy*. He is actually identified by name once only, at the top of Purgatory where Beatrice sits in judgment of him as a repentant sinner. But we must not forget that, except for this latter moment in this particular poem, an I-narrative must not necessarily be linked with the author himself where a work of art is concerned. On the contrary, a work of art constitutes a world of its own creation, in which even patently historical characters or references assume a new identity within the context of the particular art-work. The fact is that the I-protagonist wayfarer in the *Comedy* can be any man or everyman. And so the poet invites the reader to identify with the wayfarer, when in the very opening verse he refers to "*our* life." This experience of the process of coming to know God is open to any man, if he will but desire it. But if he does not, as we come to learn in the poem, then he is less than a man and even a traitor to the Creator who made him in His own image.

The wayfarer, in fact, does have the proper attitude once he has come to his senses and undergone an initial conversion, thanks to a moment of illuminating grace, in the Dark Wood of Sin. From that point on, and with proper guidance, he is not only led but also eager to be led on the subsequent journey of edification. At the same time, he is a complete and thoroughly human being, inquisitive, emotional, impatient, and demonstrative. Like the good student that he is, he looms especially large as a questing figure from beginning to end, eager to have answers to all the questions that are likely to beset any human being on such a journey, indeed in the whole course of his existence.

Beatrice

Beatrice, as we know from the beginning of the poem, is already in Heaven. We are also made aware that she is the wayfarer's former beloved before she died. We also come to know during the con-

frontation at the top of Purgatory that he subsequently allowed his eye
to stray to others following the death of Beatrice. Stepping out of the
poem for the moment, we may ask who Beatrice actually was in real
life. To this question, however, there is no certain and ready answer. It
is believed that she may have been Beatrice Portinari, who died in
1290, but this is not an absolute certainty. Nor does it really matter.
The *Comedy* itself tells us all that we really need to know. This is the
former beloved of the wayfarer. What matters is that she was truly an
inspiration, for his love relationship with her eventually led him to
God. We may note a particular circular pattern in the basic outline of
the entire journey, which is initiated and ends in Heaven. Of the three
heavenly ladies mentioned by Virgil, the Virgin Mary, Saint Lucy, and
Beatrice, it is the latter who serves as the immediate heavenly agent in
launching the journey by commissioning Virgil as initial guide, while
she herself serves as immediate goal of the wayfarer and then as guide
to lead him on the heavenly portion of the journey, introducing him to
divine knowledge and to Paradise itself. This is why at one point she is
defined as "the light between the Truth and the intellect."

As a character, she is not presented in descriptive detail, but
characterized only in general terms of ineffable beauty and brightness.
However, as we "see" her even in general, non-specific terms through
the eyes and feelings of the wayfarer, she is very much the beloved he
knew as a living woman on earth, while at the same time she assumes,
in the present context, symbolical meaning as Revelation.

Virgil

The great Roman poet of antiquity is a rich figure in the *Divine
Comedy,* as we have seen in the course of the comprehensive summary.
Beyond comment is the tribute which Dante pays him, in the initial
encounter in *Inf.* I, as his "master and author" whose *Aeneid* prompted
his long study and great love and to whose example he owes the success of his own poetic style. For Dante, Virgil was the greatest spokes-
man of the Roman Empire, which providentially effected the universal
peace that prepared the way for the advent of Christ in the fullness of
time (as prophesied in Scripture).

Also, in the Middle Ages generally, Virgil enjoyed a special status on the basis of a passage in his famous Fourth Eclogue which was interpreted as a prophecy of the Savior's birth. It was easy for Dante to view the figure of Virgil, the poet and seer of Rome, as the finest example of pre-Christian man on his own, before God's light was restored by Christ to human kind, and the loftiest achievement of human reason unenlightened by God's Word. Besides his historical self, then, Virgil, is cast as a symbol of two ideals: Rome at its best and Reason unenlightened by Faith. By having him as guide through Hell *and* Purgatory, the poet is able to cast him most effectively, even dramatically, as a character of deepest pathos who is condemned to damnation, having historically just missed the coming of Christ and the possibility of salvation. His limitations, as natural reason without grace, are especially evident with touching dramatic effect in the course of the *Purgatorio,* as we saw in the COMPREHENSIVE SUMMARY.

Saint Bernard

When in *Paradiso* XXXI Beatrice leaves Dante's side to resume her position among the blessed in the Rose of Paradise, Saint Bernard comes to take her place as a kind of third guide for the wayfarer in the third and final stage of man's approach to God. He appears as a very venerable and hoary old man, epitomizing the completely fulfilled human being who has come to know God directly. As Virgil can be taken to represent Reason and Beatrice Revelation, so Saint Bernard seems to represent the way of Intuition. These are the three guides during the three stages leading the wayfarer to the ultimate vision of God.

Because of the importance of the respective symbolic meanings which these characters embody, they may risk losing much of their human aspect for us. It must be remembered, however, that Dante himself would insist they are first and foremost their own historical selves as they had lived on earth and their fulfilled selves as we see them in the afterlife, just like all the other characters encountered on the poetic journey. (Regarding their first meaning, as the poet states in his letter to Can Grande, the literal meaning must always come first.) But to the four major characters is added the third dimension of the symbolic meanings, as mentioned. It is as though their first two meanings were expressed as a horizontal line, while the third meaning assumes a vertical aspect. In any case, this latter dimension may be summed up, with the words of Saint Thomas, in the following pattern:

> Man's knowledge of divine things is threefold. The first is when man, by the natural light of reason, rises through creatures to the knowledge of God. The second is when the divine truth which surpasses the human intelligence comes down to us by revelation, yet not as shown to him that he may see it, but as expressed in words so that he may hear it. The third is when the human mind will be raised to the perfect intuition of things revealed. . . .

What better way for Dante's poem to portray these ways than by personifying them in actual historical human figures? This is what Dante does in his characters of Virgil, Beatrice, and St. Bernard — as Reason, Revelation, and Intuition.

STUDY QUESTIONS

1. *Explain the falsity of an old indictment, based on ignorance, that Dante placed all his friends in Paradise and all his enemies in Hell.*

   Answer hints: A conspicuous exception: Dante places his dear old teacher and friend, Brunetto Latini, in Hell among the damned (*Inf.* XV). Dante was remarkably objective as a responsible Christian poet, who was trying to see from God's point of view. Explore also the poet's obvious admiration for, and virtual identity with, Ulysses, among the damned (*Inf.* XXVI). Another figure Dante might have condemned out of hand as a pre-Christian pagan we find presented as one of God's inscrutable exceptions among the saved of Paradise: Ripheus.

2. *Throughout this study guide, the* Divine Comedy *has been invariably referred to as Dante's* poem. *No mention has been made of the term* epic. *Yet many students of the* Comedy *have construed it as an epic. Explain why there may be some validity for their position.*

   Answer hints: The *Comedy* is certainly a long narrative poem. There is a central hero. And the theme is certainly a noble one, with unmistakable universality of scope. Develop and put together these elements and the total may add up to something on the order of "epic."

3. *The* Comedy *is a poem about love. Explain.*

   Answer hints: Distinguish between love and Love (with the capital letter). Follow through the figure of Beatrice as the poet's beloved lady. Examine the discussion on love in the central cantos (*Purg.* XVI–XVIII) of the poem. Synthesize.

4. *Discuss the use of recurring images in the* Paradiso *as "shadowy prefaces of the reality."*

Answer hints: Cite the many instances of circle imagery in terms of "garlands" of souls, a point of light, and circles of light and of movement throughout the *Paradiso*. Light and the circle as traditional symbols of God. Relate to the hierarchy of Angels and the degrees of blessedness ranged in the amphitheater of Heaven in sight of the unitary light of God and also the final vision of the circle image containing the mystery of the Trinity combined with the human figure.

5. *By having to descend into Hell before ascending to the light at the top of the mountain, imaged in the opening scene of the poem, the wayfarer follows an archetypal pattern of descent before ascent enacted by Christ. But the wayfarer's journey goes beyond mere imitation. It is based on necessity. Explain.*

Answer hints: The pilgrim soul must know sin before it can turn away from it. Also, it must, through this act of humility in descent, rid itself of the shackles of self-reliance. All this is part of the soul's necessary and complete edification as preparation for approaching God. In any case, the soul must have guidance along the various stages of the way.

6. *Hell and Paradise are eternal realms; Purgatory, a temporary realm. How can Dante presume to "see" not only the souls of the eternally damned in Hell, but also the souls in their glorified bodies of the blessed in Paradise?*

Answer hint: Cite the example of the Incarnation in Christ, God's Word made Flesh. Dante's poem as an imitation of God's creation. Scripture as the representation of history complete, past, present, and future, from the beginning of time to the end of time.

7. *Dante's use of Virgil and Cato has shocked many readers, who are puzzled by the contrast in treatment. Virgil, who was fairly worshiped by Dante, is located among the damned in Limbo. Cato, whose paganism is further complicated by what would appear to be the sin of suicide, is found among the saved of Purgatory. In what ways can the force of the shock be diminished?*

Answer hints: The constant allusions to Dante's journey leading to ultimate "freedom." Virgil's "intellectual" accomplishments *versus* Cato's "active" involvements. The distance that literally separates the two in Dante's cosmos.

RESEARCH AREAS

HERE IS WHERE a close reading of the *Comedy* itself and some assistance from the short, selected BIBLIOGRAPHY, below, can bear fruitful results.

1. Examine the figure of Ulysses in Homer, in later ancient classical writers, such as Cicero, and even in still later writers, such as Tennyson, and compare with Dante's Ulysses.

2. Compare the figure of Virgil as Reason unenlightened by Faith and the figure of Statius as Reason *enlightened* by Faith.

3. Survey the various sins and punishments in the *Inferno* and show how the sins to which the souls gave themselves in life now, in retribution, continue to remain with them as their very punishments in eternity.

4. Explain the "irony" of the Ulysses episode. Note that, as represented in Hell, Ulysses is not aware of why he is here. Significantly, his quiet flame contrasts sharply with that of Guido da Montefeltro in the following canto. Ulysses was a great hero who sought to pursue, along with his loyal followers, "virtue and understanding," even as a Christian is urged to do in Scripture. But Ulysses lived before, and did not know, Christ.

5. Through a careful examination and analysis of the system of "checks" and "goads" found on the ledges of Purgatory proper, show how the poet's artistry struggles nobly to reflect God's artistry.

6. Read the *Vita nuova* and trace the evolution and fulfillment of the figure of Beatrice and the poet-lover's relation to her between that early work and the *Comedy*.

7. Read Dante's *De monarchia* and compare and contrast his conclusions there with what appears to be his ideal of universal government in the *Comedy*.

BIBLIOGRAPHY

Some Translations in English

(A selection of translations in English done in various modes.)

T HE "TEMPLE CLASSICS" (London: Dent, 1899–1906, and later reprintings): *The Divine Comedy,* in 3 v.; *Convivio,* 1 v.; the Latin works, 1 v.; the *Vita Nuova,* 1 v. The only complete English translation of all the works of Dante. By Carlyle, Okey, and Wicksteed. Long a staple for having all of Dante in convenient form.

The Divine Comedy. Translated by Henry Francis Cary, with a special introduction by Charles Eliot Norton. London: Colonial Press, 1961. Originally published as *The Vision,* London: J. Barfield, 1814, in 3 v. Many editions throughout the 19th century and into the 20th. In blank verse of enduring vigor, this was the standard version for English-speaking readers throughout the 19th century.

The Divine Comedy of Dante Alighieri. Translated by Henry Wadsworth Longfellow. Boston: Ticknor, 1867. 3 v. Many later editions, e.g., in "Dolphin Books" (Doubleday, 1960–1961); and most recently, in "Modern Library" classics, paperback edition (New York, 2003–), with preface by Matthew Pearl, introduction by Lino Pertile, and copious notes. A literal translation in blank verse; in some ways a very satisfying version. First complete American translation.

The Divine Comedy of Dante Alighieri. Translated by Charles Eliot Norton. Complete edition, three volumes in one, with an Appendix by Ernest Hatch Wilkins. Boston, etc.: Houghton Mifflin Company, 1941, and later printings. Originally published in 1891–1892 in 3 v.; revised edition, 1902. Prose version of considerable beauty, with introduction, notes, and index.

The Divine Comedy: Inferno, Purgatorio, Paradiso. With a translation into English triple rhyme by Laurence Binyon. New York: Macmillan, 1933–1943. 3 v. Available in *The Portable Dante,* ed. Paolo Milano (New York: Viking Press, 1947 and later). In *terza rima,* the original rhyme-scheme.

The Divine Comedy of Dante Alighieri. With translation and comment by John D. Sinclair. New York: Oxford University Press, 1948 and later printings. 3 v. First published in 1939 at The Bodley Head. A literal translation in prose, the Italian text on facing pages, with an eclectic critical commentary on each canto.

The Comedy of Dante Alighieri the Florentine.... Translated by Dorothy L. Sayers. Penguin Books, 1949–1962. 3 v. Translated in *terza rima,* with excellent notes.

The Divine Comedy. A new prose translation, with an introduction and notes by H. R. Huse. New York: Rinehart, 1954. (Rinehart Editions, 72.) Conveniently incorporates short summary headings and essential explanatory notes, very briefly within the text itself.

The Divine Comedy. Translated, with a commentary, by Charles S. Singleton.... Bollingen Series LXXX. Princeton, New Jersey: Princeton University Press, 1970–1975. In 6 volumes, one each of the three parts — Inferno, Purgatorio, Paradiso, with Italian text and exact, literal translation in prose on facing pages; and an accompanying volume to each part, with extensive commentary and copious notes to the text. By the leading American Dantist of our time.

(Further translations continue to appear almost annually.)

Bibliography

Cornell University Library. *Catalogue of the Dante Collection* by Willard Fiske. Compiled by Theodore W. Koch. Ithaca, New York: Cornell University Press, 1898–1900. 2 v. Since the Cornell Dante collection is one of the largest in the world, its catalogue constitutes a basic bibliography.

———. *Additions, 1898–1920.* Compiled by Mary Fowler. Ithaca, New York: Cornell University Press, 1921.

Cosmo, Umberto. A *Handbook to Dante Studies.* Translated by David Moore. Oxford: Basil Blackwell, 1950. Original: *Guida a Dante* (Torino: De Silva, 1947). Excellent manual, containing a brief, classified treatment of Dante's life and works, with useful bibliographies for controlling all aspects of the subject.

Grayson, Cecil. "Gli studi danteschi in Gran Bretagna (1922–1964)." In *Dante nel mondo,* ed. Vittore Branca and Ettore Caccia (Firenze: Olschki, 1965), pp. 237–254. ("Bibliografia," pp. 242–254.) Dante studies in Great Britain, 1922–1964. The items listed are in English.

Marraro, Howard R. "Bibliografia dantesca americana dal Settecento al 1921." In *Atti dell'Istituto veneto di scienze, lettere ed arti* (Classe di scienze morali e lettere), CXXIII (1964–65), 189–277. American Dante bibliography from the 18th century to 1921. The items listed are in English.

———. "Dante negli Stati Uniti." In *Dante nel mondo,* ed. Vittore Branca and Ettore Caccia (Firenze: Olschki, 1965), pp. 433–559. "Bibliografia dantesca americana dal 1921 al 1964," pp. 455–559. American Dante bibliography from 1921 to 1964. The items listed are in English.

Pellegrini, Anthony L. "American Dante Bibliography for 1953 [initial year of annual coverage] ... 1965." In *68th–72nd Annual Reports of the Dante Society* (1954) ... 83rd *Report* (1965), and, under new title, *Dante Studies,* LXXXIV (1966) ... CIII (1985); continued by Christopher Kleinhenz, CIII (1985.... Annual register of all Dante translations, studies and reviews in any sense American. Annotated with summaries.

Toynbee, Paget. *Dante in English Literature from Chaucer to Cary (c. 1380–1844)....* With introduction, notes, biographical notices, chronological list, and general index ... London: Methuen & Co. 1909. 2 v. Useful for tracing the influence of Dante in English literature.

Biography

Barbi, Michele. *Life of Dante.* Translated by P. G. Ruggiers. Berkeley and Los Angeles: University of California Press, 1954 and 1960. A compact biography by a foremost authority.

Bergin, Thomas G. *Dante.* New York: Orion Press. 1965; also in paperback, Boston: Houghton Mifflin, 1965. A useful introduction to Dante's life and works.

Boccaccio, Giovanni, and Leonardo Bruni Aretino. *The Earliest Lives of Dante.* New York: Frederick P. Ungar, 1963, 1965. (Milestones of Thought.) Interesting as near-contemporary biography.

Gardner, E. G. *Dante.* London: Oxford University Press, 1921. A standard life and works manual by a late Victorian.

Lewis, R. W. B. *Dante.* (A Penguin Life) New York: Viking Press, 2001. Traces the life and complex development — emotional, artistic, philosophical — of the man and the poet.

Toynbee, Paget. *Dante Alighieri: His Life and Works.* Edited with an Introduction, Notes, and Bibliography by Charles S. Singleton. New York: Harper Torchbooks, 1965. A "classic" of its kind.

Background Studies

Aristotle. *Basic Works,* ed. R. McKeon, New York: Random House, 1961. Aristotelianism is a major element of Dante's thought.

Saint Augustine. *On Christian Doctrine.* Translated, with an introduction, by D. W. Robertson, Jr. Indianapolis: Bobbs-Merrill, 1958. (The Library of Liberal Arts) Useful for understanding the spiritual orientation of medieval man.

Saint Bonaventura. *The Mind's Road to God.* Translated, with an introduction, by George Boas. Indianapolis: Bobbs-Merrill, 1953. (The Library of Liberal Arts) A medieval theologian's account of the way to knowledge of God.

Curtius, Ernst Robert. *European Literature and the Latin Middle Ages.* Trans. by W. Trask. New York: Pantheon, 1953. Also a paperback reprint, Harper Torchbooks, 1963. Studies on the cultural complex in which Dante too is rooted.

Gilson, Etienne. *The Spirit of Mediaeval Philosophy.* (Gifford Lectures 1931–1932) Translated by A. H. C. Downes. New York: Charles Scribner's Sons, 1940 (® 1936). Excellent definition of Christian thought in the Middle Ages.

Huizinga, J. *The Waning of the Middle Ages.* Garden City. New York: Doubleday Anchor Books, 1954. Excellent for understanding the gradual transition from medieval to Renaissance.

Lewis, C. S. *The Allegory of Love: A Study in Medieval Tradition.* London: Oxford University Press, 1936 and later reprintings. Not specifically on Dante, but valuable for the background, particularly the first chapter, on "Courtly Love."

Orr, M. A. *Dante and the Early Astronomers.* New and revised edition. London: Allan Wingate, 1956. Excellent guide to Ptolemaic astronomy and to Dante's handling of astronomical phenomena.

Sedgwick, H. D. *Italy in the Thirteenth Century.* Boston and New York: Houghton Mifflin, 1912. 2 v. A standard history.

Taylor, H. O. *The Mediaeval Mind.* 4th ed., Cambridge: Harvard University Press, 1949. 2 v. Originally published in 1911. A classic work, extremely useful for understanding medieval modes of thought. Contains a chapter on "The Mediaeval Synthesis: Dante."

St. Thomas Aquinas. *Basic Writings,* ed. Anton C. Pegis. New York: Random House, 1945. 2 v. Valuable for understanding the background of Dante's thought.

———. *Summa Theologica*. Translated by the Dominican Fathers of the English Province. New York: Benziger Brothers, 1947. 3 v. Thomistic philosophy had the most profound influence on Dante. Well indexed.

Vossler, Karl. *Mediaeval Culture: An Introduction to Dante and His Times*. Trans. from the German by W. C. Lawton. New York: Harcourt, Brace and Co., 1929. 2 v. Reprinted in 1958 (New York: Ungar). A wide-ranging cultural-literary history; the second half is devoted to Dante. Good bibliography.

Selected Criticism
(Primarily book-length studies and collections of essays)

Auerbach, Erich. *Dante, Poet of the Secular World*. Trans. by Ralph Manheim. Chicago: University of Chicago Press, 1961. Considers Dante a key figure in the development of modern Western literature.

———. "Figura." In his *Scenes from the Drama of European Literature*, trans. by R. Manheim. New York: Meridian Books, 1959. On the "figural" principle of interpreting medieval literature, and Dante in particular.

———. *Mimesis: The Representation of Reality in Western Literature*. Translated from the German by W. R. Trask. Princeton: Princeton University Press, 1953. Paperback reprint by Doubleday Anchor Books, 1957. Of utmost significance for modern literary criticism. Contains a chapter on Dante's Farinata and Cavalcante.

Barolini, Teodolinda. *The Undivine Comedy: Detheologizing Dante*. Princeton, New Jersey: Princeton University Press, 1992. A novel approach to Dante's poem in 11 essays.

Bergin, Thomas G., ed. *From Time to Eternity: Essays on Dante's "Divine Comedy."* New Haven: Yale University Press, 1967. Seventh centenary essays by prominent students of Dante: Sapegno, Morghen, Petrocchi, Foster, Greene, and Scaglione.

Brandeis, Irma. *The Ladder of Vision: A Study of Dante's Comedy*. London: Chatto and Windus, 1960; Garden City, N.Y.: Doubleday, 1961. Six essays for the general reader, interpreting Dante's poem as poem, with moral values as well.

———, ed. Discussions *of the "Divine Comedy."* Boston: D. C. Heath, 1961. (Discussions of Literature.) Twenty essays representing an historical cross-section of critical writing on Dante by prominent scholars from Boccaccio to Singleton.

Carroll, J. S. *Exiles of Eternity: An Exposition of Dante's Inferno,* 2d ed., 1904; *Prisoners of Hope: An Exposition of Dante's Purgatorio,* 1906; and *In Patria: An Exposition of Dante's Paradiso,* 1911: London: Hodder and Stoughton. Analytical commentary by a clergyman, but quite free of moralizing.

Cassell, Anthony K. *Dante's Fearful Art of Justice.* Toronto, Buffalo, London: University of Toronto Press, 1984. Deals principally with symbolic representation of the "state of souls after death" in the *Inferno.*

De Sanctis, Francesco. *De Sanctis on Dante.* Essays ed. and trans. by Joseph Rossi and Alfred Galpin. Madison: University of Wisconsin Press, 1957. Selected Dantean essays by the nineteenth-century pioneer of modern criticism.

De Sua, William, and Gino Rizzo, eds., *A Dante Symposium* . . . (Chapel Hill: University of North Carolina, 1965). Contains A. S. Bernardo's "Dante's *Divine Comedy*: The View from God's Eye," pp. 45–58.

Eliot, T. S. *Dante.* London: Faber and Faber, 1929. Also reprinted in his *Selected Essays* (New York: Harcourt, Brace, 1932). Very influential in bringing English-speaking readers to Dante's work.

Freccero, John, ed. *Dante: A Collection of Critical Essays.* Englewood Cliffs, N.J.: Prentice-Hall, 1965. (Twentieth Century Views) Thirteen essays by first-rate contemporary critics.

Fergusson, Francis. *Dante's Drama of the Mind: A Modern Reading of the "Purgatorio."* Princeton: Princeton University Press, 1953. A contemporary analysis of the *Purgatorio.*

Gardner, E. G. *Dante's Ten Heavens: A Study of the Paradiso.* Westminster: A. Constable; New York: Charles Scribner's Sons, 1900. Analysis of the *Paradiso.*

Gilson, Etienne. *Dante the Philosopher.* Trans. from the French by David Moore. New York: Sheed & Ward, 1949. Paperback reprint as *Dante and Philosophy* (Harper Torchbooks, 1963). Not easy reading, but a very rewarding study of Dante's developing attitudes towards philosophy.

Grandgent, Charles Hall. *Dante.* New York: Duffield, 1916. General introduction to Dante by a prominent American Dantist.

Grayson, Cecil, ed. *The World of Dante: Essays on Dante and His Times* (For the Oxford Dante Society) Oxford: The Clarendon Press, 1980. Ten topical essays by various scholars.

Hollander, Robert. *Allegory in Dante's* Commedia. Princeton, New Jersey: Princeton University Press, 1969. Employs the fourfold allegorical interpretation of the Bible compounded with Scriptural "universal history."

Limentani, Uberto, ed. *The Mind of Dante*. Cambridge, England: At the University Press, 1965. Seven essays on various aspects of Dante's work and thought by Sapegno, McNair, Foster, Boyde, Limentani, Cremona, and Brand.

Mazzeo, Joseph Anthony. *Medieval Cultural Tradition in Dante's "Comedy."* Ithaca, N.Y.: Cornell University Press, 1960. On some leading conceptual patterns of the tradition, such as "hierarchy" and light metaphysics.

Mazzotta, Giuseppe. *Dante, Poet of the Desert: History and Allegory in the Divine Comedy*. Princeton, New Jersey: Princeton University Press, 1979. Reads the poem as a dramatized vision of universal history on the structural pattern of Exodus, with the metaphorical desert marking our estrangement from the world.

Musa, Mark, ed. *Essays on Dante*. Bloomington: Indiana University Press, 1964. Nine essays on various aspects of Dante's poem by contemporary Dante scholars.

Passerin D'Entreves, A. *Dante as a Political Thinker*. Oxford: Clarendon Press, 1952. Clear analysis of Dante's political thought as evidenced in his works.

Reade, W. H. V. *The Moral System of Dante's Inferno*. Oxford: Clarendon Press, 1909. A clear, useful analysis.

Santayana, George. *Three Philosophical Poets: Lucretius, Dante, Goethe*. Garden City, New York: Doubleday Anchor Books, 1953. Originally published in 1910 by Harvard University Press. The essay on Dante has been often cited and frequently reprinted.

Sayers, Dorothy L. *Further Papers on Dante*. London: Methuen, 1957. Also, New York: Harper Brothers, 1957. The eight lectures bear more on the poetic aspects of the *Comedy* and are more heterogeneous than the first series.

―――. *Introductory Papers on Dante*. London: Methuen, 1954. Also, New York: Harper Brothers, 1954. Eight lectures for the non-specialist.

Singleton, Charles S. *Commedia: Elements of Structure* (Dante Studies, I). Cambridge: Harvard University Press, 1954. Four interrelated studies and an appendix analyzing various levels of meaning in the *Comedy* by the leading American Dantist of our time who set a fresh direction in interpreting Dante.

―――. *Journey to Beatrice* (Dante Studies, II). Cambridge: Harvard University Press, 1957. Focuses on the *Purgatorio,* the development of the action and meaning on various levels.

―――. *An Essay on the "Vita Nuova."* Cambridge: Harvard University Press, 1949. A milestone in Dante criticism.

————. "The Vistas in Retrospect." In Modern Language Notes, LXXXI (1966), 55–80. Brilliant interpretation of Christo-centric form in the *Divine Comedy.*

Toynbee, Paget. A *Dictionary of Proper Names and Notable Matters in the Works of Dante.* Oxford: Clarendon Press, 1898. A new edition of this indispensable work prepared by Charles S. Singleton, published in 1968.

Whitfield, John H. *Dante and Virgil.* Oxford: Blackwell, 1949. Treats of a central relationship in the *Comedy.*

Wicksteed, P. H. *From Vita Nuova to Paradiso.* New York: Longman's, Green, 1922. Good on the development of Dante's political and religious thought.

Williams, Charles. *The Figure of Beatrice.* New York: Noonday Press, 1961. A fervently written guide to Dante's allegory.

NOTE. There is now available *The Dante Encyclopedia.* Ed. Richard Lansing *et al.* New York and London: Garland Publishing . . . 2000. 1006 pp. A fundamental reference for Dante, his works, and related topics.

History of Italian Literature

De Sanctis, Francesco. *History of Italian Literature.* Trans. by Joan Redfern. New York: Harcourt, Brace and Company, © 1931. 2 v. Also, London: Oxford University Press, 1930. Reprinted, New York: Basic Books 1960, ©1959. 2 v. Written in the 19th century by a pioneer of modern literary criticism.

Whitfield, John H. *Short History of Italian Literature.* Penguin Books, 1960. (Pelican A445.) An essayistic treatment.

Wilkins, Ernest H. A *History of Italian Literature.* Cambridge, Mass.: Harvard University Press, 1954. Factual literary history, with helpful synchronic references to developments outside Italy.

GLOSSARY-INDEX

NOTE: EDITIONS AND TRANSLATIONS of Dante's *Comedy* come furnished with indexes and/or glossaries of varying scope. Listed here are only proper names and other matters of interest which are actually mentioned in the COMPREHENSIVE SUMMARY. For complete coverage in depth, the reader is referred to the authoritative Toynbee Dante dictionary and to *The Dante Encyclopedia* (see BIBLIOGRAPHY).